The making of American politics 1750-1850

M.J. Heale

Longman
London and New York

To my father and the memory of my mother

Longman Group Limited London

*Associated companies, branches and representatives
throughout the world*

*Published in the United States of America
by Longman Inc., New York*

First published 1977

Heale, M.J.
The making of American politics, 1750-1850.
Bibliography: p.
Includes index.
1. United States — Politics and government — Colonial period, ca. 1600-1775. 2.
United States — Politics and government — Revolution, 1775-1783. 3. United States —
Politics and government — 1783-1865. I. Title.
JK116.H4 1977   320.9'73   77-24250
ISBN 0-582-48735-8
ISBN 0-582-48736-6 pbk.

Set in VIP Times
and printed in Great Britain by
Richard Clay (The Chaucer Press) Ltd,
Bungay, Suffolk.

Contents

Preface

A French visitor to the United States in the 1830s discerned in the American 'a new political and physiological phenomenon, a hitherto unknown variety of the human race'. Whether American physiology was unique seems doubtful, but in the mid-nineteenth century Americans and foreigners alike were remarking on the novelty of the republic's political arrangements. European travellers were variously enchanted, amused, affronted, and outraged by the obsession which so many Americans had with politics, by the ubiquitous party spirit and the bitterly partisan press, by the ceremony and pageantry of the great torchlight processions, by the crude efficiency of the political machines and the arcane workings of the nominating conventions, by the uninhibited debates in Congress and the flamboyant stump speeches at the polls, by the mobilization and participation of millions of electors, in short, by the American way of politics. The election celebrations which he witnessed, wrote the same fascinated Frenchman, were the 'episodes of a wondrous epic which will bequeath a lasting memory to posterity, the memory of the coming of democracy'.[1]

The purpose of this book is to sketch the evolution of the American system of politics from its roots in the colonial past to its relative maturity in the 1830s and 1840s. The Americans who signed the Declaration of Independence had once been proud subjects of the English king, members of political communities which necessarily owed much to the English connection. In the mid-eighteenth century the English system of government served as the principal model for the evolving colonial polities, which in some ways were becoming more like the elite structures of the Old World at this time. Yet the American environment and the men and women who peopled it were also making their own contributions to the political patterns of these communities, and in 1776 Americans were suddenly released to develop a system of politics answerable to the imperatives of the New World. Traditional beliefs, attitudes, and customs were not lightly shed, and it took two or three generations of Americans to work out the political implications of the declaration that 'all men' were 'created equal', that all were endowed 'with certain unalienable rights', and that governments derived 'their just powers from the consent of the governed'.

By the mid-nineteenth century American politics had assumed a recognizably modern appearance. It was generally accepted that governments drew their legitimacy directly from the people, that all (white) men should possess equal political rights, irrespective of economic circumstance or social station, and hence that the majority should rule – subject to the constraints of a written constitution. This democratic (if racist and sexist) ideology had been converted into an imperfect reality by the American party system, which was acquiring a degree of bureaucratic permanence. The major political parties gave the avowedly equal individuals of this great political nation a sense of identity and community, conveyed their aspirations upwards through the polity, and provided the mechanisms whereby their aggregated demands could be brokered, accommodated or defused. By offering the voters a choice of candidates and platforms, the two-party system enabled the majority to choose the men and the measures by which the nation would be governed, though this limited choice was often unacceptable to minorities and campaign promises could not always be kept. The American system of politics, then, had already acquired many of the features with which it would always be associated, such as national nominating conventions composed of quarrelsome state delegations which ultimately resolved their differences under clouds of patriotic rhetoric, political bosses who made deals and dispensed patronage, congressmen who delivered speeches for the benefit of the folks back home in Buncombe County, and a politically-active people who wallowed in the incessant hullabaloo and turned up at the polls in extraordinary numbers.

An infinite number of influences, both tangible and intangible, had interacted together in the shaping of this remarkable system of politics, and this book can only hope to introduce the reader to some of the more important of them. Americans owed their representative institutions in no small part to their English origins, and selected strands of English constitutional thought continued to condition American political perceptions until well into the nineteenth century. The age-old assumptions that political order required some sort of hierarchy and that the 'better sort' should rule were also not easily shaken off, even in a political society in which most white men had the vote. A libertarian suspicion of power and a patrician desire to protect government from popular passions were both reflected in the American Constitution, itself a major determinant of American political forms, which had to be fashioned within its comprehensive embrace.

The distinctive configurations of American society and the abundant economic resources of the country inevitably powerfully influenced the evolution of American politics. Even before the Revolution such traditional ruling authorities as a hereditary aristocracy or hierarchical church establishments were non-existent or weak in the New World communities, which were composed virtually entirely of 'commoners'. But if American society was relatively undifferentiated in this sense, it was highly variegated in another, being composed of a host of different national, ethnic, and religious groups. The regional variety of the vast continent meant that the American people were divided also by sectional tensions. After 1776 Americans thus had to fashion a system of politics answerable to the needs of a people who were at once both undifferentiated and diverse. They were also a resourceful people, in more ways than one. As George Washington himself remarked with pardonable simplification in 1788, even 'the lowest class of people' could expect to be happy in America, because of 'the equal distribution of property, the great plenty of unoccupied lands, and the facility of procuring the means of subsistence'.[2] Americans were early a nation of property-owners, and they looked to government to protect that property and to provide the conditions in which individuals could acquire and accumulate it. Actually, an increasing proportion of Americans were propertyless, and some were unfortunate enough to be property themselves, and deprived minorities often suffered acutely in this land of abundance. Nonetheless, the independence that was made possible for many white men by the relatively broad distribution of property, the competitive and contentious spirit which was engendered by the presence of so many different interest groups, the opportunistic temper which was encouraged by the ready availability of land and the expansive economy, together with the liberating potentialities of the Protestant faith, combined to nurture an individualistic or natural rights political philosophy which in Europe would be labelled liberal.

After Independence Americans of all political persuasions were thus committed to creating a government designed to protect individual liberties, but they nonetheless disagreed sharply over the form the republican polity should take. Some long remained unconvinced that liberty was compatible with democracy, at least in its more unrestrained forms, and they tended to look to an energetic government to maintain order. Such attitudes were variously betrayed by the nationalists of the 1780s, the Federalists of the 1790s, and the Whigs of the 1830s. This tradition emphasized the need for an enlightened, capable, and active leadership to sustain the republic. It often appealed to men of a continental or cosmopolitan outlook, particularly to those who identified progress with the growth of commerce and industry, forces which to them held the promise of a powerful, prosperous, and dynamic Union, possessed of the capacity to protect freedom and to reconcile the varied interests of the people. Resisting this was a tradition associated with the Anti-Federalists of the 1780s, the Jeffersonian Republicans of 1800, and the Jacksonian Democrats of the 1830s, which nourished a conviction that too much government – particularly central government – was inimical to republicanism. The men who articulated anxieties of this sort tended to see in governmental consolidation and commercial growth the threats of new forms of aristocracy, and they preferred to rest the security of the republic on the self-governing ability of the people. Their philosophy has often been labelled agrarian, for they seemed to assume that liberty and equality were best attained in a society of sturdy farmers and small producers, and they tended to associate progress with the westward advance of the republic rather than with a dynamic economy. This Jeffersonian-Jacksonian tradition, with its powerful egalitarian thrust, was more successful politically than the Federalist-Whig tradition, which ultimately had to accommodate itself to the democratic realities of the American political world. Conversely, the potent economic forces which were transforming America were equally inescapable, and it fell to the Jacksonians to demonstrate how business enterprise could be accommodated to republican – and egalitarian – principles.

The conflict between these contrasting political persuasions was given a special urgency by the conviction that America's very *raison d'être* was at stake. The first colonists had brought with them the desire for a better life, and the Revolution had rekindled the ambition to fashion the perfect society on American shores. This dream of a political society which would serve as an example and reproach to an imperfect world long retained its potency, so that Americans had to live with the all but intolerable burden of the knowledge of their special destiny. The promise of American greatness triggered both hope and fear, an optimistic pride in the anticipated secular utopia and corrosive doubts about Americans' capacity to achieve it. This divided temperament may have contributed to another characteristic of the American political animal, his tendency to espy subversive designs whenever the republican mission seemed in trouble. Even as they came to accept the fact of party competition and the necessity of compromise and conciliation to the complex American polity, many Americans remained disposed to spot an un-American intent behind every political mask.

In the mid-nineteenth century to be 'un-American' frequently meant to be 'pro-British', a mark of how far American political culture had changed since the days when the colonial elites had sought to emulate English forms. To a degree, the story of how colonial Englishmen were transmogrified into nineteenth-century Americans is the story of how a traditional political order, in which local community ties were strong and in which elites ruled by virtue of their high social status, was turned into the political order of the mass society, in which popular parties sought to forge new supra-local loyalties, enrolling the restless individuals of a numerous people into great political associations of equals. The patrician values, immemorial customs, and deferential habits which had sustained the traditional polity were only slowly eroded, but in the early turbulent decades of the nineteenth century the American system of politics came finally to be organized on the principle that the majority – of white men – could and should rule.

In a book such as this, the author's principal debts are necessarily to the many scholars from whom he has learned. Some measure of my obligation to their publications is indicated in the references, which have been used mainly to give the sources of quotations, and in the select bibliography. I am also grateful to those friends who read particular chapters and offered their advice – Geoffrey Holmes, Michael Mullett, and Alasdair Kean. I am especially indebted to Bob Bliss, whose comments improved the first nine chapters. Donald Ratcliffe and John Ashworth helped me on particular points. Some of the material used in the book was gathered during a year in the United States, which was made possible by an award from the American Council of Learned Societies, by the hospitality of Rutgers University, and by the University of Lancaster's enlightened attitude towards sabbatical leave. Finally, I must thank Sian Lounds for her impeccable typing of the manuscript.

M.J.H.

Part 1

Anglo-American origins

The primary example of political society that American colonists had before them as they searched for ways of governing themselves in the century before 1763 was that of their respected parent. Consciously and unconsciously, willingly and unwillingly, the English settlers of the New World carried a vast amount of political baggage with them, in the form of assumptions, customs, ideas, institutions, practices, convictions. It was widely believed in this Anglo-American world, for example, that a hierarchical social structure, held together by custom and deference, was a prerequisite of political order. In the good political society a 'speaking aristocracy' ruled for the benefit of the whole community with the willing assent of a 'silent democracy'. This holistic conception of politics, with its implicit denial of a role for political parties, was to inform political discourse in England and America until well into the nineteenth century.

The American colonists were also profoundly influenced by English constitutional thought and practice, particularly the more radical Whig and 'Country' varieties, for the idea that the people had a right to consent freely to the laws by which they were governed, and the assumption that an overweening executive represented the chief threat to liberty, suited admirably their own dependent position within the British Empire. This constitutional heritage encouraged Americans to develop their own representative assemblies and conditioned their perceptions of political life, so that they emerged from the colonial period with considerable experience of self-government and a lasting conviction that the price of liberty was eternal vigilance. Liberty was virtually inseparable from property – the possession of which gave independence – in the conventional wisdom of the period, and in both England and America political rights were thus effectively confined to those with a 'stake in society'. But where this provision excluded most Englishmen from the political nation, it included most colonial men, who could thus generally pursue their demands and express their grievances within their more-or-less responsive political systems. This and other conditions peculiar to the New World societies tended to militate against hierarchical and deferential values and to promote a more individualistic ethic, but not sufficiently to prevent the emergence of fairly stable colonial elites, who aspired to lead their societies after much the same fashion as England's gentlemen. These elites, however, commanded fewer instruments of control than did England's rulers, and the interaction of Whiggish forms with the New World environment frequently resulted in their division into rival factions, so that at least some Americans were able to enter nationhood skilled in the arts of competitive politics.

Chapter 1

The politics of Old England

'In him we justly admire the old country gentleman, faithful to his King without servility, attached to the people without democracy.'[1] These words written about a respected Cornish member of Parliament capture something of the flavour of the political world of mid-eighteenth-century England. It was a hierarchical world in which each man had his place, in which each was expected to offer loyalty both to those above him and to those below him. The much-vaunted political order of eighteenth-century England was maintained not so much by coercion from above – though coercion was employed on occasion – as by a common acceptance of the reciprocal obligations between men occupying different stations. Patronage and deference, not military might or party organization, supplied the cement of English politics in the age of Walpole and Newcastle. Such forces sufficed to provide a measure of coherence to a political system in which active participation was confined to a few.

English society in 1750 can be thought of as a pyramid. At the top was the king, a little uncomfortable in his role by virtue of his German origins. More authentically English were the aristocracy and the gentry, ranging from the great lords, with their strings of inherited titles and large landed estates, to the relatively humble – though sometimes extremely wealthy – baronets and knights, esquires and gentlemen. The vast third estate of commoners was composed of two fairly distinct social orders. First there were the graduated ranks of the 'middle sort', freeholders and farmers, merchants and manufacturers, clerks and clergy. And at the base of the pyramid were the 'lower orders', themselves subtly differentiated into a multiplicity of descending grades, from artisans, soldiers and sailors to labourers, paupers and vagrants. To men of all ranks this great human chain of being was but the natural order of things. No less an authority than divine providence had 'distributed men into different ranks' and had placed the poor 'under the superintendency and patronage of the rich'.[2]

The belief that social distinctions were providential or accidental in origin served to camouflage the fact that status was largely determined by wealth. More than anything else it was landed property which conferred dignity, and the commoner who acquired a large enough estate could usually expect a title. It was thus possible for a family to rise or fall in rank. The great magnates naturally commanded the most respect, but property of any size conferred some prestige, whether it consisted of the freehold of the yeoman farmer, the commercial wealth of the merchant, or the humble cottage of the hard-working labourer. Property ensured independence, which is to say individual liberty, or so it was held, although it did not free a man from the obligation to respect his betters. The most despised element in the population were those without property, the paupers and vagrants who were wholly dependent on others, and they were often treated as virtual outcasts of society, denied social position and political rights.

If wealth largely determined status, the different ranks in society were held together by patronage and deference. A great political figure might procure governmental, clerical or military offices for his relatives, friends and supporters, and consider it his duty to do so. The village squire might be gratified to assume responsibility for the education of the talented son of a local farmer, a merchant might oblige his family by giving an apprenticeship to a nephew, and a landlord might waive the rent of tenants who had fallen on hard times. Although certain groups like the yeomanry might look to one another for support, the ties in this society were probably more often vertical than horizontal. A man turned naturally for aid and protection not to others of his own class, as tends to be the case in industrial society, but to some superior who was personally known to him, to the local squire, to an important relative, to a friendly senior in his profession. In this sense, England was a land of village communities, most people's loyalties and attachments being essentially local and familial in character. Patronage was regarded as an obligation on those with rank and position within these (ideally harmonious) communities – it was their duty to look after their relatives, friends, neighbours and subordinates, and many a harassed patron found the duty a wearisome one. In return, those who were so favoured accorded the patron their respect, supported his political ambitions, or deferred where appropriate to his wishes. In this sort of society power inevitably rested largely with those at the top, but they had to use it carefully, for they too had to respect the rank of their subordinates. Many men considered it an honour to be given a post by a distinguished patron, and they were proud to give him their loyalty, but they might well respond with an indignant refusal to any demand for absolute obedience. The relationship between patron and client was most frequently described as one of 'friendship', a euphemistic description though one which was not entirely without merit.

Deference characterized politics at every level. It was incarnate in the low bows that the elder Pitt was famous for giving the king (it was said that his nose could be seen through the back of his legs), and was expressed in the support that the independent members in Parliament usually gave to the necessary business of the king's government, and in the willingness of ordinary electors to support the gentry at the polls. The politics of deference worked to the particular advantage of the landed interests, but it meant that their position rested more on persuasion than on coercion. Few questioned the right of their social superiors to exercise political authority. Yet deference did not mean subservience. Candidates were expected to show a proper regard for their constituents, to protect their interests, to cultivate the support of their leading men and to 'treat' the voters at election times. Sometimes the voters did rebel when they felt they were being taken too much for granted and returned a candidate of their own, as the townsmen of Lewes did in 1768 in opposition to the wishes of their patron, the Duke of Newcastle, who was outraged at their 'base and ungrateful behaviour.'[3] Not all Englishmen respected their betters, and obedience might also be induced by coercive techniques, such as by the enactment and sometimes ruthless enforcement of laws in defence of property.

Ties of patronage and deference, then, together with some use of repressive legislation and legal procedures, promoted the hegemony of the landed aristocracy and gentry and made possible a highly stable political order. What made the hold of the great magnates even more secure was a system of political thought which linked political rights to property, accorded the hereditary aristocracy and landed gentry an indispensable role in the polity, and celebrated order and the *status quo*. By the mid-eighteenth century the English constitution, like the structure of English society, seemed to have been accorded a divine sanction.

Whatever God really thought of the English constitution, eighteenth-century mortals, English and foreign, inordinately admired this smoothly-functioning machinery. Montesquieu called it 'this beautiful system', George III echoed that it was 'the most beautiful combination ever framed', while an American editor described England's government as 'the most compleat and regular, that has ever been contrived by the Wisdom of Man'.[4] The unique accomplishment of the English, it was held, had been in devising a monarchical system of politics which preserved freedom and restrained power without sacrificing order. This view of the political process assumed that men were naturally frail and unreliable creatures who needed to be protected from one another. Since men were often found to be 'malicious, insolent, and easily provoked', their lives and their property could only be protected by the rule of law and by a political structure which imposed checks on the powerful.[5] Somehow the English, against all the odds, had constructed such a system.

The beauty of the English system was held to reside in its mixed nature, in the ingenious balance achieved between the great interests of the realm. Political theorists from Aristotle through Charles I to Sir William Blackstone had identified three basic forms of government by which men were ruled: monarchy or rule by a single person, aristocracy or rule by a few, and democracy or rule by the many. Each was said to

have its own peculiar virtues and vices. Monarchy provided unity and
order but was apt to degenerate into tyranny, aristocracy provided
wisdom and ability but was apt to degenerate into a factious and selfish
oligarchy, and democracy brought liberty and virtue but was apt to
degenerate into anarchy and licentiousness. The genius of the English,
as Charles I had pointed out to Parliament, had lain in devising a
unique system which combined 'the conveniences of all three, without
the inconveniences of any one'.[6] The English had apparently succeeded where other countries had failed because of the fortunate
structure of their society: the great social divisions in England
corresponded almost perfectly to the three idealized types of
government. Men of the eighteenth-century thought of English
political society as composed not of classes in the modern sense but of
three great estates, the crown, the nobility, and the common people.
(The common people in this perspective included the varied ranks of
the 'middling sort' and largely excluded the propertyless.) Each of
these estates entered into the government of the realm, the crown in
the person of the king, the nobility through the House of Lords, and
the common people less directly via their representatives in the House
of Commons.

England, then, could claim to have the best of all possible worlds.
Laws could only be made with the consent of each estate in Parliament.
Unity and vigour in the government were provided by the king as head
of the executive, but he was prevented from becoming a tyrant by the
watchdogs of the other estates; the House of Commons ensured the
survival of the liberty of the people, but liberty could not become mob
rule because of the restraints of the Lords and the crown; and the
Lords acted as a balance between the king and the Commons,
mediating any confrontations between those embodiments of power
and liberty and providing the benefits of their wisdom and experience.
This system of government, then, preserved both liberty and order by
ensuring that no single interest acquired power over any other interest.
Yet while they checked one another, the monarchical, aristocratic, and
democratic elements each had something valuable to contribute. 'Like
three distinct powers in mechanics, they jointly impel the machine of
government in a direction different from what either, acting by itself,
would have done   argued Blackstone in 1765, 'but at the same time in
a direction partaking of each, and formed out of all; a direction which
constitutes the true line of the liberty and happiness of the community.'[7] It was the ingenious equilibrium in the English constitution which
inspired the reverence for it, as the rather different but equally vital
balancing mechanisms later enshrined in the American Constitution
were also to be venerated. The object of constitutions, in English and
American eyes, was to divide and contain power.

The alluring simplicity of the theory of the English constitution
served to disguise its many weaknesses. One perennial difficulty lay in
determining the right balance between the different interests. Since

executive authority rested with the crown alone while legislative authority rested primarily with the nobility and the political representatives of the people, any conflict between the estates was likely to take the form of a tug-of-war between the king and Parliament. In imposing certain restraints on royal authority, in providing for the independence of Parliament, in securing for that body a firm hold over finance, and in increasing the king's ministers' answerability to it, the English Whigs (and even some Tories) sought to ensure the supremacy of the legislative branch in the country's system of government.

The Whigs held that legislative power lay ultimately in the people. The liberty of Englishmen was guaranteed because they made their own laws via their representatives in Parliament. According to the most advanced Whig theory (though it was far from being universally subscribed to), the people themselves had brought government into existence by making a compact – or social contract – with one another and with the king in order to secure protection both for their persons and their property. The liberty that was nourished by England's mixed constitution lay in the protection of life and property from arbitrary attack. This equation of liberty with the protection of property was central to Whig thought and carried important implications for the civil polity. The 'people' that the House of Commons represented were those with a 'stake in society', those with some property of their own. The basic English suffrage law was that of 1430, which confined the right to vote for county members to 40-shilling freeholders, a limitation which was justified on the grounds that the propertyless were politically unreliable and that in any case the taxes that Parliament levied were normally on land. Tenants and workmen could be made to vote as their landlords and employers instructed them, but a freeholder could cast his vote fearlessly. Only the possession of property, especially landed property, was held to ensure a man's political independence. Political participation was thus effectively confined to the privileged few, a feature which made English politics profoundly different from the emerging political systems in the American colonies.

The judiciously mixed constitution, the supremacy of the legislative branch, and the restriction of the political nation to the propertied classes did not of themselves produce stable government. While the much-admired stability of English politics in the eighteenth century was often attributed to the nation's ingenious constitutional arrangements, a number of other conditions also operated in favour of harmony. One was the weakening of the great divisive issues of the seventeenth century. The disruptive constitutional and religious questions had both been resolved by the settlements of the period 1688–1720, which had set clear limits on royal authority, had safeguarded the position of the Church of England and had extended toleration of worship to Protestant dissenters. The consensus achieved in Britain's civil and religious constitution was further protected by the relatively homogeneous nature of the social bases of her political institutions. Parliament had emerged as the primary organ of government, and both Houses in effect represented the landed interest, although a number of members in the Commons from great commercial centres like London, Liverpool, and Bristol could speak for trade. While landowners ranged from the powerful aristocrats with their great estates to small yeomen farmers working their own freehold, all had a common interest in landed property. As participants in a predominantly agrarian economy, they did not expect very much from the central government, whose principal duties were protecting the realm, maintaining law and order, and promoting commerce. Later in the century, when the industrial revolution was picking up speed, new demands were to be made on government by new interest groups, but the relatively undiversified economy of preindustrial England served to minimize political strife.

Parliament in the mid-eighteenth century, then, was not deeply divided by ideological issues or by fiercely-competing economic interest groups. Men did not normally enter it to promote a programme, a policy or a cause. Being a member of Parliament was not normally a career in itself as it is today, but more often a social obligation or a stepping-stone to higher things. The sons of peers often sat in the Commons as a mark of the prominence of their families and to prepare themselves for the Lords. Some men entered Parliament in search of social advancement or to further their careers in the army, the navy or the law. The financially insecure sometimes secured parliamentary seats and offered their services to the government in the hope of being rewarded with sinecures, pensions or remunerative offices in the gift of the crown. Some men, of course, went to the Commons in pursuit of political power, while others gracefully accepted seats because they were the leading men of their county, respected landowners who were acting more out of a sense of *noblesse oblige* than of personal gain. In the absence of polarizing issues and at a time when the activities of government were very limited, most members of Parliament – and certainly the bulk of the backbench 'independents' – were usually more interested in their own parochial concerns than in the issues of state.

Nonetheless government, however limited, had to function, and some kind of coherence had to be imposed on the political system. Order of a kind was provided in the eighteenth century by a number of extra-constitutional developments. The Glorious Revolution had made Parliament the focus of the English political system, but the king was still the head of the government, a situation which tended to enhance the political authority of the men who formed the link between the two, the ministers. The king retained the right to choose his own ministers, but to be politically effective they needed also to be acceptable to Parliament, of which they were members. The difficulties of the first two Georges in comprehending the English system of politics also tended to shift power away from the crown itself and towards the ministry. A 'cabinet council' of the leading ministers had taken shape late in the previous century, but even this became too large for efficient government and an 'inner' cabinet slowly emerged. Although its meetings were intermittent, this in time began to consider business not referred to it by the king after he had ceased to attend it. The cabinet, consisting of the great offices of state, thus gradually if imperfectly established itself as a central organ of government, still lacking cohesion and authority but generally trying to coordinate business and to proffer advice to the crown. At the head of the cabinet the king was replaced by the prime minister, another novelty unknown to the formal constitution. Sir Robert Walpole is usually the first to be credited with the title of prime minister, in recognition of the dominance he achieved between 1721 and 1742. Enjoying the support both of the king and of the greater part of the House of Commons, Walpole cemented his authority by his skilful use of his office of First Lord of the Treasury, which put much crown patronage in his hands. The emergence of the prime minister, like that of the cabinet, helped to bring a degree of unity to the eighteenth-century administration, though both processes were far from complete.

The ministers who were chosen by the king needed to retain the confidence of Parliament to survive, and to secure this they employed the varied techniques of patronage and persuasion. The politics of deference played as vital a role in the Palace of Westminster as they did at constituency level. One ingredient in the process of building a parliamentary following was the crown 'influence' which ministers had at their disposal. Some Commons seats were under the direct control of the ministry, for their tiny electorates contained several officeholders whose jobs depended on the government, while other small electorates were bought with money. The support of a larger number of M.P.s was cemented by the judicious distribution of crown patronage, in the form of offices, pensions or contracts for them or for their relatives or friends. Perhaps some 150 or so members of Parliament – out of a total of 558 – were secured to the ministry by the use of crown influence in the mid-eighteenth-century, although many of these men were supporters of the government anyway and places were given to them in recognition of services rendered rather than as bribes.[8] The ministers could usually add their own personal followings to the crown placemen. A wealthy peer might own a number of 'rotten boroughs' in the Commons and be connected with other members of Parliament by ties of friendship and family. Ministries in effect were often coalitions of such groups or 'connections', although their personal 'influence' could never match that of the crown. But even the king and the 'connections' together could not normally command a majority in the House of Commons, and the ministry needed a yet further source of support. This was provided by the independent country gentlemen. A group of perhaps 150 men representing the county and larger borough constituencies, the country gentlemen were large landowners who had no need of crown patronage or aristocratic patrons. They were proud of their independence, but the deferential society had left its mark on them too, for just as they expected the loyalty of the freeholders who had elected them, so they too conceived it to be their duty as loyal Englishmen to support the king's government whenever they could. When a ministry lost the confidence of the country gentlemen, as Lord North's did in the 1780s, its days were numbered.

The success of an eighteenth century administration, then, rested largely on its powers of persuasion. Once it had the confidence of the king, it had to win and maintain the support of a majority in Parliament, particularly in the House of Commons, by the parliamentary oratory of some of its leading members, by the use of 'influence', and by demonstrating to the large number of independent members that it was governing competently. By contrast, in the contemporary American colonies, where government patronage was limited and independent country gentlemen rare, administrations often failed to secure majorities in the local legislatures. In fact, although English politics were highly stable in the sense that government was dominated for much of the century by men from similar backgrounds and with similar views, individual ministers themselves were rather insecure. The ministries of Walpole and Henry Pelham were exceptional in their longevity, and below the level of prime minister even their composition changed from time to time. A government could never predict with much accuracy the division of the House of Commons on a particular issue, and if it found its majority falling some of its ministers might have to be replaced. Even skilful patronage managers like Newcastle suffered from a constant sense of insecurity and were ever espying or imagining plots to unseat them. Unlike their modern successors, eighteenth-century prime ministers were not the leaders of parties which could assure them of safe majorities in the Commons. The Hanoverian succession and the gradual fading of the old issues had rendered less vital – though not meaningless – the old distinctions between Whig and Tory. There were fairly solid groupings, but most men in politics called themselves Whigs and competed between themselves (rather than against Tories) for the privilege of holding office. Perhaps a more relevant distinction was that between Court and Country, but even that did not impose much coherence on parliamentary behaviour. The placemen and other M.P.s who regularly supported the king were often called the 'Court party', while the independent members and those who for whatever reason regularly found themselves in opposition were dubbed the 'Country party', but they were not parties in any modern sense. The title Court or Country described a man's working relationship to the administration – whether he was tied to it or was aloof from it – and to a lesser extent his political attitudes and ideas. In neither case did it imply membership of an organized political group. Ministers were not placed in power by a dominant party and they could not command an automatic majority in Parliament. They were selected by the king and they survived by the arts of management and persuasion and on sufferance of the House of Commons.

To most contemporaries it was but right that government should be dependent on the goodwill of Parliament rather than on the support of a party. In constitutional theory, governments took their authority from the king, and it was the duty of the legislature to keep a watchful eye on the royal prerogative. Further, the conventional wisdom of the period perceived little virtue in party anyway. With the political nation so narrow, it was possible to see the state as an organic whole, a corporate structure with but a single interest, the common good. It was the duty of statesmen to identify the public good by reasonable discussion among themselves and then to promote it, rising above the individual and particularist interests which assailed them on all sides. In such a political culture, it was readily assumed that the affairs of government fell on the 'natural leaders' of society, that is those possessing the land (and hence the independence), the education, and the experience necessary for playing a statesmanlike part in public life. There was no room for party in this conception of the ideal political order. Parties were said to undermine the consensus, to produce turmoil and anarchy, and to replace the good of the whole with the narrow interests of a faction. In theory at least, the king was meant to recruit his ministry from the best and wisest men in the realm, who were meant to promote the common weal with the disinterested support of independent-minded members of Parliament. Eighteenth-century politics, of course, were never like this, and a few writers were beginning to acknowledge the value of limited party conflict between members of the elite, but the theory gave some sanction to the patrician political style of the Whig grandees, who expected but could not command the support of the House of Commons.[9]

The consensual ideal also informed the thinking of many of the more severe Country critics of eighteenth-century administrations. If the theory left no room for party it also left no room for patronage. To a number of men of widely differing persuasions the British constitution was patently failing to operate as it should. Radical Whigs, carrying forward the libertarian tradition of the seventeenth century, complained that the independence of Parliament was being undermined by the influence of the crown. Also in opposition were the ex-Tories, whose most eloquent spokesman was Henry St. John, Viscount Bolingbroke, and they harped on the same theme, concentrating their fire on corrupt ministers. The basic charge of both groups was that the celebrated equilibrium of England's mixed constitution had been upset. The balance between the three estates, the monarchy, the aristocracy, and the Commons, had been shifted in favour of the monarchy, which had enlarged its powers and was encroaching on the other estates. Or, put another way, the primacy and independence of the legislature were being threatened by the pretensions and machinations of an overweening executive. To the Country critics the English polity was suffering from two kinds of decay or corruption, the technical corruption implicit in the upsetting of the constitutional balance and the moral corruption implicit in the erosion of the virtue of members of Parliament and the people at large. Both forms of decay represented a threat to English liberty, which could not survive the loss of the right balance between the estates or of the virtue of the people. This conviction that a people could be robbed of their freedom by various forms of degeneration or subversion was to cross the Atlantic and to condition the political perceptions of several generations of American leaders.

The most influential of the radical Whig writers, at least for their impact on the American colonies, were John Trenchard and Thomas Gordon, the authors of a series of newspaper articles of the early 1720s which were published as a book entitled *Cato's Letters*. Like others they rejoiced in England's ingenious constitution. 'No nation in the world enjoys the *liberty* which *England* enjoys', wrote 'Cato' proudly, attributing this fortunate state of affairs to the checks and balances in the mixed system of government.[10] But the balance was in constant peril, particularly from the self-interested designs of the king's ministers. By corrupting the other branches of government they could gain uncontrolled power, which is to say establish a tyranny, and there were signs that they were doing just that. The representatives of the people in Parliament were being bought by crown offices, pensions, and other forms of patronage, while the people themselves were being corrupted by the distribution of money and favours at elections and by the depraved example of their superiors. Having thus seduced and distracted those who were meant to watch over them, the ministers added to their power by introducing schemes to enrich themselves and impoverish the people, such as a foreign war, high taxes and a national debt, and, when their usurpations finally provoked unrest, a standing army to complete their control. Most of these themes had been made familiar by the seventeenth-century libertarians, but Trenchard and Gordon wove them together into a compelling indictment of Walpolean government. A sinister and diabolical conspiracy, located in the Court, was about to deprive Englishmen of their ancient liberties and impose on them a military despotism. This belief remained alive throughout the century among the Country radicals, whose endless variations on the theme were eventually to be recast by the English and American critics of George III.[11] On the eve of the American Revolution, for example, and in the wake of the Wilkesite agitation, James Burgh's *Political Disquisitions* insisted that the conspiracy had already succeeded and that liberty was lost.

Another vehement opponent of ministerial government was Lord

Bolingbroke, the one-time Jacobite whose merciless attacks on Walpole appeared regularly in *The Craftsman*. Crown influence in the Commons, he argued, was more effective than an army in destroying British liberty. New taxes, increased revenues, and the civil list had greatly enlarged the financial resources of the ministers and hence the opportunity for corruption. The king was almost as much a victim of this process as Parliament, according to Bolingbroke, who located the source of the evil in 'prime' ministry or 'Robinocracy', both terms of abuse and the latter a reference to Sir Robert Walpole. The Robinarch contrived to keep the three estates, monarchy, aristocracy, and commoners, dependent on him. Nominally a minister, he was 'in reality . . . a *sovereign*, as despotic, arbitrary a sovereign as this part of the world affords . . . '.[12] He kept the favour of the king by flattery and by misrepresenting the real concerns of the people, and he bound Parliament to him by the distribution of honours, favours, promises, and bribes. Ministerial patronage itself was an old phenomenon, but what now made it particularly dangerous in Bolingbroke's eyes was the new system of finance which had grown up since the Revolution. Bolingbroke, like some other Country figures, nourished a sentimental attachment to the old social order of the landed gentry, an order which was being eroded by the rise of commerce (to which he gave a guarded welcome) and by the emergence of a class of monied men (to which he did not). The monied interest and the ministry were aiding and abetting one another at the expense of the landed interest, or so he suspected. Ministers were borrowing in anticipation of revenue and then imposing higher taxes, which drained money away from the landed classes while creating a new corps of subservient officials and larger public funds with which to advance the interests of a corrupt ministry and its allies in the banks and counting-houses. To Bolingbroke, English liberty was being threatened not merely by the use of the royal influence in the Houses of Parliament, but also by the new financial structure which put powerful weapons in the hands of wicked ministers, who were using them to destroy the independence of the yeomen and landed gentry of England.[13]

Bolingbroke's answer was for a Patriot King to liberate his people from the ministerial leeches who were draining the life out of them. The king should dismiss the corrupt ministers, appoint wise and virtuous men in their place and inaugurate a harmonious reign in which government would be raised above party and faction. Bolingbroke thus reasserted the ideal of a cohesive and party-free political order, in which public-spirited statesmen led by a Patriot King and supported by an independent Commons governed in the interests of all. The functions of such a government would be limited, and in this respect Bolingbroke contributed towards that Anglo-American political tradition which was hostile to powerful and positive government. Bolingbroke did not succeed in unseating Walpole, but his writings and those of similar opposition theorists influenced later generations of

Englishmen and (more importantly) Americans, who continued to espy threats to liberty in ministerial patronage and a commercial money power and who continued to cherish the holistic yet elitist vision of a consensual political world.[14]

Despite their mutual distaste, the ministries of the mid-eighteenth century and their critics shared certain assumptions. Both, for example, saw themselves as upholders of the balanced constitution of 1688. The complaint of the opposition spokesmen was not that there were fundamental flaws in the constitution but that the ministers were perverting it. Both thought of the political nation as being confined to men of property and standing, and neither advocated a redistribution of wealth, although Bolingbroke was unhappy about the rise of commerce. Both assumed that leadership in politics would be provided by a social elite, and both assumed that the people would accept the leadership of men who had demonstrated their capacity for government. As Ian Christie has written of the radicals of the late eighteenth century, they were 'no democrats'; rather, their ideal was 'a broad, propertied oligarchy, in which the lower orders should clearly know and accept their place . . . '.[15] Both the ministries and their critics were talking about a political world which was held together by deference, by the loyalty given by subordinates to their superiors in the great social chain of being, whether that loyalty was generated by patronage or by patriotism.

In the last resort, both perceptions of the eighteenth-century political order were aristocratic, for both served the interests of those at the top of the social pyramid. In the endless charges and counter-charges about the respective powers of the king and the Commons little was said about the aristocracy, the real holders of power. Aristocratic patrons abetted the attacks on the crown, for they did not want an over-powerful monarchy which might curb their privileges, as they solemnly seconded the periodic royal complaints about the pretensions of the Commons, for they feared democracy even more than royal tyranny. A monarchy which was limited in power and a common people which accepted their subordinate role enabled the aristocracy to rule through the arts of patronage and persuasion. Whatever the radicals had said about the constitution being undermined by the growth in the power of the crown, it was really the aristocracy which had invaded both the other estates. The influence of the crown had been diminished by the Glorious Revolution, but many of the king's ministers, generals, and admirals were still supplied by the aristocracy, and the early Georges, as Hanoverians, were obliged to rely for advice on political matters on their English courtiers. Walpole was the only commoner in his full cabinet for over ten years of his administration. The aristocracy had made even greater inroads into the third estate, owning several Commons' seats outright and supplying candidates for others. In the second half of the eighteenth century about a fifth of M.P.s were the sons of peers or were themselves Irish peers who did not qualify for seats in the Lords.[16] The aristocracy in large part had tamed both the king and the Commons. The politics of deference of eighteenth-century England, then, underpinned the hegemony of the landed aristocracy. England was ruled by 'the rich and well-born', in the words of one American revolutionary who never lost his admiration for the old country's system of government. The combination of property, patronage, deference and lordly coercion served to make possible a political order which was noted for its stability. In large part this stability rested in the narrow basis of the political nation, for such features as the limited franchise and pocket boroughs virtually insulated the government from the wider society. But stability did not mean stasis. The dramatic growth of industry and of cities in the second half of the century, the wars with America and France, and the emergence of pressure groups outside Parliament ultimately combined to put impossible strains on the old system. Royal and aristocratic patronage were to be progressively whittled away in the late eighteenth and early nineteenth centuries, making ministries more dependent on public opinion and less on the king's favour for support. In this increasingly complex economic and political world a degree of unity was provided by the strengthening of the institutions of prime minister and cabinet. As the parochial preoccupations of the eighteenth century gave way to new and divisive national issues, and as the functions of government increased, so political authority came to be increasingly exercised by men at the nation's capital, by experienced parliamentarians, whether nobles or commoners. As the House of Commons became more answerable to the electorate in the nineteenth century these political leaders had to fashion new instruments of management, and ultimately political parties came to replace patronage and deference as the primary means of ordering politics.

But on the eve of the American Revolution all this was still far in the future. To most people the aristocratic and deferential world of eighteenth-century England still seemed fairly secure. Yet already there were occasional intimations of mortality, as when cries of 'Wilkes and Liberty' ruffled the patrician calm of the House of Commons. The common people of Middlesex, it seemed, wanted to be represented in the House of Commons by a candidate of their own choice instead of one chosen by the king's ministers. 'I wish we do not soon see quarrels of a greater complexion than squabbles for places and profit', wrote a troubled Horace Walpole as he peered into the uncertain future.[17]

Chapter 2

Politics in colonial America

The impressive example of political stability and gentlemanly rule set by England in the mid-eighteenth century was only imperfectly imitated in her possessions overseas. In the thriving colonies on the North American continent the loyal subjects of the king had indeed introduced many of the political ideas, institutions, and customs that had served the mother country so well, but often with less than orderly consequences. One leading scholar has described colonial politics as 'a constant broil of petty factions struggling almost formlessly . . . for the benefits of public authority',[1] a description which exaggerates the shapelessness of political life in the colonies but draws attention to its disputatious nature. Ironically, it was the transplanting of English constitutional forms into the American wilderness which was in part responsible for the emergence of this disconcerting political turbulence. As in England, political influence still tended to rest with local notables and gentlemen of standing, but the factional nature of colonial politics rendered their position less secure. And in the few colonies where factional alignments reached back into the electorate and produced serious confrontations at the polls, they served to erode traditional habits of deference and pointed the way to the party competition of the future.

The assumptions about political society that the colonists brought with them were for the most part anything but novel. Even as they were on the high seas the first settlers of Massachusetts Bay had been told by their leader John Winthrop that 'God Almightie in his most holy and wise providence hath soe disposed of the Condicione of mankinde, as in all times some must be rich some poore, some highe and emminent in power and dignitie; others mean and in subieccion.'[2] Whatever the Puritan mission was to be, it was no part of its design to repudiate the pyramidical order long sanctioned by tradition, and ministers and political leaders in all the colonies continued to preach acceptance of one's place in the world and obedience to one's superiors. But the colonists were introducing their traditional ideas and customs into a new and potentially transforming environment. The social and political systems that emerged in the colonies were hybrid creations, the result of complex interactions between the Old and New Worlds. One set of influences conspired to pull colonists away from traditional patterns of thought and behaviour. Thus the absence of an aristocratic estate and the weakness of other feudal institutions, the highly variegated nature of the population, the vitality of colonial religious life, the abundance and ready availability of land and the expansive nature of the colonial economy all tended to militate against the perpetuation of hierarchical forms. On the other hand, the survival of traditional habits of thought, the creation of well-integrated local communities, the increasing stratification of society and the consequent emergence of indigenous elites, the ardent emulation of English governmental bodies and the importation of Whig ideals all served to pull the inchoate colonial polities towards the English model. Indeed, to a surprising degree the 'good old cause' prospered in the American environment, in certain respects more vigorously than in England.

Patriotic Englishmen though many of them were, the colonists themselves almost unwittingly created a number of novel features in their embryonic communities. For one thing, the men and women who settled in America were not a true cross-section of English society. For another, the geography and geology of North America made their own impressions on economic development and political structure. Both because of the unrepresentative nature of the settlers and because of the peculiarities of the American wilderness and its resources, the colonial societies were bound to develop distinctive characteristics of their own.

The most conspicuous element missing from colonial society was, of course, a hereditary aristocracy. Neither the British royalty nor the nobility sought to establish themselves in person in the American colonies, and absent too were bishops, manor courts, licensed monopolies and – in general – widespread tenancy. As one English official later noted, such conditions tended to impair whatever feelings 'of subordination that property, ancestry or dignity of status . . . naturally excited' among Englishmen at home.[3] In terms of the idealized English social order, only commoners migrated to the new land, and one of the most compelling problems that the colonial experience was to bequeath to later generations of Americans was how to provide for orderly government in such an undifferentiated society. But if Americans were not separated by the traditional social orders, they were divided in other ways. Many of them, after all, had not even come from England. The king's other subjects, Scotsmen, Welshmen, Scotch-Irishmen, and Celtic Irishmen had left their homes in disproportionate numbers, while various European groups, most notably Germans, Dutchmen, French Huguenots, and Swedes, also sought their fortunes in the New World, giving to American culture a diversity that it would always retain. The New England colonies, ever wary of strangers, remained the most homogeneous in ethnic composition, while New York and Pennsylvania became the most diverse. The southern colonies left an indelible stamp on American society by importing large numbers of black slaves to work their plantations, although no colony was innocent of slavery. America's only hereditary class rested at the bottom of the social structure and not at the top, and was to prove as difficult to remove as any aristocracy.

The American colonies, then, or at least the more heterogeneous of them, had to develop political systems which would enable this array of peoples to live with one another, a task made no easier by the religious animosities that often existed between them. The Puritans had carried Congregationalism to New England, Anglicanism remained the approved religion in the South and in New York, the Scotch-Irish immigrants spread the Presbyterian faith through the middle colonies and the frontier areas of the South, while the Germans contributed a confusing variety of Protestant sects. English and Welsh Quakers established themselves in Pennsylvania and New Jersey, and the tolerant middle colonies proved similarly alluring to the English Baptists, although they were also to be found in Virginia and indeed throughout the eastern seaboard. The degree of religious diversity should not be exaggerated, since almost all the denominations were Protestant, and, indeed, over nine-tenths of the American churches belonged to the 'left wing' of the Protestant faith, or to the Puritan-Calvinist-Reformed tradition. The American colonies were settled by the dissenting sects spawned by the British and European Reformations, but these sects also vigorously dissented from one another as well as from the Old-World establishments. Ethno-religious conflict, which has always been a feature of American political history, thus made an early appearance in the colonies, as in Pennsylvania where the Quakers and the Scotch-Irish Presbyterians tended to occupy opposing political camps. If religious diversity did not necessarily serve the cause of tolerance, it at least made toleration a practical necessity in the middle colonies. The dissenting sects were also little inclined to afford much respect to governing authorities not of their own faith.

There was also perhaps an important psychic difference between the Old and the New Worlds. Among some colonists at least there was a sense that they were creating something better, a quest for perfection which generated hope and fear. The mission of the early Puritans had been to establish a Bible Commonwealth which would act as a beacon to the rest of mankind. Similarly idealistic but rather more secular were the sentiments with which the trustees blessed the Quaker experiment in West New Jersey: 'Thus we lay a foundation for after ages to understand their liberty as men and Christians, that they may not be brought in bondage, but by their own consent; for we put the power in the people.'[4] Neither the Puritan nor the Quaker communities fulfilled the ideals of their founders, but the sense of mission never quite died out, later generations of Americans inheriting the belief that the New World was destined to render some signal service for mankind. However this was interpreted, it tended to make Americans both an optimistic and an anxious people, for the very act of nursing a vision of a unique and glorious mission evoked a dread lest it be denied. As John Winthrop had told the first Puritans, if they failed in their purpose 'we shall be made a story and byword through the world'.[5] This idea that a special destiny awaited Americans, together with the resultant anxiety, were to become lasting features of American political culture. This commitment to the future also served to weaken Americans' respect for the prescriptions of the past.

If the character of colonial immigration itself in some measure militated against the re-creation of traditional political orders in the colonies, the American environment was also to help shape the new societies in distinctive ways. The abundance of land and other natural resources in particular powerfully influenced American development. In England's 'tight little isle' land was concentrated in a relatively few hands, and with it wealth and social status, but in the colonies it was relatively easy to acquire, so that the majority of white men held some kind of stake in society. 'It was the best country in the world for people of small fortunes', wrote one often-quoted traveller.[6] The possession of land conferred on the owner a high degree of independence and an interest in the preservation of property. The preconditions for the individualistic ethic which was to characterize American political life in the nineteenth century thus existed long before Independence, and the colonial experience ensured too that the protection of private property would remain a primary objective of any system of government in America. The phenomenal expansion in the colonial economies in the course of the eighteenth century also encouraged Americans to believe that they too had a right to the active pursuit of wealth. The colonial societies were never static, and although economic opportunities varied greatly according to time and place, it was never easy for any social elite to preserve a monopoly of economic and political power. Old wealth was often threatened by new, as in Rhode Island in the mid-eighteenth century, where the supremacy of the farmers and merchants of Newport was challenged by the rise of Providence, which provided a rival group of merchants with interests of their own, and the politics of the province became largely dominated by a power struggle between the two. The relatively broad distribution of property in the colonies, together with rapid geographical and commercial expansion and the opportunities and entrepreneurial spirit it brought, thus tended to weaken the authority of the traditional holders of power.

The individualistic dynamic inherent in Protestantism also encouraged a disrespectful spirit among some Americans. One event which served to undermine respect for tradition was the Great Awakening. This remarkable revitalization of piety, accomplished by a series of explosive revivals, began in New Jersey in the 1720s, spread to the other middle colonies and New England in the 1730s and 1740s, and eventually to the South, where the Baptists continued to ignite revivals through the 1760s. For the first time men and women throughout the colonies shared a common experience, one which perhaps served to foster an awareness that they were all Americans. What the Awakening did was to touch many ordinary people. To the evangelists men and women could not be saved from everlasting perdition simply by subscribing to a creed and observing church ritual; a profound religious experience was necessary – the individual had to be converted by the direct action of the Holy Spirit. This emphasis on individual responsibility and on the direct relationship between the individual and God served to give the movement an essentially democratic thrust, despite its general adherence to the doctrine of predestination. People found that a trained ministry was not essential to bring about such a religious experience, and itinerant lay preachers appeared. When the orthodox clergy attempted to resist these innovations, the 'New Lights' and others galvanized by the Awakening rebelled against them. The very dynamic of the revival encouraged ordinary men to criticize established authority and was eventually to help make possible the break with England. Habits of deference were beginning to break down, and to survive in politics the leading men found it increasingly expedient to comply with popular wishes. In the words of one Connecticut preacher, there was now 'a levelling and seditious Spirit prevailing, and an Impatience of all Rule and Restraint'.[7]

The peculiar characteristics of the men and women who settled America and of the environments in which they found themselves thus tended to conspire against the indefinite survival of custom and deference. These restless peoples had left behind them the lords spiritual and temporal who had been their traditional political guides, but had brought with them their own distinct and diverse national, ethnic, and religious characteristics. In this sense, the divisions in the more variegated colonial societies might be described as vertical rather than horizontal, people being separated more by nationality and sect than by rank. Many settlers also brought with them a sense that the New World communities were not wholly bound by the past, that some special drama was to unfold on the American continent. The dissenting Protestant sects brought with them too a suspicion of elaborate ecclesiastical hierarchies, which was strengthened by their renewed vitality in the mid-eighteenth century, and their emphasis on the conversion experience highlighted the role of the individual in his quest for God. The wide distribution of property and political rights, and the rapid economic and geographical expansion, together with the resultant political and economic power struggles, further served to weaken those traditional loyalties which had cemented the English political order and prepared the way for a politics of competing interests and individuals.

But even as the colonists were listening to the liberating call of the American wild, they continued to feel the magnetic pull of Old England. Two features in particular served to restrain the revolutionary potential of the American environment and to perpetuate traditional values. One was the increasing stratification of the colonial societies and the eventual emergence of fairly stable elites, who discovered a natural interest in the preservation of hierarchical forms and in the cultivation of a system of politics revolving around property, patronage, and deference. Their interests were nicely served by the second feature, the importation of English political institutions and ideas, both by the imperial authorities and by the colonists themselves. The introduction of English constitutional forms into the American colonies did not of itself produce political harmony, any more than the growing social stratification produced order, but together they helped to create a political culture in which Englishmen could feel more-or-less at home, even if at times at odds with their fellows. Indeed, the contentiousness of colonial politics can be traced in part to the success of this constitutional transplant. The interaction of the English freehold qualification for the suffrage with the American environ-ment, for example, meant that most white men held the vote, a circumstance which made colonial elites more vulnerable than the landed aristocracy of England. But in the middle of the eighteenth century the elites were in command. Like the English gentry, they nourished the ideal of an organic political order, over which men of substance, status, and experience presided with the willing support of their subordinates. Their constitutional assumptions too were Whig-gish: that there should be 'balance' in the government, that the legislative branch nonetheless should have primacy, and that the political nation should be confined to those with a 'stake in society'.

The establishment of English governmental forms on the American continent was a slow process, but by the mid-eighteenth century it was possible for the colonists to argue, in the words of a New York lawyer, that 'we are under the same constitution with the people of England'.[8] Superficially the resemblances were quite marked. Quite apart from such traditional English features as town councils, magistrates, and the jury system, the very structure of colonial government embodied the English concept of a mixed constitution. At the head was the governor, appointed by the crown in most colonies, with the power to summon and dissolve the local legislature, to veto legislation, and to control public expenditure. In fact the governor was a much more active head of the executive than eighteenth-century monarchs, his political as opposed to his constitutional role perhaps more approximating that of prime minister. He was assisted in his duties by a council, which usually consisted of twelve leading men of the colony appointed by the crown. This shared with the House of Lords the characteristics of being the upper legislative chamber and the highest judicial body, but it also possessed executive duties and its smallness and non-hereditary nature made it more resemble the English privy council. Protecting the liberties of the people was an elected assembly, which by the eighteenth century had effectively established its right to make local laws. As in England, no one of the branches of government held complete power; each in theory acted as a check on the arbitrary impulses of the others in a liberty-preserving equilibrium. The nature of the hierarchy – governor, council, assembly – bore more than a passing resemblance to the model of king, lords, and commons, and certainly encouraged Americans to think of themselves as governed by English constitutional forms. 'It is from and under the English Constitution, we derive all our Civil and Religious Rights and Liberties:' insisted the Stamp Act Congress of 1765.[9]

The initial insecurity of the colonial elites perhaps drove them on to imitate Old-World political forms. Some recent scholars have argued that they made a more-or-less deliberate attempt to 'Anglicize' colonial society and politics in the course of the eighteenth century.[10] Indeed, Americans of all ranks probably felt the attraction of the familiar. Conscious of their lowly provincial status and uncertain of their future in their strange new land, Americans might win a degree of reassurance by surrounding themselves with traditional institutions. The emergent elites in particular sought to buttress their positions by wholeheartedly embracing the political ideas and practices of the mother country. They were naturally receptive to political and social theories which conferred dignity on men of property, and equally receptive to those which emphasized the role of representative institutions in the protection of individual liberties, for the colonial assemblies were the arenas in which the elites were both to strengthen their own political influence and to make the diverse colonial political systems more like that of England. But a number of other influences also served to pull colonial politics towards the English model. Many colonial offices, for example, were in the gift of the British ministry, and if Americans wanted them they had to play the game of politics according to English rules. Further, the periodic friction between the colonial assemblies and the imperial authorities itself encouraged Americans to develop a structure of government closely resembling the English. Thus, in asserting their claim to look after their own affairs, the colonists insisted that they were entitled to the same rights and liberties as Englishmen at home, including the right to their own law-making bodies with the same powers and privileges as the English Parliament. The lure of the English political tradition, then, proved irresistible, particularly those aspects of it which taught how power could be restrained in the interests of individual freedoms.

The rise of the assembly was perhaps the most crucial constitutional development in the American colonies in the hundred years before 1763. It was the mechanism through which the colonial elites sought a degree of autonomy, and its emergence as a vital political force was made possible by the negligence of the British government and the imperatives of Whig ideology. The British supervision of colonial politics was not notably vigilant or systematic. Indeed, preoccupied as they were with European problems, the scramble for patronage and domestic politics, the ministers' lack of interest was equalled only by their ignorance of colonial affairs. One colonial in London complained with some feeling and much accuracy of the 'little knowledge of (or indeed inclination to know) American affairs, among most of those concerned in the Administration'.[11] Taking advantage of this ministerial indifference, the colonists developed their own organs of government, particularly the assemblies which were elected by the Americans themselves and were large enough to contain many members of the elites. The writings of the Parliamentarians of the mid-seventeenth century, of the Whigs of the Glorious Revolution, and of the English radicals of the eighteenth century were all mined extensively to strengthen the colonists' own claims to a form of parliamentary government. The assemblies, insisted the colonists, did not exist simply by permission of the king; rather, the English settlers had brought with them their traditional constitutional right to consent to the laws by which they were governed.

Gradually, if erratically, the assemblies (and the elites which dominated them) enlarged their powers, using the same weapon in their struggles with the governors as the House of Commons had in its struggle with the king, the right to levy taxes. In their efforts to establish their constitutional parity with the House of Commons the assemblies closely modelled their forms on that body, appointing such officers as speakers and sergeants-at-arms and claiming the same parliamentary privileges. A measure of autonomy was implicit in the considerable control they established over their own composition, including the right to admit and expel members. To a large extent the assemblies did come to act as colonial parliaments, and while the imperial authorities denied the theory behind this analogy (preferring to see the assemblies as dependent bodies like English town councils and maintaining the right to veto their measures), they were powerless to prevent the practice. The Massachusetts assembly was almost describing a fact as well as explaining a theory when it told Governor Hutchinson that 'this house has the same inherent rights in this province, as the House of Commons has in Great Britain'.[12] From the colonial period Americans were to inherit the conviction that vigilant representative assemblies were at the heart of good government.

To an extent, indeed, several American colonies came closer to observing the Whig ideal in their governments than did mid-eighteenth century England. The legislatures in general jealously guarded popular liberties from governmental encroachment, functioned as checks on the executive, and sometimes became the primary organ of government. Although colonial governors could still claim powers that the king had surrendered in England, such as the right to veto legislation and to prorogue and dissolve assemblies at will, their effective powers were much less, for they could not normally count on the support of the legislatures. In England the king's ministers survived with the support of both the independent country gentlemen and the placemen in Parliament, but the colonial assemblies contained few men who considered it their patriotic duty to support any competent government and most governors possessed only limited patronage sources with which to buy allies. Hence governors and assemblies continued to clash with one another in a way that king and Commons no longer did. The price of preserving old constitutional principles was a measure of political instability.

Like the Whig grandees of England, the colonial gentry were consolidating their own power as well as restraining the royal prerogative by their emphasis on legislative supremacy. They were able to cling to Whiggish ideas because these served their own patrician interests. The assumption remained that the function of an assembly was to protect the liberty and property of the people from the arbitrary impulses of the executive, not to give all men an equal voice in government. As in England, therefore, the political nation was confined to property-holders, for only they would have the independence to make a free choice in an election, and they were the ones with a 'stake in society', that is property on which taxes might be levied. In New York assembly members were required to be 'elected by the major part of the freeholders of the respective counties and places', and in other colonies too suffrage provisions tended to follow the English freehold qualification.[13] As in England, also, towns and counties looked to their leading men to represent them in the assemblies, which were filled with prosperous farmers, merchants, successful lawyers, and large planters. Community loyalties remained strong. The treating of voters, the lax conduct of elections and the disinclination of many men to exercise their right to vote all helped to perpetuate the rule of the elite. Frequently contests did not take place, as in Maryland where there was usually little or no opposition in assembly elections and the same men were often repeatedly returned. In Virginia contests were quite common, but even the most adamant critics of the idea that an aristocracy ruled in that colony admit that 'candidates . . . came from the upper half of the property holders', and were usually slaveowning planters.[14]

The gentlemen of the American colonies, then, largely succeeded in repeating the accomplishment of the gentlemen of England in gathering political power into their own hands. But they were relatively insecure elites, in part because American conditions tended to protect the imported constitutional ideas and practices from subversion. The absence of rotten boroughs and of placemen meant that representatives were more answerable to their constituents than to wealthy patrons. Their electorates were huge by Old-World standards because of the wide distribution of property and could not be safely ignored, as the wealthy Virginian Landon Carter once found when he lost his assembly seat, due, he thought, to his failure to familiarize himself 'among the people'.[15] Further, although colonial voters often stayed at home on election day, particular issues could trigger off considerable popular interest from time to time. Thus several representatives lost their seats in the Massachusetts House of Representatives in 1740-41 for opposing the popular land bank scheme, which was designed to provide the colony with a needed supply of paper money. The growing pains of the rapidly expanding colonies could thus inject divisive issues into their politics.

Political divisions among the elites were also encouraged by the triumph of the representative principle in the colonies. In England, the different estates were represented in Parliament, but many boroughs did not have their own representatives in the House of Commons. The common people of the realm, it was said, were 'virtually' represented by others of their own kind in the House, and it did not matter much if large parts of the country were not allocated seats. In the colonies, by contrast, as new towns and counties had been created by the spread of population, they had tended to be given representation in the assemblies. There were more representatives in relation to the population than in England and fewer areas were excluded. Hence it was possible to think of a legislator as the spokesman for his community, and the theory of direct representation was being developed in America even as it was being dismissed in England. In nine colonies the deputy was required to be a resident in the community he represented, and his constituents sometimes took it on themselves to instruct him whether to attend the assembly and how to vote in it. Local attachments were always to remain strong in American politics. Generally, most colonials continued to defer to the political leadership of local men of standing, but the degree to which the representative principle was being applied could ultimately only serve to weaken the authority of the patrician elites. In such a political milieu the gentry also found difficulty in maintaining unity, for the plethora of distinct economic, regional, and religious interests in a colony could invade and divide an assembly.

The interaction of English constitutional forms with the American environment thus often promoted a politics of turbulent factionalism, which contrasted sharply with the placidity of English political life in the mid-eighteenth century. But factionalism was not universal, and some major colonies, such as Virginia and Massachusetts, succeeded in achieving a high degree of internal cohesion, at least until the disruptive approach of the Revolution. Yet even where factionalism obtained, it was not necessarily a sign of serious political instability. Indeed, the struggle between the governor and the assembly apart, a measure of stability was achieved in most colonies as the shifting, impermanent kaleidoscope of groupings that had once plagued them disappeared. What has been called 'stable factionalism' was fairly common by the 1750s, that is a system of politics characterized by competition between two or more fairly permanent interest groups with relatively coherent followings.[16]

These factions did not normally represent distinct classes in the electorate; rather, they were normally led by prominent men, sometimes joined to one another by family ties, who looked for support from all economic classes. Mid-eighteenth century New York was one example of a colony whose politics were marked by conflict between fairly coherent factions, which were led by the great families but which were in some measure responsive to the demands of a restive electorate. The great merchant houses of the De Lanceys and their New York City connections helped to confer on the family both high social position and considerable political power, and they led a faction which secured some popular support among the colony's many Anglicans and in the commercial counties at the mouth of the Hudson. Their great rivals, the Livingstons, owed their prominence in part to their great landed estates, and they tended to win support among Presbyterians and other dissenters and in the upper reaches of the Hudson valley. There was no clear demarcation between the two factions, the De Lanceys also numbering large landowners and Presbyterians in their ranks and the Livingstons some powerful merchants and Anglicans, and both were obliged to look for support among the public at large, resorting to campaign handouts and the newspaper press to broaden their appeal as far as possible. In this way, it has been suggested, the politics of New York (and of Pennsylvania too) could be regarded as relatively 'modern' in character, anticipating the voter-oriented and party-dominated political systems of the nineteenth century.[17] If the patrician hegemony of Georgian England is taken to represent the 'traditional' style of politics, New York's factional competition at the polls might be seen as a transitional stage to a more 'modern' political system. This point should not be pressed very far, however, for the New York factions were still part of an eighteenth century political world, the great families exercising their authority over them in informal and proprietorial ways.

Stable competition between elite-led factions also characterized the politics of several other colonies by the mid-eighteenth century. But in some colonies factional strife was replaced by the hegemony of a unified ruling elite, demonstrating that there was no neat evolution from 'traditional' to 'modern'. In Virginia the small freeholders apparently submitted willingly to the rule of the great planters, who were knit together into a cohesive oligarchy by family ties and common interests. Each county was assumed to have its own distinct – and homogeneous – character, and it was taken for granted that the interests of its magnates and lesser gentry were virtually identical with those of the county as a whole. The leading planters thus almost naturally occupied the seats in the powerful county courts and represented their communities in the assembly. Traditional techniques and values also survived in Massachusetts, where Governor William Shirley in the 1740s was able to draw many of the leading men into a governing oligarchy by the use of patronage, favours, and deftly-conceived policies. The members of the assembly themselves were in some measure protected by the deference accorded to them by their constituents. Assemblymen were elected by the townships whence they came, and in these small communities the leading offices and the best pews in the meeting-houses tended to go to men of substance, at least to those whose public-spiritedness and sound morality had earned them the respect of their fellows. As John Adams later noted, local offices in New England were not infrequently held by the same families for a number of generations. The deference that the 'silent democracy' showed towards the 'speaking aristocracy' in both Virginia and Massachusetts played perhaps an even more vital role in preserving order in those colonies than it did in England, where coercion might be resorted to when willing obedience failed.[18]

The political systems of the colonies could never be perfect microcosms of the mother country, but by the mid-eighteenth century the family resemblances were marked. The increasing stratification brought about by economic development resulted in hierarchical social orders dominated by elites, which sustained their pre-eminence by their wealth, their aristocratic trappings, and the respect of their subordinates. Social status also conferred political position, and the elites assumed command of the local and central governments, much like the landed gentry in England. If this pyramidical sociopolitical order made possible the persistence of many of the values and practices of the Old World, the introduction of English constitutional forms reinforced the similarities. What perhaps is remarkable is the extent to which Whig ideas and institutions conquered the American landscape and its people. As a Philadelphia newspaper told its readers in 1758: 'Whether you be *English, Irish, Germans,* or *Swedes*, whether you be churchmen presbyterians, quakers, or of any other denomination of religion, whatsoever, you are by your residence, and the laws of your country, freemen and not slaves. You are entitled to all the liberties of Englishmen and the freedom of this constitution.'[19]

The re-creation of much of English political culture in the New World was accomplished in spite of – and in certain ways because of – the presence of conditions hostile to ancient loyalties. Even after Independence, for example, Americans continued to cling to the belief that order required hierarchy, although the relatively undifferentiated nature of their own society and its heady mixture of peoples would seem to render anachronistic the notion of a vertical chain of harmonious beings. The pyramidical and holistic concepts of politics favoured by the elites also seemed to be ill-suited to those features of the colonial societies which tended to enhance the independence and self-reliance of each man, such as the broad distribution of property, the expansive economic opportunities, and the individualistic thrust of Calvinistic and evangelical Protestantism. Yet organic images retained a vital force, in part perhaps because they promised the comforts of fellowship to the men and women striving to subdue the American continent, and they were given legitimacy by the conventional wisdom of English political thought, by mercantilist assumptions about a single national interest, and by religious traditions which emphasized the community as well as the individual. And for as long as Americans remained within the embrace of the British Empire, they could only turn to England for their models of social organization and political behaviour.

Yet the incongruity between the configurations of colonial society and the principles of English political culture meant that any break with the mother country might well be followed by the fashioning of a dramatically new system of politics. Since the colonists had for the most part left the incrustations of feudalism behind them when they had sailed from Europe, the rejection of the English monarchy would leave them with little alternative but to establish a government of the people – there was no one else to rule. Nonetheless, the full implications of republican and majoritarian principles were to take several decades to manifest themselves, in part because of the versatile nature of the American elites. Because they were not a clearly separate estate like the hereditary lords of England, the elites could themselves lead the republican cause when the time came with perfect propriety, without a crippling sense of being traitors to the class they had so long aped. Further, they could offer the advantages of considerable experience in government, a reassuring belief in the supremacy of the legislative branch, and a distrust of the executive, and a measure of skill in practical politics. There seemed to be no reason, at least in the eyes of the elites, why they should not retain political command. Few Americans in 1776 were prepared to equate republicanism with democracy.

Part 2

The making of the American republic (1763-1789)

It was 'as Englishmen' that the colonists first resisted the sinister encroachments of the British government, and in a sense the Revolution was begun in an attempt to defend the political ideas and institutions taken from England. But the act of Independence in large part freed Americans from those pressures which had encouraged them to emulate English forms and incited them to seek new kinds of political organization better adapted to American conditions. Even before 1776 the American political nation had been remarkably extensive and active, and the excitements and hardships of the revolutionary era enlarged and invigorated it yet further, rendering even more conspicuous the fact that these energetic common people were a 'headless' society, without king, lords or bishops to guide them.

The alternative to immemorial practice proved to be a government which took all its authority from the consent of the people. But it took time to test the novel implications of republican theory and to devise a system which would work. Americans had carried from the colonial period a strong political identification with their local communities, and this, allied with the popular pressures which were now unleashed, always threatened to disrupt any general system of government. The attempts to fashion a political system to accommodate these diverse forces brought to the surface tensions which were to become lasting features of American politics, such as those between nation and state, between north and south, between 'cosmopolitan' and 'localist' perspectives, and those which resulted from the survival of slavery and of the remnants of established churches in an avowedly free society. The quest for stable republican institutions was also hampered by the heritage of Whig libertarianism, which had left Americans with a distrust of power in all its forms, though particularly of executive power, and a conviction that liberty was easily lost. The protection of liberty (and hence of property), not the establishment of democracy, remained at the heart of revolutionary republicanism. This facilitated the political survival of members of the old elites, well-versed as they were in Whig principles and well-schooled in practical politics, though they lost their virtual monopoly over American public life. The danger was, however, that no governmental body would exercise effective political control, such were the constraints that the first constitutions put upon power. But by 1789 a Constitution had been devised which provided a framework within which a national political system could develop. Americans came to accept this written compact as the supreme law of their land, constraining even popular legislative bodies, and later generations were to be united by a worship for it and divided by fears that it too could succumb to subversion.

Chapter 3

The spirit of 'seventy-six

'To anticipate the future glory of America', wrote a Massachusetts clergyman in 1773, 'is ravishing and transporting to the mind'.[1] John Winthrop had once been similarly transported by the praise and glory he believed awaited the Puritan commonwealth, and the idea had persisted in colonial thought that some special destiny was reserved for the American people. The revolutionary excitements of the 1770s rekindled and were in turn sustained by this millenial faith, as Americans came to believe that Providence had chosen them to carry the banner of liberty for the human race. The new nation was to show a depraved world how men *should* live together. Colonial Americans had once reverently admired England's balanced constitution as the best bulwark of freedom, but in the troubled years after 1763 they had come to see it as subverted beyond redemption, and by 1776 they had reached the conclusion that only a republican government could properly secure men's inalienable rights. Yet Americans did not embark on their great experiment without trepidation, for republics were themselves notoriously vulnerable polities. A form of government which did not rest on military force or corruption could only rely on the virtue of the people to sustain it, on their willingness to subordinate their selfish desires to the public good. It remained to be seen whether Americans were selfless enough to carry out the historic task that Nature's God had assigned them.

In a curious way, then, the revolutionary mission reinforced some of the oldest of political premises, even as it demanded that Americans seek quarantine in the New World environment. The individualism which was later to characterize American life may have had its roots in the political, social, and economic conditions of the colonial period, but the republican imperative ran counter to the individualistic ethic. The very word republic, as Tom Paine pointed out, meant 'the *public good*, or the good of the whole,' and throughout the revolutionary struggle and for a generation and more thereafter American leaders continued to purvey organic images of the good political society, calling on American citizens to put aside their private quarrels for the republican cause.[2] This version of the republican creed offered some comfort to America's gentlemen, for it invited Americans of all ranks to put trust in one another.

But although republicanism was compatible with patrician leadership, the inspiriting events of 1776 released Americans to seek their own political destiny. No longer were they to be subject to British supervision, and the many subtle pressures which had compelled colonists to appropriate what they could from the society and politics of Old England were suddenly much weakened. The physical and psychological constraints of colonial dependency abruptly ceased to shape American development; in a way rare in history, it fell to this awed generation of Americans to decide for themselves how they and their heirs were to be governed. The challenge was a utopian one, and as such could only be approached with both high hopes and great fears. That confident republican mentor Tom Paine again sensed something of this. America could be 'as happy as she please', he insisted, while conceding that 'If there is any true cause for fear respecting independance(sic), it is because no plan is yet laid down. Men do not see their way out --. . . .'[3]

The removal of the traditional governing authorities in itself made concerted planning difficult. The American societies were possessed of patriotic elites with expertise in government, but they lacked distinct orders whose historic task it was to rule. Political authority thus almost necessarily reverted to the people themselves, and popular forums of all kinds began to make decisions affecting the public welfare, from the elected state legislatures, through town and county meetings, to the innumerable extra-legal committees and associations which had sprung up well before Independence. As state leaders struggled to transform the old assemblies into workable governments, they found their authority frequently defied by local groups and communities. The 'Green Mountain Boys' of the hinterland of New York and New Hampshire thumbed their noses at the governments of those states and carved out for themselves the even newer state of Vermont. Popular pressures were added to centrifugal pressures, as when the artisans of Philadelphia in 1779 forced the town meeting to try to counter inflation by controlling commodity prices. The resistance to British rule thus unleashed a host of particularistic and popular forces, the containment of which was to become – and would always remain – a central function of the American political system. But they also legitimated that system – the movements of the revolutionary era served to define republicanism as a system of government in which all authority rested directly on popular assent.

The extensive but hitherto relatively quiescent political nation inherited from the colonial period thus became more self-aware and assertive in these years. The surviving members of the old elites themselves abetted perhaps even more than they resisted the politicization of the common man, for they needed to arraign the people behind them in their defiance of the British crown. The flight of thousands of loyalists also opened up unprecedented opportunities for new men in politics, and new political configurations appeared in several states. To a degree, the old contests between different patrician factions were replaced or joined by alignments in which the commercial and landed gentry tended to be pitted against men representing more parochial and less privileged interests. The politicization of the American people also encouraged, and was encouraged by, the fashioning of constitutions which sought to adapt the more valuable lessons of Whig history to the peculiarities of the American social and political environments. Old ideas and New-World circumstances both served in particular to enhance the role of the popular branch of government, and power came to rest primarily in the state legislatures, which themselves were made more representative of population.

In thus seeking to make the people the fountain of all political authority, however, the American revolutionaries were erecting safeguards for liberty rather than advancing democracy in any modern sense. Indeed, many of them believed that gentlemen of property and standing would have an invaluable and even essential role to play in a republican polity, which would need to be protected from a descent into anarchy and licentiousness. But in the event the separate states could not resolve all the problems of republican government themselves. The thrust of early American republicanism was to divide and even to dissipate power, so that even many state legislatures lacked the authority to govern effectively, let alone the first national government. Americans were to find the experience of creating a system of politics adapted to their new status to be a divisive and frustrating one. 'Independency', John Adams had observed at the outset, 'is a Hobgoblin of so frightful Mien that it would throw a delicate person into Fits to look it in the Face.'⁴

In 1776 the members of the Continental Congress which had assembled at Philadelphia formally rejected the rule of the British king, but they could not so easily free themselves from the hold of English ideas. As Bernard Bailyn and Gordon S. Wood among others have recently shown, the American revolutionaries were in some measure acting out the imperatives of English libertarian thought. In England, as we have seen, the Country critics of ministerial corruption had remained a minority, irritating gadflies buzzing around the head of the Whig establishment. But in America, where virtually the entire political order (apart from the royal appointees) could be regarded as being 'in opposition' to the British ministry, English opposition thought had long been the conventional wisdom. From *Cato's Letters* and from the writings of Bolingbroke, James Burgh, and others, colonial and revolutionary Americans learned that in England the celebrated mixed constitution was being subverted by the machinations of the king and his ministers, who were allegedly wiping out the liberty of the people and the independence of the Commons by the use of bribery and patronage and by the manipulation of the national debt and excise taxes. This image of a political order in which liberty was fast receding before the power of a voracious ministry immensely appealed to American colonists intent on protecting their own privileges. Further, as they became persuaded that liberty was dying out in England, they reached the ironic conclusion that they, the American colonists, were the last surviving champions of English rights.

Not all colonial leaders interpreted the world about them in such stark and dramatic terms, of course, but this kind of mentality was sufficiently strong among influential Americans in the decade before 1775 to invest almost every imperial action with a sinister design. Given the high taxation and the national debt under which the mother country laboured, it seemed only reasonable to the Grenville ministry that the colonies should share in the costs of their own defence, to which end it introduced the Stamp Act of 1765. A tax which had been imposed on them without their consent, however, could only seem to Americans to have a 'manifest tendency to subvert the rights and liberties' they had so long enjoyed, and they united in strong resistance.[5] Each successive measure of the British government then seemed to fulfil the radical prophecy of a ministerial conspiracy to reduce America to servility. The Declaratory Act, asserting Parliament's supremacy over the colonies, and the Townshend Acts, imposing a series of import duties, seemed further to strike at colonial rights, and the stationing of British troops in Boston in 1768 revived the old fears of a standing army, that traditional symbol of tyranny. When the British government was eventually obliged to respond to colonial resistance by closing the port of Boston and virtually repealing the Massachusetts charter, it misguidedly supplied the last compelling proof of an apparent intent to reduce Americans to slavery, by military force if necessary. The 'acts and measures . . . adopted since the last war', complained the colonial leaders when they met together in the Continental Congress, 'demonstrate a system formed to enslave America'.[6] The only course left was rebellion, a rebellion which was begun, as Gordon S. Wood has noted, not so much against the British constitution as on behalf of it.[7]

The American Revolution, then, was undertaken in defence of rights inherited from England and of political institutions modelled on those of England. It was also made possible by an intellectual heritage which warned that liberty-preserving constitutions were the constant victims of subversion, a conviction that was to become deeply embedded in American political culture. It was 'as Englishmen' that the deputies at the Continental Congress first laid formal claim to their 'rights and liberties', although as the breach widened Americans increasingly insisted that they were speaking of 'natural' rights, given by God to all men everywhere.[8] The Revolution was a movement which could be – and was – supported by men of all ranks, for its initial object was independence from the corrupted and corrupting mother country rather than a redistribution of power and influence within American society. Those members of the colonial elites who were not tied to the imperial administration sensed in the break with England an opportunity to enlarge their own power, and planters encumbered by large debts to British merchants and American merchants impatient at the restrictions of the mercantilist system also saw powerful material advantages in Independence. Members of the lower classes nursed resentments against England too, such as workmen whose wages had been undercut by British soldiers taking part-time jobs and American seamen who had been pressganged into the British navy. Grievances and ambitions of many kinds, then, helped to enlist the sympathies of Americans of all ranks to the cause of Independence. But the structure of colonial politics could not be preserved intact. For one thing, the sudden removal of royal government meant that new governments had hastily to be created in the midst of war; for another, the configuration of libertarian ideas appropriated from England, while compatible with patrician rule, turned out to have some very radical applications. However fervently they embraced the revolutionary cause, the old elites could not be sure of winning and maintaining control of the destiny of the nation.

The break with England itself prompted Americans to reconsider the nature of political authority. If the colonists' very absorption of aspects of English political culture had contributed to the confrontation, the accomplishment of Independence ironically pointed them in a new political direction. Many of the influences which had prompted the colonial gentry to emulate English political forms were now removed, and were replaced by a growing nationalism which demanded that Americans cultivate their own brand of politics. Patrician leaders themselves early realized that the only practicable alternative to a monarchical system of government was one which took its legitimacy from popular consent. Yet there is no doubt that many revolutionaries continued to hold to the concept of a polity in which order was maintained by some sort of hierarchical structure. In the first flush of revolutionary fervour, it was possible to believe – or at least to hope – that a virtuous and enlightened people would willingly choose their own hierarchy, that they would elect as their rulers men capable of rising above faction and discerning the interest of the whole, which was to say 'men of education and fortune'.[9] In looking for a political system suited to American circumstances, gentlemanly revolutionaries thus resurrected an old model of republican government, one in which political order would be maintained by the authority of a natural aristocracy and the deference of the common people. As some of them recognized, democracy and deference were in a sense compatible with one another, indeed were necessary to one another if order were to be preserved in the New World polities. 'There must be decency and respect and veneration introduced for persons in authority, of every rank, or we are undone', wrote John Adams in 1776. 'In a popular government this is the only way of supporting order . . .'[10]

But in the tumult of revolution no elite could readily impose its own blueprint for government on a refractory people. The issues raised by the audacious American bid for independence inevitably further heightened political consciousness and enhanced contentiousness among an already restive people. Waging war on the British opened a veritable Pandora's Box of perplexing problems for the harassed revolutionaries. What to do with the loyalists? How to construct state and national governments? How to control rapidly rising prices? How to pay for the war? How to distribute public land and how to tax private land? Whether to issue paper money and/or to establish banks? Whether to provide public support for education and to end it for religion? These were among the issues which agitated the state legislatures of the 1770s and 1780s. The economic problems in particular touched the welfare of almost every member of the community, drawing more interests than ever before into the political process. In several state legislatures the long-powerful elite groups which represented commercial, urban, and creditor interests now found themselves faced with emergent oppositions of loose voting blocs whose members were associated with small farming, rural, and debtor interests. This polarization – separating the 'cosmopolitan' from the 'local' – was far from complete, but it was one which was destined to reappear many times in different forms in American history. Thus one Virginian found that the wartime House of Burgesses was 'composed of men not quite so well dressed, not so politely educated, nor so highly born as some Assemblies I have formerly seen . . .', and the researches of Jackson T. Main have established that the proportion of men of moderate means rose dramatically in several state legislatures in these years.[11] Where ordinary farmers accounted for only about twenty-five per cent of the New York legislature before the war, for example, they reached forty-two per cent after it, while in Virginia the proportion rose from perhaps thirteen per cent to twenty-six per cent.

The entry of new men into politics was reflected in the state constitutions which were drawn up in this period, some of which tried to erect barriers against the disturbing forces of change and others of which in effect accepted and promoted the new order. In South Carolina, for example, the wealthy low-country planters led by conservative Edward Rutledge succeeded in perpetuating their own rule. A 'pure democracy may possibly do, when patriotism is the ruling passion;' Rutledge offered in 1776, 'but when the state abounds with rascals . . . you must suppress a little of that popular spirit.'[12] The new constitution gave a few token seats to the western parishes, but the eastern parishes remained grossly over-represented in the lower house, a quarter of the state's population controlling two-thirds of the seats. High property qualifications for the senate, governorship, and privy council also served to cement the control of the wealthy coastal rice planters and Charleston merchants. Not that they were not good Whigs. In accordance with English liberal Whig theory, the authority of the executive was greatly curtailed and political power was vested primarily in the legislature.

If South Carolina continued to sustain the old English equation of landed property and political power, New York put renewed emphasis on the old concept of a balanced constitution. The constitution of 1777 made a clear distinction between the assembly and the senate, assuming, as Robert R. Livingston later observed, that different orders in society were 'necessary to a steady government'.[13] The assembly was to be the popular branch, with seats apportioned roughly according to population, and voting for it was substantially liberalized. The senate, by contrast, was designed to be a much more exclusive body, a provision confining its electorate to freeholders worth £1,000 clear of debt barring over two-thirds of the state's adult males, and the creation of only four senatorial districts giving an advantage to candidates whose reputations were widely known. The legislature thus represented the small freeholders and tenant farmers in one branch and the larger landowners in the other, and these popular and propertied branches acted as mutual checks. The governor was also elected by the £1,000 freeholders, for it was intended that he should act as a check on the legislature, and he was given more power than was normal in the revolutionary era to be able to do this. With a lower house sensitive to the demands of the small farmers and an upper house sensitive to the pressures of the trading interests and commercial agriculture, New York could be said to have achieved its goal of a balanced political order.

But New York's ingenious constitution did not satisfy all its citizens. In the backcountry region which is now Vermont, Ethan Allen and his brothers led a revolt against the uncooperative New York authorities. The reasons for this movement were complex, among them being the speculative ventures of the Allens, but the relatively conservative constitution of New York provided something against which popular opinion could be readily mobilized. These spirited frontiersmen and land speculators quickly established their independence and proceeded to erect a defiantly democratic government. Pennsylvania had already enraged American conservatives by adopting a highly democratic constitution, and the Allens secured a copy and – with a few changes – made it their own. This meant a popularly-chosen unicameral legislature, for which no property qualifications for membership were required and in which power was concentrated. Popular control over it was further ensured by requiring its meetings to be public, its votes to be recorded, and its proceedings to be published. An elected governor and executive council reviewed bills and carried out the legislative will. As in Pennsylvania too, most judges and magistrates were also elected by the people. In two instances the Vermont constitution was even more innovatory than that of Pennsylvania. The latter's taxpaying qualification for the vote was replaced by a provision giving it to all men who took the Freeman's

Oath, so that Vermont became the first state in which the franchise was not clearly tied to some kind of financial stake in society. Further, Vermont established a militia system in which all but the most senior officers were elected by the people. The Vermonters, in short, had established a political system in which the popular element was all-pervasive. Property was in no way represented and the constitution was not 'balanced'. Little of English forms of government survived.

The variations in the constitutional provisions from state to state make it difficult to generalize about the new governments. South Carolina's conservatism was parallelled in Maryland, New York's balance of people and property was also enshrined in the Massachusetts constitution, and Vermont's radicalism had been anticipated by Pennsylvania. In some states the surviving members of the old elite had retained virtually complete control, in others they were obliged to share their power with new men, and in yet others the popular elements swept all before them, at least for a time. Nonetheless, the political confusions, variations, and changes of these years could not quite obscure certain patterns. English assumptions about political order had not yet been shaken off. The democratic constitutions of Pennsylvania and Vermont (and of Georgia) were the exceptions which pointed up the rule that most states continued to link political rights to property, made some sort of attempt at a balanced constitution, and continued to tolerate a gentlemanly office-holding elite. Thus their decision to establish governors and senates, however little power these were given, was at least in part the result of the traditional notion that the 'democratical' elements in the government should be restrained as well as the executive. The traditional conception of a hierarchical governing structure was reflected in the way in which a man's political capacity was assumed to relate to his wealth. The voter formed the base of the political pyramid, and while six states either lowered property requirements or replaced them with a taxpaying qualification, seven did not, and in any case the suffrage everywhere (save Vermont) was still confined to those with some sort of property, however little. Office-holders were required to possess yet more property than the voters. North Carolina, for example, preserved the hierarchical conception of the polity by requiring that assembly-men possess 100 acres, senators 300 acres, and the governor landed property worth £1,000. Such provisions helped to keep offices in the hands of local and state notables.

Most of the new state constitutions, then, were not models of egalitarian democracy. Their central object remained the Whiggish one of protecting individual liberties and constraining power, and it was widely accepted that an unrestrained democracy was more likely to imperil than to further these ends. But this is not to suggest that the constitution-makers were hostile to the notion of popular sovereignty. Rather the reverse. The English Whigs had always held that legislative power lay ultimately in the people, that the liberty of the people depended on the degree to which they controlled the law-makers, and the American revolutionaries moved swiftly to carry this doctrine to its logical and sometimes uncomfortable conclusions. Their quarrels with the royal and proprietary authorities and their immersion in English opposition propaganda having convinced them that the main threat to liberty was an overweening executive, the new constitutions located power primarily in the legislatures (insofar as they located it anywhere), leaving the governors as little more than figureheads, most of them being denied even the right of veto. In the legislatures, too, power was tipped towards the lower houses, especially in relation to money bills. Even the judiciary was subjected to a degree of popular control, for judges were normally appointed by the legislature or the governor, both of which, of course, were themselves elected. The doctrine of the sovereignty of the people was most conspicuously honoured in the provision for the annual election of the assemblies – in Rhode Island the assembly was actually elected twice a year! The men who determined government policy were thus obliged to present themselves to their electoral masters at frequent intervals – thus a crippling constraint was placed even on legislative power. The object of this was not so much the furtherance of democracy as the protection of liberty, for history had shown that long-serving parliaments could become corrupt and despotic. 'Where annual election ends, tyranny begins' had been an old cry of English radicals. Men of the revolutionary era deeply distrusted power in all its forms, an antipathy which they built into their constitutional designs and bequeathed to all later generations of Americans.

Yet the obsession with protecting popular rights weighted the new governments heavily in favour of the 'democratic' element, and some Americans at least began to argue that popular sovereignty should mean majority rule. Even before the Revolution American legislators were much closer to their constituents than were their counterparts in England, and the revolutionary imperative required that the people be even better represented in legislative bodies. Thus suffrage qualifications were further lowered in some states, but perhaps more important were the attempts to make representation in the state legislatures fairer than it had been in the colonial assemblies. Hence in several states more seats were allocated to the western districts, Pennsylvania and North Carolina in particular doing justice in this respect. But not only the western areas were better represented. In some states, as in Massachusetts, the relatively dense population of the eastern seaboard had been under-represented in the old assembly, and when seats were roughly allocated according to population they were to send more delegates to the legislature. As J.R. Pole has pointed out, the existing elites were often prepared to support the majority principle, under which each electoral district was to contain equal numbers of voters, because wealth as well as population was concentrated on the commercial seaboard.[14] As long as artisans and labourers continued to accept the political leadership of the rich merchants and lawyers of these eastern communities, that is, as long as a hierarchical and deferential social order survived, all ranks could unite in the demand for the representation of numbers. By the end of the revolutionary era the several states had moved a long way to recognizing that all (white) men should have an equal voice in the making of law. Such features as small constituencies, the reasonably equitable distribution of seats, and the absence of rotten boroughs provided a very different base to political life to that which obtained in England. The degree to which the representative could be made answerable to the voters was to affect American political development profoundly. He was still seen as the protector of the liberties of the people and the interests of his community, rather than as the champion of the common man, and as such was expected to be a person of some substance. But once the American elites had accepted the majority principle their continued survival depended on the sufferance of their subordinates.

The emergence of majoritarianism, then, was more the product of a Whiggish desire to free men from the arbitrary control of others (and of practical electoral politics) than of a desire to effect equal opportunities or the equal distribution of power. The ascendancy of the lower houses of the legislatures and the triumph of the representative principle would have been applauded by English libertarians, as would the bills of rights appended to many of the state constitutions, which enshrined some of the most famous of Whig principles, such as the freedom of speech and the freedom of the press. The bills of rights themselves were evidence that the restraint of power remained the central objective of American revolutionaries. And like their Old World counterparts, most American liberals continued to assume that some sort of balancing mechanism was necessary in government, that the political nation should be confined to those with a stake in society, and that office best went to men of standing. But in reacting against the executive tyranny and corruption which allegedly subverted the English constitution, and in summoning the American people to their cause, the old elites had been forced to share their power with new men and had been obliged to accept systems of government which were perilously responsive to popular whims.

The revolutionaries' commitment to libertarianism rather than to levelling radicalism was also shown by their relative lack of interest in economic reform. Despite conservatives' complaints about the self-interested behaviour of debtors in the state legislatures, there was no serious attempt to redistribute property or wealth. The estates of the fleeing loyalists were indeed confiscated – Pennsylvania appropriated an estate valued at nearly £1 million from the Penns – and were frequently broken up, being sold in smaller lots to speculators or farmers, but the lands of wealthy patriots remained untouched. The continued respect for property rights was subsequently demonstrated by the measures taken to afford a degree of compensation to certain of the loyalists who had lost their estates. The abolition of feudal relics like quitrents also underlined the assumed connection between liberty and property – the free man was the independent man, enjoying absolute control over his own property and owing service to no one. The one form of property which was not readily compatible with the libertarian doctrines of the Revolution was slavery, which now stood cast in bold and embarrassing relief. 'Every Argument which can be urged in Favor of our own Liberties will certainly operate with equal Force in Favor of that of the Negroes:' pointed out northerner Ebeneezer Hazard in 1777.[15] To many northerners there was an obvious solution to this dilemma. The radicals of Vermont outlawed slavery in their state constitution, a fairly painless measure since there were apparently less than fifty blacks in the region at the time. Similarly, the Supreme Court of Massachusetts interpretated that state's constitution as having abolished slavery, and other northern states moved to adopt gradual – sometimes very gradual – emancipation schemes. But Massachusetts could dispense with 5,000 slaves more readily than Virginia could dispense with 200,000. The southern planters found themselves unable to release their grip of their great armies of slaves, and instead began to address themselves to the difficult task of proving that slavery was after all compatible with the ideals of the Revolution. The survival of slavery in a society committed to the inalienable rights of man remained a source of tension both within the South and between the South and the rest of the Union.

If slavery could not be easily reconciled with the revolutionaries' goal of individual freedom, nor could the maintenance of religious establishments. In Virginia the planters demonstrated their libertarianism by casting out the Church of England. To Thomas Jefferson and James Madison, well-versed in the rationalism of John Locke and the Enlightenment, toleration – as opposed to religious freedom – was not enough, for to give official sanction to any creed was an invitation to the persecution of others, as seemed to be proved by the vicious treatment accorded to many Baptists in prerevolutionary Virginia. Indeed, the best guarantee of religious liberty, they came to believe, lay in a multiplicity of sects, none of which was in a position to impose its will on others. When the legislature finally adopted Jefferson's Bill for Establishing Religious Freedom in 1785 Virginia became the first state in modern history to renounce any governmental claim to interfere in ecclesiastical affairs. Men could worship how they pleased without any kind of civil disability. The lesson that pluralism and liberty went together was to be remembered by Madison when he helped to fashion a political system for the new nation.

Yet the Virginians' disestablishment of the church and their rationalistic definition of religious freedom exerted relatively little influence on other states. In New England the movement for the separation of church and state stemmed from other roots and was less universal in its demands. The established Congregational churches of

Massachusetts and Connecticut strongly supported the patriot cause, but they saw little reason to sever themselves from the state, despite the resentments of other sects, from whom the pressure for separation came. The Baptists in particular were now numerous, and although they were formally exempted from religious taxation they were subjected to repeated harassment. The Baptist leader Isaac Backus pointedly remarked on the inconsistency of demanding political liberty without granting 'that dearest of all rights, equal liberty of conscience', a position which led him to deny that 'the civil power has a right to set one religious sect up above another'. The dissenting sects failed in their immediate campaigns to separate the Congregational churches from the state in Connecticut and Massachusetts, where taxes for their support continued to be levied until well into the nineteenth century, but ultimately it was their brand of religious freedom that was to prevail in America. Isaac Backus, for example, did not believe that particular churches should be tied to the state, but he tended to see the Protestant faith and republicanism as mutually supportive. 'No man can take a seat in our legislature till he solemnly declares, "I believe in the Christian religion and have a firm persuasion of its truth",' he noted approvingly in 1783.[16] Like most of his fellow revolutionaries, he apparently saw no great harm in imposing disabilities on Roman Catholics and did not object to the Protestant version of the scriptures being taught in state schools. In this sense it was the nonconformist pietism of Backus rather than the rationalism of Jefferson which conditioned the American position on the relationship between church and state. In a variety of formal and informal ways the several states continued to cherish the Protestant faith, such as by appointing Protestant chaplains to their legislatures. But it was not too difficult to reconcile this with the revolutionary cause, for Protestantism and the spirit of freedom were traditionally associated with one another, as in England's Glorious Revolution of 1688. Protestantism and republicanism were both held to cherish individual rights and to deny the legitimacy of authoritarian forms. Eventually all the American sects were to recognize that their proper position in the American polity was as voluntary associations, that is as independent religious denominations rather than as churches supported by the state.

As the slave masters and Congregational clergy were discovering, the imported libertarian doctrines could be pressed to some rather disturbing conclusions. Most Americans shied away from the anarchic notion that the truly free man owed obedience to no earthly authority, but it never entirely disappeared from American political discourse. The American commitment to the notion of popular sovereignty also remained a source of potential trouble. In England sovereignty was said to reside in Parliament, in which each of the three estates was present. In America sovereignty was increasingly assumed to reside in the people at large, as was recognized in Massachusetts when the new constitution was legitimized by a popularly-elected convention. The idea that the majority of the people could make and unmake constitutions was a novel, exhilarating yet frightening one, for only the self-restraint (or public virtue) of the people could protect such a polity from anarchy.

If the American political systems had been less than orderly before the Revolution, the developments of the war years did little to induce greater stability. The generals and congressmen directing the war effort despaired at trying to get the temperamental state governments to act together. The ruinous inflation and the inevitable speculation served to undermine confidence in the capacity of the authorities and in the virtue of the people. The annual election of the state legislatures, while it may have been designed to prevent them from sinking into corruption, had the effect of making laws changeable and policies unpredictable. The weakening of those bodies which were meant to check the power of the assemblies, together with the (albeit imperfect) emergence of the majority principle and the dependence of the representative on his constituents, made governments responsive to popular currents and threatened the political pre-eminence of the social elites. Gentlemen were troubled by the way in which new men could push themselves to the front in this uncertain environment. The continued if sporadic attempts of back-country areas to take affairs into their own hands and of urban crowds to impose their will on municipal authorities called into serious question whether that 'respect and veneration . . . for persons in authority', which John Adams had said was so essential to popular government, really was sufficiently strong to contain the particularistic and populistic pressures of revolutionary America. Before 1781 such fears tended to be held in check by the overriding need to secure final military victory over the British. But as they emerged from the years of war the political leaders of the new states looked with deepening apprehension at the institutions they had created. As the New England divine Jeremy Belknap grumbled in 1784, 'democratic government' was 'to say the least . . . extremely inconvenient'.[17]

Chapter 4

A quest for republican security

By about 1780 the euphoria which had gripped so many revolutionaries in the early days of Independence was fast evaporating, and there was widespread agreement among men in public life that the American experiment in liberty and self-government was going badly astray. The disparate political and economic courses pursued by the several states, the apparent disregard for law and authority, the machinations of merchants and financiers, the unnerving rate of inflation, and the unpredictable and capricious nature of the state legislatures combined to produce the impression of a country close to anarchy. Much remained to be done before the republic was secured.

Winning the war with Britain indeed seemed an easy task compared with that of finding and fashioning a general system of politics answerable to the nation's peculiar needs. If Americans were to survive as one people – or perhaps to become one people – they would need a government with the capacity to maintain union and order without excessive force. One brute fact of American life was the sheer size of the active political nation, both numerically and geographically, and any system of government would need to be capable of accommodating and containing the consequent popular and particularistic demands made upon it. Republican institutions would also need to be reproducible, for the American people were beginning to move out of the old states and into the fresh lands in the West and they had no wish to replace one colonial condition with another. At the very least, too, a central governing authority would have to respect the rights and sensitivities of the states, but would also need the capacity to maintain its integrity against the encroachments of both state and foreign governments.

The tortuous search for such a political system in the 1780s exposed a number of tensions which were to became lasting features of American political life. One was that between national and states rights principles, the appropriate balance between which would long remain an issue of contention. A measure of sectional antagonism was also disconcertingly evident in these years, an ominous mistrust between northern and southern states. Yet another variety of American conflict, already discernible within several states but now revealing itself in a broader arena, was that which warily poised men of continental or 'cosmopolitan' interests and viewpoints against those whose primary attachments were local or parochial. These overlapping tensions had their ideological dimensions, though sustaining them too were some very real economic and financial interests, much of the political conflict of the period being related to the settlement of the private and public debts that had accumulated during and after the war. Within states debtors and creditors confronted one another in court rooms and legislative chambers, and in the country at large the state and central governments wrestled with the problem of which was to assume responsibility for the national debt. The struggle for the possession of this debt was in a sense a struggle for control of the destiny of the nation, for whichever governmental body or bodies emerged with greatest financial responsibilities could also hope to win political dominance.

The ultimate goal of several of the economic and financial measures attempted in this period was thus political. Those men in favour of a greater centralization of power in particular looked to economic integration as a means of achieving a harmonious political order in the union as a whole, a strategy which was to be imitated by nationalistic leaders on later occasions in American history. In the 1780s the attempts to refashion the American political system by working within the existing governmental framework failed, and eventually the advocates of change resorted to a bloodless rebellion of their own. What they needed to carry them to victory in this popular republic, they finally recognized, was the aid of the American people.

The gentlemen who debated the state of the nation in the 1780s had inherited from the classical political theorists and from English Whiggery a cluster of assumptions and beliefs which helped to cast in bold relief the threats they spotted on the American political landscape. They had been taught that liberty was best protected by a government divided into separate branches which acted as mutual checks, and as they had once seen the celebrated equipoise of the English constitution destroyed by an overreaching executive, they now believed that the new state constitutions had permitted the pendulum to swing perilously far in the reverse direction. In the context of traditional political theory, to say that the balance in a government had been tilted in favour of the lower house – or popular branch – was to say that the democratic element had gained too much power. Thus the patricians' complaints about democracy did not represent a call to exclude the people from government, for they recognized the indispensability of a popular branch; all they wanted were 'sufficient checks against the democracy'.[1] Legislative tyranny and democracy were to them virtually interchangeable terms. The disillusionment of many American political leaders with legislative government was linked to their diminishing faith in public virtue, which had always been regarded as so essential to a government elected by the people. The very fractiousness and particularism of American public life in the

1780s were in themselves seen as proof of a serious moral erosion, for if the people really were virtuously submerging their private interests in the public good harmony should have prevailed. From this perspective, the local politician who appealed for popular support was a 'demagogue' bent on dividing and subverting the republic. Disapproving patricians were now concluding that a people who were not born virtuous must have virtue thrust upon them. 'The best republics will be virtuous and have been so,' wrote John Adams. 'But we may hazard a conjecture, that the virtues have been the effect of the well ordered constitution, rather than the cause.'[2] A system of checks and balances and a government of laws would restrain individual ambitions and enable the republic to survive. Constitutionalism thus raised almost to the level of ideology was also to become a lasting feature of American political culture.

The separate state legislatures themselves seemed increasingly unlikely to establish such a government of laws. Indeed, it was their behaviour which was doing so much to persuade patrician leaders that vice was fast replacing virtue in American public life. 'Frequent Interference with private property and Contracts, retrospective Laws destructive of all public Faith . . . ,' mourned Virginia's George Mason in 1783, 'and flagrant Violations of the Constitution must . . . occasion a general Depravity of Manners, bring the Legislature into Contempt, and finally produce Anarchy and a public convulsion.'[3] To most politicians the only effective remedy for such depravity was a stronger central government, which might be achieved either by revising the existing constitutional framework or by constructing a new one. But whatever was done, it needed to be done to the centre. While visiting Boston in 1784 Thomas Jefferson found 'the conviction growing strongly that nothing can preserve our Confederacy unless the band of Union, their common council, be strengthened'.[4]

The most determined champions of a stronger central government were those who might be characterized as the cosmopolitan elite. The men with a national vision tended to be those whose revolutionary service had involved them in continental rather than state affairs, such as George Washington and his young *aide* Alexander Hamilton, or those whose business interests had given them extra-local attachments, such as the wealthy Philadelphia merchant Robert Morris. The central political struggle of the 1780s was not so much between aristocracy and democracy as between cosmopolitanism and localism. A city merchant or a large-scale commercial planter was more likely to think continentally than a backwoods subsistence farmer, so the cosmopolitan-localist polarization took on some of the characteristics of a class conflict. A high proportion of the well-to-do naturally lived in urban and commercial farming areas, had attended college away from their own homes, had served as officers in the continental army or had held office in Congress or in the Confederation government, experiences which tended to pull them into the nationalist camp. But wealthy men and prominent political leaders did not necessarily become nationalists. Those who had built powerful positions for themselves in state politics, such as John Hancock in Massachusetts and George Clinton in New York, were fearful that their own authority might be diminished by a stronger central government. And men of lowly socioeconomic status were not necessarily aligned against the cosmopolitan elite. Urban workmen often sided with their rich merchant neighbours in the nationalist cause, perceiving advantages for themselves in a closer commercial union. Those with a cosmopolitan outlook, then, were drawn from men of all ranks – as were their opponents – though they encompassed a disproportionate number of the wealthy.

Before the revolutionary era the only central supervision of American affairs had been provided by the British authorities. In 1774 the defiant colonies had sent delegates to a Continental Congress to coordinate their resistance, and one task that fell to Congress after Independence was that of drafting a scheme for a general government. The resulting Articles of Confederation allowed each state to retain its prized individual sovereignty, while delegating certain functions to a Congress in which each state had one vote. The revolutionaries' intense suspicion of executive power was reflected in the failure to create a separate executive, both legislative and executive authority being vested in Congress. The resistance to British rule had also bred a suspicion of a distant central authority, and Congress found itself at the mercy of powerful state legislatures, which had grave preoccupations of their own. The lack of an effective taxing power was one of Congress's most serious constraints, making it dependent on the voluntary contributions of the states, and for this and other reasons its deficit increased every year. Its mounting debts did little to win it public confidence.

Nonetheless the accomplishments of the Confederation government were considerable. It was no mean attainment to survive the exhausting years of war and to conclude a victorious peace with Britain. Perhaps even more significant for the future of the American nation was the government's success in establishing its authority over the western domain. Before the Revolution British claims in North America had extended at least to the Mississippi, and with the removal of crown authority those states with ill-defined frontiers sought to press their boundaries westward. Other states, like Maryland and Rhode Island, could make no such claims, for they were bounded on the west by existing states, and they argued that the western territory rightfully belonged to the United States as a whole. The dispute over the western lands was made no easier to resolve by the rival claims·of land companies and individuals who had been speculating in the area since before the Revolution. The landless states (and the speculators in them) insisted that the western territories be ceded to Congress, Maryland in particular refusing to ratify the Articles of Confederation until this had been done, and under the exigencies of war the vital cessions were made. Congress thus became responsible for the western domain, which, it soon learned, it could use to pay off its debts.

Unlike the British, Congress and the states encouraged westward expansion, and in the 1780s thousands of Americans pressed into the virgin lands beyond the mountains, particularly into the area bounded by the Appalachians, the Ohio River, and the Mississippi. It fell to Congress to determine how this region was to be governed, a momentous decision which would set a precedent for any new territory settled by the American people. The Northwest Ordinance of 1787 finally decreed that western Americans too could aspire to statehood, that indeed as many as five states if necessary could be carved out of that particular area to join the original thirteen. At first the Northwest was to be administered by a governor appointed by Congress, then it would acquire a legislature, and when an area within it had acquired a free population of 60,000 it could be admitted to the Union as a state 'on an equal footing with the original States in all respects whatever'.[5] The Northwest Ordinance thus laid down the procedure by which most future states would be admitted to the Union. Whatever the inadequacies of the Confederation government, it had at least provided for an orderly method of opening up the West and indeed of enlargening the Union itself. It had guaranteed that American institutions were reproducible across the continent.

But the Confederation Congress's ultimate success with the western lands came far too late to redeem its reputation. If anything it raised more unsettling questions, for a system of government which could not always persuade thirteen states to work together seemed unlikely to cope with a yet larger number. But the continental-minded had been convinced of the need to strengthen the central government long before the Northwest Ordinance, before even the war had been won or the Articles of Confederation finally ratified. In the dark days of 1780, as the British army marched northwards, there was even talk of making George Washington dictator, and the nationalists secured a major victory when Congress created the post of Superintendent of Finance, and appointed the Philadelphia merchant Robert Morris to it. For two years the Confederation government and the nationalist cause were to centre largely on him.

Under Morris's leadership, the nationalists sought a constitutional amendment to give Congress the power to levy import duties, and they also supported his scheme to establish a national bank. These measures represented an ambitious attempt to change the nature of the Confederation, for their combined effect would be to strengthen the central government and to attract the influential support of the monied classes to it. At the heart of Morris's strategy was an attempt to secure control of the public debt. Like others of his generation he equated political power with the power of the purse – the rise of Parliament and of the colonial assemblies had been made possible by their control over finance. Both the central and state governments had borrowed liberally to fight the war, and the accumulated debt could in theory be repaid by either. Whichever government, national or state, established responsibility for the continental debt would have to be given power to raise money, and other powers could be expected to accrue. Morris even tried to increase the debt, sending out agents to appropriate for the national government a host of unsettled claims. 'A national debt, if it is not excessive, will be to us a national blessing,' wrote Alexander Hamilton to Morris. 'It will be a powerful cement of our union.'[6] The history of the decade after 1781 can largely be written in terms of the struggle for possession of that debt.

The nationalists' first priority was to give the Confederation government more power to collect money, and in 1781 Congress recommended to the states an amendment to the Articles to provide for a five per cent duty on imports, to be collected by federal officers and to be used only by Congress. The object of the 'Impost of 1781' was to give Congress funds to enable it to pay off the debt and to render it less dependent on the states. In 1781 also Morris presented his plan for a Bank of North America, the stock of which would be sold to private investors throughout the Union, but which would act also as the financial agent of Congress, lending it money and hopefully supplying the circulating medium of the country. He wrote a circular letter to the nation's wealthy men, urging them to buy shares and promising that the bank would be an agent of stability. One of its objects, he told John Jay, was 'to unite the several states more closely together in one general money connection and indissolubly to attach many powerful individuals to the cause of our country by the strong principle of self-love and the immediate sense of private interest'.[7] By winning for Congress control over the national debt, by establishing an impost, and by creating a national bank, Morris hoped greatly to increase the powers of the central government, whose strength would be further enhanced by the support of the monied men who owned the continental securities and bank shares. But Morris's attempts to secure greater political integration through financial integration were ultimately confounded. The impost amendment required the consent of all the states and most of them agreed readily enough. But in the fall of 1782 the radical Rhode Island legislature unanimously rejected it. Soon after the Virginia legislature also defected and the nationalist programme was in ruins.

But by now military hostilities had ended, and as Americans turned to the problems of peace their dismay with the Confederation intensified. In part this demoralization was the product of an economic depression which had been occasioned by the disruptions of the war and separation from Britain. The racing inflation of the war years had led Congress in 1780 to call on the states to abolish paper money, and most of them had complied. The war had also drawn much specie into the country, and with the return of peace merchants began to use this to pay their overseas debts. This meant that hard money was leaving the country at the same time as the states were contracting the supply of paper, and the shortage of both kinds of money deepened the depression. An increasing number of people found that they could not pay their debts, and their demands that the state legislatures resume paper money or other easy credit policies grew more insistent. The army of debtors, however, owed its existence in a sense to the large corps of creditors, who had no intention of allowing the currency to depreciate without a fight. Many creditors were wealthy merchants, but others were moderately successful farmers, professional men, and small traders, for in the days before banks, insurance companies, and stock exchanges, the private loan was a popular form of investment. Both debtors and creditors were sufficiently numerous to wield a certain political power, and the struggles in the state legislatures became bitter. The tensions between these embattled interests were greatly exacerbated by the problem of taxation. With the return of peace the states were obliged to impose heavy taxes in order to pay off their accumulated debts, taxes which were often unjustly distributed and were in any case difficult to meet in a period of money shortage. In Virginia, for example, a tax of one shilling an acre was levied, so that poor farmers scratching a living from thin soil had to pay as much, acre for acre, as wealthy planters on rich land. The poll tax was another regressive form of taxation adopted by some states, such as Massachusetts, where the politically influential merchants of the eastern seaboard used it to shift much of the tax burden onto the mass of small farmers. The army of debtors was being enlarged so that the governments could pay off *their* debts, and as these accumulated in the hands of speculators an ugly temper disfigured the political life of several states.

Other groups too were finding that the state and central governments could not adequately meet their demands, and were becoming exasperated by the volatility of state laws and policies. Manufacturing industry advanced quite rapidly in the 1780s and pressed for tariff protection against British goods, but when some states imposed higher tariffs than others employers and their workmen alike agreed that there was some virtue in the idea of a stronger central government. Protective tariffs were not always welcomed by merchants, but they too had their reasons for favouring some trade regulation. Many were in acute financial distress, partly because of the loss of British markets, and they pressed the state governments to retaliate by putting restrictions on British shipping. But again British ships simply took their custom to states where restrictions were lighter. What was needed, many merchants concluded, was a government capable of regulating trade on a national level.

Other issues added to the disillusionment of many Americans with their governmental institutions. The limited authority of Congress was demonstrated in the difficulties it experienced in preventing foreign nations from infringing American rights, an incapacity which hurt both national pride and the material interests of certain merchants and farmers. The British irritatingly continued to occupy forts and trading posts in the Northwest, despite the Treaty of Paris. Even less friendly were the actions of Spain, which still held Florida and the Gulf Coast and which decided to hamper America's advance westward by closing the mouth of the Mississippi to American commerce. This was a serious blow to trans-Appalachian settlers who needed the Mississippi network to float their goods to market, and John Jay was dispatched to treat with the Spanish minister. He returned with a proposal which was acceptable enough to many northerners, commercial privileges in Spain in return for the abandonment of the Mississippi, but it outraged westerners and their southern allies, who secured its defeat in Congress. Sectional voting had already unhappily appeared in Congress in the 1770s. This affair dangerously intensified sectional antagonisms and deepened the convictions of nationalists that only a stronger central government could save the Union.

Yet even as the economic depression and the pretensions of foreign nations broadened the support of the nationalists, their goal seemed more distant than ever. The crucial battle for possession of the national debt was being won by the states. The certificate-holders began to apply to their own states for redress when Congress was unable to pay them, and Pennsylvania, New York, and Maryland formally assumed responsibility for the federal debts owed to their citizens. By 1786 about one-third of the continental debt had been taken over by the states, and the Confederation government seemed in danger of withering away. Already attendance in Congress was incomplete, and the weakness of the nationalists in it was underlined in 1785 when the Superintendant of Finance was replaced with a Board of Treasury dominated by states-rights advocates. Even more dispiriting to the continental-minded was the embarrassment over the foreign debt. Already Congress had been obliged to suspend the payment of interest on wartime loans from France, and in a few years' time (1793) it would be faced with the even greater problem of beginning to pay off the principal of its foreign loans. Even many of those who had resisted the nationalizing plans of Morris and his allies conceded that Congress needed some sort of taxing authority and there was widespread support for a revised version of the impost. Again most states readily consented to an impost amendment, but it needed only one obstreper-ous state to wreck the scheme, a role which this time fell on New York. By the end of 1786 the future of the Confederation seemed in jeopardy.

The commercial and cosmopolitan interests also seemed to be losing ground at state level. The battles between debtors and creditors were being won distressingly often by the former. The depression and the heavy taxes had reduced many small farmers, artisans, and small planters to desperate straits, but the new state constitutions had given these classes an influence in the legislatures, where their agitation was intense, and by 1786 seven states had re-established some form of paper money. In most cases the currency held its value reasonably well, but that issued by Rhode Island and North Carolina depreciated swiftly. The Rhode Island legislature printed £100,000 in paper money, which it made available as loans to freeholders and declared as legal tender in payment of private debts as well as taxes. Creditors were understandably outraged at being obliged to accept what would soon become depreciated currency and many merchants closed their stores in protest. Riots broke out and the agrarian-dominated legislature passed an act imposing fines on those who refused to accept the money at face value and loss of citizenship for a second offence. Some harried Providence merchants took the only course open to them by fleeing the state. Such was the havoc caused that the enforcing acts were eventually repealed in December 1786, but not before Rhode Island had become notorious throughout the country for its fiscal irresponsibility. For conservatives everywhere Rhode Island became a horrifying symbol of democratic government, proof that popular rule really did threaten property. The excessive dependence of the legislatures on selfish and erratic popular pressures was similarly demonstrated in most other states, or so some men felt, by their enactment of laws to suspend payment of taxes and to protect debtors.

Yet even a government dominated by the commercial and creditor interests was no more capable of maintaining social order, as the disheartening example of Massachusetts showed. There the creditors had prevailed on the state authorities to redeem the debt certificates at about twice their market value, and the high taxes which resulted were so distributed as to fall heavily on the farmers. Many merchants themselves were being hard-pressed by British and other creditors at this time, but to the debt-ridden farmer it seemed that he was being squeezed in order that payments could be made to the wealthy mercantile interests who had presumably bought up the public debt. Laws were passed to enforce the collection both of taxes and of private debts, the property of debtors was seized and sold and many were consigned to jail. Popular resentment in western Massachusetts was particularly directed at the courts, which were being used to collect debts for creditors, and in August 1786 groups of armed farmers closed the courts in a number of counties. The state government responded by raising troops and marching them west, and the so-called rebels were soon dispersed. Shays's Rebellion had not really amounted to much, but this example of armed insurgency against a republican government horrified conservatives throughout the nation. 'We are all in dire apprehension that a beginning of anarchy with all its calamitys has approached', wailed Virginia's Henry Lee, 'and have no means to stop the dreadful work.'[8]

But they did have a means, even if an extra-legal one, and some nationalists were exploring it even before Shays's Rebellion. The Articles of Confederation could not be revised, but perhaps the people could be induced to replace them, as they had replaced the British government with their own state governments. Republican theory held that the people could make their own governments and constitutions. This had been the justification for the extra-constitutional conventions and congresses of the Revolution, as it had also been the justification for the adoption of the Massachusetts and New Hampshire constitutions by popularly-elected conventions. The idea of a convention to draw up a new constitution had been mooted frequently in the 1780s, and it gained favour with the deepening crisis of 1786. In January of that year the Virginia legislature invited the states to send delegates to a convention at Annapolis to discuss commercial problems. After a few days the convention disbanded with the report that little could be done about commerce until other parts of the federal constitution were changed, and it suggested another convention to be held in Philadelphia in 1787 to 'render the constitution of the federal government adequate to the exigencies of the union. . . . '[9] At first the call of the Annapolis Convention was widely ignored, but then reports of the lawless horrors of Daniel Shays and his luckless associates began to reach patrician ears. 'I beleave that the Tumults here, in this State will Alarm the other States;' predicted one perceptive citizen of Massachusetts, 'and by that Means Congress will Soon have Suffict Powers For the Benefitt of the Whole.'[10] Several state legislatures now hastened to elect delegates to the proposed convention, and in February 1787 Congress finally gave its blessing to the project.

The cosmopolitan elite had finally won a major victory after years of repeated failures. The sense of crisis of 1786-87 had finally persuaded enough of the nation's leading men that decisive action was necessary to combat the anarchic forces of localism and particularism. Deeply disturbed by the instability that they sensed around them, they determined to make one last effort to restore a balanced constitution, to create a central government capable of maintaining order, and to vest political power in men of experience and standing. But this reassertion of Whiggish forms, they finally realized, could only be accomplished with the aid of that most powerful of all allies, the will of the people.

Chapter 5

An American Constitution

A reverence for constitutions is perhaps a characteristic of the English-speaking peoples. At any rate, the idealized English constitution of 1688 had once commanded the highest admiration from Englishmen and Americans alike, and in due course the American Constitution of 1787 was to invoke a similar awe on both sides of the Atlantic. It was William Ewart Gladstone who was to bequeath one of the more memorable phrases about the American Constitution, which he described as 'the most wonderful work ever struck off at a given time by the brain and purpose of man.'[1] To those like Gladstone nourished in the tradition of Whig liberalism, the American Constitution could indeed be seen as a fitting successor of the constitution of 1688, inheriting the task of protecting freedom by the restraint of arbitrary power. The arbitrary power in the American case, it is true, was more theoretical than actual, but the Founding Fathers were at one with Old World theorists in agreeing that the concentration of power in a single body was an invitation to tyranny.

But it was not simply as an instrument for protecting the freedoms of the American people that the Constitution gained the respect of later generations. Some have seen in the Constitution a democratic commitment to popular government. Its first words are 'We the People', and it was ratified by the people in popularly-elected conventions. Others have admired (or abhorred) the Constitution for the limitations that it places on majority rule and for the way in which in the early years of the republic it facilitated the leadership of the rich, the well-born, and the able. Yet other commentators have commended the hard-headed pragmatism embodied in the Constitution, viewing it not as a logical explication of any single theory of government but as a series of realistic and workable compromises between contending sets of interests and principles. All of these interpretations of the making of the Constitution have some validity. The framers did want to base their new government on the consent of the governed, they equally wished to protect it from popular passions, and they were determined too to fashion something that would work, whatever its philosophical inconsistencies. In the event, they succeeded in creating a system of government of remarkable ingenuity, one which, among other things, succeeded in reconciling the principle of popular sovereignty with the maintenance of patrician leadership.

And, as we shall see, the Constitution they constructed would also serve well enough in the more democratic age to come.

The fifty-five men who assembled at Philadelphia did so with a determination to save the republic. Some, of course, wanted to save the country from the convention itself, whose purpose they mistrusted. But most of the delegates located the nation's perils elsewhere. Gouverneur Morris, a New Yorker parading as a Pennsylvanian, deplored the way in which 'the great objects of the nation had been sacrificed constantly to local views'. Virginia's Edmung Randolph opened the proceedings in Independence Hall with the observation that the 'chief danger arises from the democratic parts of our constitutions'. Even George Mason, the author of Virginia's celeb-rated Bill of Rights, identified the two great 'evils of our republican system' as 'the danger of the majority oppressing the minority, and the mischievous influence of demagogues'.[2] The republic was in imminent peril, or so many of the country's leading men were insisting, and the subversive forces were localism, demagoguery, democracy, legislative tyranny, and a selfish and factious spirit. In their minds, of course, all these were closely-related phenomena.

The essential complaint of these gentlemen was that parochial issues were being put before the common good of the Union. The several evils which they so deplored could all be identified primarily with local and state attachments. It followed that the best hope of achieving stability lay in establishing a more vigorous government at the centre, powerful enough to restrain divisive and particularistic pressures. Implicit in this line of reasoning was also the assumption that authority in such a government was likely to come to rest on men of standing and experience, for 'the local demagogues' would be unlikely to command the support needed to carry them to national office.[3] This was as it should be, it might have been argued, for only the cosmopolitan elite had the continental vision necessary to rise above selfish and local considerations and to rule for the good of the whole. But the case for a stronger national government was not self-evident, and in a period when distant government was associated with authoritarianism, it would not be easy to prove that the nationalists' schemes were compatible with the popular doctrines embraced so fervently during the Revolution. This was not simply a theoretical problem, for any system of government constructed at Philadelphia would need broad public support to survive. For another, it was part of conventional political wisdom that the republican form of government functioned best in a limited territorial area, such as in the ancient and medieval city-states. The nationalists had to persuade themselves and their colleagues that a general government could maintain its authority over an extensive area and a diverse people and yet remain both stable and genuinely republican. James Madison and his like-minded friends at Philadelphia had thus set themselves a truly awesome task. Quite apart from accommodating the varied interests of the different states, they had to construct a system of politics which would restore balanced government, put office into the hands of gentlemen of talent and virtue, win the consent of the people, and encompass a mighty continent.

The constitutional edifice fashioned at Philadelphia was not 'struck off at a given time' in quite the ready way that Gladstone's phrase seemed to imply. The Constitution took four long summer months to hammer out, and its shape was determined as much by bargain and compromise as by reason and political theory. The larger states like Virginia and Pennsylvania wanted a more consolidated central government, with a bicameral legislature in which both houses reflected the distribution of population. Small states like New Jersey and Delaware feared that they would be overshadowed in such a Union, and they tried to turn back the 'Virginia Plan' with a hastily-devised 'New Jersey Plan', which was essentially a revised version of the Articles of Confederation. The deadlock was only broken – and the convention only survived – by an engineered compromise which gave the separate states an equal voice in the Senate and provided that representation in the lower house be according to population. But the so-called 'Great Compromise' also included other features. The framers came to reluctant terms with slavery by allowing a slave to be counted as three-fifths of a person for the purpose of determining the allocation of representatives. As a palliative to the North, direct taxation was also to be determined on the same basis. Many of the northern delegates detested the concessions over slavery, which Gouverneur Morris described as 'the curse of heaven', but without them some southern states could not have been induced to stay in the Union.[4]

These features, of course, were unique to the American Constitution, as was the peculiar distribution of power between the central and state governments. The nationalists had wanted to give primacy to the central government, arguing that Congress should have the power to veto all state laws, but in vain, and their victory was a limited one. In a sense, the old federal system was not destroyed; rather, a national system was introduced to co-exist with it. The statutes and treaties of the United States were declared to be 'the supreme Law of the Land', and Congress was given a wide range of enumerated powers, one sweeping clause giving it the right to levy taxes, to repay the public debt, and to provide for 'the common Defence and general Welfare of the United States'. The national government would thus be one of some weight. But the states too retained considerable independence. The powers of the national government were to be confined to those clearly listed, and, as an early amendment soon spelled out, all other powers were 'reserved to the States respectively, or to the people'.[5] Unlike the English Parliament, then, Congress was not the source of all legislative authority. The American system of government was a hybrid creation, simultaneously national and federal (or confederal) in shape, in which the central and state governments shared power between them. A new equipoise had been discovered with which to protect republican liberty.

The need for balance indeed exercised the minds of the framers at almost every stage. Most of them took it for granted that the national government itself would have to be a 'balanced' government, although the overpowering model of the English constitution caused difficulties for them. The British government, Charles Pinckney pointed out, 'contains three orders of people distinct in their situation, their possessions and their principles', while the United States contained 'but on order that can be assimilated to the British Nation – this is the order of Commons'.[6] In the national government, as elsewhere in American life, men were still looking for means to reconcile their hierarchical assumptions about political stability with a social condition which militated against hierarchy. Some conservative delegates flirted with the idea of creating a kind of aristocracy of property to be represented in an upper house, and even Madison wondered how stability would be preserved if and when government became dominated by the representatives of the propertyless masses. Eventually the framers resolved on a new kind of balance, one of governmental powers instead of social orders. Yet even this in a curious way reflected the influence of the English constitution. Montesquieu, whose *Spirit of the Laws* was immensely influential in the United States, had thought that he had detected a separation of the executive, legislative, and judicial powers in England, and he had attached great importance to this as a device for promoting liberty. Americans seized on the doctrine of the separation of powers as one way of preserving both freedom and order in their undifferentiated society, but it is doubtful whether they realized how far they were departing from Old-World practices. The establishment of a separate judiciary, for example, was to have a major effect on American political history, for the Supreme Court came to serve as the final court of appeal on the constitutionality of both federal and state laws. The British Parliament tolerated no such independent judgement over its actions.

The executive was also to be more divorced from the legislature than was the case in England. The lesson of the state and confederation governments seemed to be that provision must be made for an independent executive branch capable of withstanding legislative pressure. In reasserting the old idea of a balanced constitution the framers thus came to modify the Whig doctrine of legislative supremacy. The convention finally agreed on an executive department headed by a single person, the president, chosen for a four-year term not by the legislature but by a specially-constituted set of electors. (Each state was entitled to as many electors as it had representatives in Congress, and could choose them however it wished.) This would give

him, as Madison said, 'a free agency with regard to the Legislature'.[7]
He was to be allowed substantial powers to execute the law, he was also
to serve as commander-in-chief and his independence was to be
protected by allowing him the right of veto. But although these
provisions ensured that the president would not be emasculated after
the manner of the early state governors, it was also agreed that the
president should not possess enough power to enable him to bend
Congress to his will. In this respect the distressing example of England
was very much in the framers' minds, for as one of them said, crown
patronage was 'the source of the corruption that ruined their Govt.'.[8]
Hence the delegates decided to deny executive officers seats in
Congress (thus averting the evil of 'placemen') and to limit the
patronage powers of the president, most of whose appointments had to
be confirmed by the Senate. The gentlemen at Philadelphia were
determined that the American Constitution should not suffer the fate
of the degenerated Whig constitution of 1688.

If the legislature was to be protected from the executive, it was also
to be protected from itself. The convention agreed to replace the old
Congress with a bicameral legislature, in which each house would act
as a watchdog on the other. That the classical conception of a mixed
constitution still hovered in the minds of the delegates is suggested by
the composition of the House of Representatives, which was clearly
meant to be the popular branch of the government. Members were
apportioned according to population and they were elected every two
years directly by the people, that is by those who were entitled to vote
for the lower houses in the states. (The powers thus given to the states
in relation to congressional – and presidential – elections meant that
the states as political units were powerfully to influence the development of American politics.) These representatives were the only
federal officers to be popularly chosen. The framers evidently
recognized the desirability of a popular branch, but they were
determined that it should not stand by itself. 'The first branch,
originating from the people, will ever be subject to *precipitancy,
changeability,* and *excess* . . . ', warned the irrepressible Gouverneur
Morris. 'This can only be checked by *ability* and *virtue* in the second
branch.'[9] The convention finally decided on a Senate which would be
composed simply of two men from each state, chosen by their state
legislatures for terms of six years. This ingenious arrangement
preserved the principle of the equality of the states, so dear to the small
states, and gave hope that the Senate would indeed be composed of
men of talent and experience. Like the British House of Lords it was
meant to provide a 'stable institution in the government'.[10]

By the time their work was complete the gentlemen of Philadelphia
had achieved their principal goals. They had constructed a political
system which, they could reasonably hope, would restore the
governmental balance they so much desired, would function well over
an extensive territory, would probably serve to exclude demagogues

and the meaner sort from high office, and was compatible with the doctrine of popular sovereignty. The remarkable device which did all this was the principle of representation, and it was this which finally made the American system fundamentally different from other forms of government. Only the American system of government, according to Tom Paine, was based 'wholly on the system of representation' and hence it was 'the only real republic in character and practise, that now exists'.[11]

What Paine meant was that the American system was one in which the people delegated prescribed governing powers to their chosen representatives, and that all the officers of government were their agents. In this sense the resemblance of the hierarchy of president, Senate and House of Representatives to king, Lords and Commons was illusory, for the president and Senate did not speak for separate hereditary classes. There had been talk of making the Senate the chamber of property-owners, as was the case in a number of states, but in the American political environment it was really only possible to justify the establishment of a president and Senate on the grounds that they too represented the people. This argument was already being used to justify bicameralism and separate executives at state level. Later generations would find the universal application of the representative principle unremarkable, but to the Founding Fathers it was a revolutionary breakthrough in political science. Never had a government existed in a populous nation in which all branches stemmed from the people and just the people. The uniqueness of American politics, in Madison's words, was to lie in the delegation of the government . . . to a small number of citizens elected by the rest'.[12] The principle of representation thus both recognized the doctrine of popular sovereignty and legitimized the distribution of powers.

The device of representation also provided an answer to Montesquieu's influential judgement that large republics were liable to destroy themselves through their own imperfections. James Madison was well aware of the multiplicity of different interests in the American Union, but this in itself, he thought, could be a source of security rather than of danger. His views were spelled out in his famous tenth *Federalist*, part of the series of papers that he wrote with Alexander Hamilton and John Jay to persuade New Yorkers of the virtues of the Constitution. In a small and fairly homogeneous community, he pointed out, it was relatively easy for a majority to come together to oppress the rest, but extend the sphere and 'you make it less probable that a majority of the whole will have a common motive to invade the rights of other citizens'.[13] A pure democracy could not operate over a large territory, but a republic, based upon the scheme of representation, could well preserve a veritable empire of liberty.

The lesson of religious history in eighteenth-century America, that the best guarantee of religious freedom was a multiplicity of sects, had not been lost on Madison, who now perceived that political liberty too might rest on a multiplicity of social interests. Thus, 'a rage for paper money, for an abolition of debts, . . . or for any other improper or wicked project, will be less apt to pervade the whole body of the Union than a particular member of it. . . . '[14] The republic would thus be protected from the divisive effect of party, because the inevitable local factions would themselves be hopelessly separated from one another. The very diversity of the Union would serve to frustrate any potential tyranny of the majority, and the system of representation would collect and filter the views and interests of this sprawling country.

Further, the process of representation had the incomparable merit in the eyes of the framers of tending to put government into the hands of the 'better sort'. For, as Madison explained, it would serve 'to refine and enlarge the public views, by passing them through the medium of a chosen body of citizens, whose wisdom may best discern the true interest of their country. . . . '[15] The system of indirect elections for senators and president in particular should keep those offices in the hands of notables and deny them to party and factional upstarts. The complex arrangements for the election of the president, it was argued, provided 'a constant probability of seeing the station filled by characters pre-eminent for ability and virtue'.[16] Ability and virtue were not the monopolies of men of standing, of course, but only they were in a position to display their talents. The patrician elite was well aware of the advantages of the large constituency to men of their own class. Richard Henry Lee, an opponent of the Constitution, believed that because of its small size even the House of Representatives would give the ordinary people little voice in the national government, for 'In the nature of things, nine times in ten, men of the elevated classes in the community only can be chosen'.[17] The principle of representation was ideal for the purposes of the delegates at Philadelphia, for it at once recognized the sovereignty of the people while putting leadership into the hands of the cosmopolitan elite.

The constitutional convention, then, had constructed an ingenious system of politics, one which reconciled the interests of large states and small states, of free states and slave states, which provided for a vigorous national government as well as active state governments, and which restored balance and stability. It promised to span a continent, it was wholly elective in form, and it afforded the nation's gentlemen a good opportunity for exercising power. So, at any rate, the delegates at Philadelphia might hope, but it was one thing to write a constitution and quite another to secure its adoption.

Now the nationalists embarked on their most audacious course. Enlisting the libertarian doctrines of the Revolution, they argued that since the people were the fountain of all political power, they had the capacity to lay aside the Articles of Confederation in favour of a new instrument of government. If the gentlemen at Philadelphia had adhered to the stipulated procedure, they would have presented their work as a series of amendments to the existing Articles, but they knew that they could never win the required consent of every state legislature. Instead they proposed to have the new Constitution ratified by state conventions, which, it was to be hoped, would be 'expressly chosen by the people'.[18] For the first time in history, the people as a whole were to give their express consent to the national institutions by which they would be governed. The convention further decided that only nine states needed to ratify the Constitution for the new government to come into being, hence finally abandoning the Articles' paralysing principle of unanimity.

Then the battle was joined. In newspapers, pamphlets, state legislatures, conventions, and public meetings across the Union the merits of the proposed Constitution were argued at length. An early *coup* for the nationalists was to appropriate to themselves the supposedly popular name of Federalist, a title which falsely implied that they were against a consolidated government, and which obliged their opponents to accept the equally misleading label of Anti-Federalist. Thereafter the Anti-Federalists seemed to be out-manoeuvered at almost every step in the game. The Federalists had the great majority of newspapers on their side, and such was their commercial power that they were sometimes able to force hostile newspapers to moderate their criticisms. The Federalists, whose core consisted of the old nationalists who had been fighting for a stronger central government for years, were more cohesive, better-organized and better-financed than their opponents. They also occupied a better strategic position. Many Federalists had private reservations about the proposed national government, but they knew that what had been agreed at Philadelphia was the best that circumstances could allow, and now they campaigned unequivocally *for* the Constitution. The Anti-Federalists were on less certain ground. Some clung tenaciously to the Articles of Confederation and damned the Constitution as an affront to the 'spirit of republicanism',[19] others admitted that the Articles were inadequate and favoured some strengthening of the central government, and a crucial group was prepared to accept the Constitution subject to certain amendments. The Anti-Federalists were never able to close ranks sufficiently to turn back the Federalist assault. Men whose attachments and interests were primarily local, the Anti-Federalists were impeded from emerging as a powerful political movement by their very parochialism.

But for several months the American people were treated to a public debate on the nature of the government they were being invited to live under, a debate which early displayed some of the continuing characteristics of American political discourse. The argument over the Constitution could only be an argument over the nature of the American republic, over what America was meant to be, and the impassioned patriot – whatever his views – all too readily identified his political opponents with hostility to the American mission itself. Both Federalists and Anti-Federalists were tempted to see themselves as the saviours of the republic, protecting it from the subversive activities of their adversaries, who, whether wittingly or otherwise, were embracing dangerously unrepublican – or un-American – doctrines. Many Anti-Federalists espied the sinister creatures of monarchy and aristocracy lurking behind the plain words of the Constitution. Patrick Henry complained of its 'awful squinting; it squints towards monarchy', while a sardonic Pennsylvanian preferred his dubious loyalty to 'this our royal government'.[20] The Federalists for their part insisted that it was their opponents who were 'the enemies of liberty, and the secret abettors of the interests of Great Britain'.[21]

Threading its way between the bursts of rhetorical outrage was a more reasoned discussion. The Anti-Federalists in particular charged that the Constitution would impose an over-powerful consolidated government on the country, and, as every eighteenth-century theorist knew, it was in the nature of power to expand at the expense of liberty. The Federalists themselves betrayed the strength of the continuing popular suspicion of strong and distant government by not so much defending the need for it as by emphasizing the limitations on it. At most they might concede with Madison that the government was of a 'mixed character', that is 'neither a national nor a federal Constitution, but a composition of both'.[22] Some opponents of the Constitution saw a sinister design in the failure of the convention to attach a bill of rights to it (such bills being common in the state constitutions), and even many of its supporters regretted this omission. In some states it became clear that only such an explicit guarantee of individual and state liberties against an encroaching government would secure ratification. Reluctantly the Federalists conceded the battle and in so doing they won the war. In June 1788 New Hampshire became the ninth state to ratify the Constitution, and soon after the indispensable states of New York and Virginia fell into line.

The 'better sort' had finally secured a government of their own design, and in doing so demonstrated that the politics of deference were not yet dead. In state after state the Federalists were identified with men of wealth and standing, as Jackson T. Main and others have demonstrated. But as was to be the case with many political contests in American history, the divisions over the Constitution were probably more related to geography than to class. In general the eastern seaboard, the cities, and the commercial farming areas tended to be Federalist, while isolated and subsistence farming areas tended to be Anti-Federalist. In Pennsylvania, for example, Gouverneur Morris saw the Federalists' problem to be to overcome 'the cold and sower temper of the back counties'.[23] The Constitution did not divide the rich from the poor so much as it divided commercial and metropolitan areas from rural and undeveloped areas. But since much of the nation's wealth was concentrated in the commercial areas, this cosmopolitan-backwoods dichotomy naturally took on the appearance of a class struggle.

The success of the Federalists in recruiting the support of eminent landlords, merchants, and lawyers gave them a considerable advantage in an age when deferential habits still survived. Heading the list of the Constitution's influential friends were the two great American heroes Benjamin Franklin and George Washington, whose benedictions reassured many that the framers had after all been true to the Spirit of '76. A vital group in the state conventions were those who had been elected as Anti-Federalists and later changed sides, sixty or seventy men in all, and about half of them are said to have been relatively obscure figures, capable perhaps of being overawed by the mass of wealth and standing arrayed behind the Constitution. 'The *better sort*', said Melancton Smith of New York, 'have means of convincing those who differ from them'.[24] The strong Federalist support in the cities suggests that urban workmen too were still identifying with their community rather than with their class. In New York City, for example, the Federalists won over ninety per cent of the votes cast in the election for the ratifying convention, the craftsmen, artisans, and tradesmen voting with the merchants, financiers, and lawyers for a central government capable of promoting commerce and manufacturing. As Alexander Hamilton had predicted, the city's artisans and mechanics were disposed 'to bestow their votes upon merchants and those whom they recommend', for the merchant was 'their natural patron and friend'.[25] Rural voters too continued to defer to the established leaders of society. In Virginia the nationalists John Marshall and Edmund Randolph were elected to attend the ratifying convention by an Anti-Federal county, whose residents presumably felt that weighty political decisions were best entrusted to prominent public men. The low turnout in the elections for the ratifying conventions was perhaps a final sign of deference. Some four-fifths or even more of the white men in the country did not even go to the polls, content, perhaps, to leave the issue of the structure of the nation's political system to the men they expected to operate it.

So what John Jay called 'the better kind of people' had re-established their authority.[26] They had secured a form of government which, they hoped, would reconcile popular sovereignty with patrician leadership. As political theorists, they had moved a long way from the celebrated English model, constituting a government which was wholly elective, which derived its authority entirely from the people through the principle of representation, and which was neither entirely national nor entirely confederal in form. The Constitution made no specific mention of property qualifications for voting or even for office-holding and it explicitly forbad titles of nobility. Further, the Constitution itself was declared to be the fundamental law of the land, which would bind even Congress. Hence the Old Whig notion of the primacy of the legislature was replaced by the notion of the primacy of the written Constitution, a reverence for which was destined to become an important feature of the American political tradition.

But the Founding Fathers had not entirely cast off the Whiggish heritage. Their central quest remained that of devising a political system which would preserve freedom and restrain power without sacrificing order. They once more accepted that men were unreliable creatures who needed to be protected from one another, and that power therefore had to be divided against itself. Liberty and order were to be preserved by achieving the right equipoise between the different branches of government. Like their English peers, too, they continued to assume that this balance was ever in peril, and they attempted to build into their Constitution various safeguards against the kind of degeneration that the English version had allegedly undergone. And they still continued to adhere to a holistic or organic view of political society, in which the general interest was best discerned by men of independence, experience, and virtue, who determined public policy by reasoned discussion between themselves. In pursuit of this vision of patrician harmony, the framers devised a system of government which would facilitate responsible leadership, frustrate party, and limit the access of local figures to high office. In a system of free elections, Alexander Hamilton argued confidently, continuing to picture society in hierarchical or vertical terms, 'the representative body, with too few exceptions to have any influence on the spirit of the government, will be composed of landholders, merchants, and men of the learned professions'.[27] But it remained to be seen whether the Constitution really would inaugurate a republic in which a 'speaking aristocracy' ruled with the express consent of a 'silent democracy'.

Part 3

Politics in the
early republic (1789-1815)

It was to be many years before Americans freed themselves from their old political customs and from the weight of English example. The politics of the early republic constituted an unstable mixture of traditional values and novel practices. Political leadership still tended to fall on notables, particularly in the national arena, partly perhaps because of the filtration process imposed both by the Constitution and by self-appointed nominating caucuses. The survival of property qualifications for voting and for office, however modest, also reflected an assumption that governments represented more than just people and that political leadership might reasonably be exercised by men of substance. But probably more important in perpetuating patrician rule was the attitude of the electorate itself, which, although extensive and active, does not seem to have been aroused much against 'the better sort'. At any rate, American politics continued to be substantially leader-oriented, and political authority tended to become concentrated in the legislatures. At the national level the republic seemed to be evolving something like a parliamentary system, as Congress gained an ascendancy over the executive branch.

But this period also witnessed a significant modernization of the political process, most notably in the emergence of a competitive two-party system. In the national capital men of different persuasions resorted to the weaponry of party in order to protect the newborn republic, and at local level bitter confrontations divided old communities and did much to weaken the hold of custom and deference. Yet the old conviction that parties were illegitimate survived and contributed to the early collapse of the first American party system. Nonetheless these primitive parties left their mark. The Federalists helped to establish a viable federal government, possessed of important financial powers and responsibilities, and their measures opened the way to a dynamic industrial and commercial economy. The Federalist political vision itself was rejected, for it seemed to rely too much on paternalistic assumptions and English models. The Republicans contributed the lasting conviction that republican liberty was best preserved by trusting the people and distrusting government and a demonstration that a goodly measure of pragmatism was necessary for success in American politics. The early party battles also served to transmit to later generations the ancient premise that constitutions (and hence republics) were subject to degeneration, and the conclusion that Americans had constantly to guard against subversive forces – or un-American activities. The difficulty of conceiving more than one interpretation of the republican polity was also revealed by the strength of sectional feelings in this period, especially by the secessionist tendencies of those who believed that the federal government was betraying the republican cause. But a precarious unity was in the end maintained, and by 1815 the holistic ideal of a republic free of serious party and sectional strife seemed close to realization.

Chapter 6

The Federalist design

Rip Van Winkle, on awakening from the long sleep which had caused him to miss the revolutionary excitements, tottered back to his village where he encountered an inn sign on which he recognized 'the ruby face of King George', whose red coat had been repainted blue and buff, whose sceptre had been replaced by a sword, and whose name had been changed to 'GENERAL WASHINGTON'.[1] Washington Irving, viewing the American past from the secure vantage point of Regency England, was able to write of it with a certain whimsical irony, but to an earlier generation the metamorphosis of King George into President George was not a matter for levity. The American people may have thrown off the rule of Britain but they had not liberated themselves completely from the past, and British precedents and practices continued to exert a powerful hold over the minds of the builders of the new nation. Some, like Alexander Hamilton, remained unabashed admirers of the British system of government, and wanted to emulate it, while others, like Thomas Jefferson, pointed to contemporary Britain as a lesson in what to avoid. But whether they revered or reviled their disowned parent, American leaders of all persuasions found themselves unable to free themselves completely from her hypnotic spell.

British influences took a variety of forms. First, there was the cluster of assumptions and ideas inherited from English political thought. Many Americans continued to see the central problem of politics as that of protecting liberty against the inevitable encroachments of power and they continued to assume that the remedy lay in a balanced constitution. Their ideal political order was one which the English Whigs of 1688 would have found congenial, one in which the political nation was identified with the holders of property, particularly land, and in which an enlightened patrician elite ruled with the consent and for the benefit of all. Further, some Americans were impressed with the material accomplishments of eighteenth-century Britain, with the way in which she had combined political stability with economic vitality and imperial expansion. If the Whigs of 1688 had restored liberty to England, they had also laid the foundations of her economic greatness by establishing such institutions as the Bank of England and a sound system of public credit, or so it now seemed to men on both sides of the Atlantic. And however much or little respect Americans might accord to Whig ideas and current British practices, there was one brute fact which they could not escape – that most American trade was still with Britain and her colonies. The complex economic and financial network of the prerevolutionary era, by which Americans had been supplied with foreign markets, manufactures, and investment funds by courtesy of British merchants and bankers, had been largely re-created since 1783. America's destiny was still intertwined with that of Britain.

Many Americans also continued to be impressed in spite of themselves by the orderly development of parliamentary government in Britain. Alexander Hamilton envied the energy imparted to British affairs by the executive, now more than ever coming to be dominated by the prime minister rather than the king. The British cabinet, too, had become a fairly strong institution by the late eighteenth century, seemingly demonstrating that order could be imposed on the muddle of British politics by a group of powerful men at the centre. The industrial revolution, the war with America and France, the financial reforms of William Pitt the Younger, and the incapacity of the king had all contributed something to the flowering of ministerial government, in which the nation's affairs were directed by men whose ability, social standing, political convictions, and public services had earned for them the confidence of the rich and the well-born in Parliament. The Philadelphia Constitution had explicitly rejected the British model of parliamentary government by separating the executive from the legislature, but for at least a generation after 1789 American leaders found themselves – both consciously and unconsciously – imitating some of the traits of Mother England. Both the Federalists under Alexander Hamilton and the Republicans under Thomas Jefferson and James Madison experienced the mimetic pull of British forms, most notably in a tendency to overcome the inconveniences of the separation of powers by creating Americanized versions of ministerial or parliamentary government. In the long run, however, the American people and their continent were to demonstrate that they could not be managed by such Old-World devices.

In the opening months of 1789 the complex mechanism so carefully constructed at Philadelphia still existed only on paper. One constitutional system had already failed to win the allegiance of enough of the American people, and there was no guarantee that the new one would work any better. But the great majority of American political leaders determined to do what they could to translate the blueprint into a viable form of government. Most of those who had been at Philadelphia joined the new government in either an elective or an appointive capacity, and both houses of the first Congress proved to be overwhelmingly Federalist in composition – only a handful of Anti-Federalists were elected. George Washington, feeling older than his fifty-seven years and yearning for the peace of Mount Vernon, was once more pressed into active service, this time as his country's first president. Alexander Hamilton once spoke of Washington as '*an Aegis very essential to me*', but he was also an aegis very essential to the new government, for only he had the towering authority that was needed to stamp it with legitimacy. 'You only can settle that political machine,' Lafayette wrote to Washington from France. 'It is to little purpose to have *introduced* a system', echoed Hamilton, 'if the weightiest influence is not given to its firm *establishment*, in the outset'.[2] Washington did not have the most subtle mind of his age, but he did command the confidence of his countrymen, and he brought to his new office a sound common sense, an unshakable integrity, a calm and deliberate nature and a massive presence. His awkward aloofness seemed even to add to his stature, for few ordinary mortals cared to be familiar with the great man. (Gouverneur Morris for a dare once slapped Washington on the back and was quickly reduced to a humiliated silence by the general's icy stare.) Washington, better than anyone, typified the patrician style of politics of the eighteenth century, not actively seeking public office but gravely accepting it as a duty incumbent on leading men.

The widespread desire among the American elite to augment the prestige of the national government was further displayed in the debate over titles. Washington's decision to mark his inauguration by delivering an address before Congress – itself an echo of the King's Speech before Parliament – created an obligation on that body to reply, but how was the chief magistrate to be addressed? John Adams, who for years had emphasized the need to cultivate a feeling of respect among the people for their agents in government, seized the opportunity to press for a high-sounding title. 'His Highness' was advocated by some, and Washington himself was said to favour 'His Mightiness', tempting one congressman in a frivolous moment to propose 'His High and Mightiness'.[3] The monarchical overtones of all such titles again revealed how difficult it was for Americans to conceive of a head of state who was not a sort of substitute king, and the parallel was reinforced by Washington's own august persona and liking for ceremony. But if the new president was to be a republican king, Congress eventually decided that it would be better not to admit it and conferred on him instead the formal title 'The President of the United States', soon to be transmuted into the simple dignity of 'Mr. President'.

A faint and imperfect image of the British style of government also glimmered behind Congress's organization of the executive department. The Constitution was silent on what government departments might be needed and how they were to be headed, and it was not even clear that any such departmental heads would be answerable to the president. Many people had assumed that the country would in effect be governed jointly by the president and the Senate, and if it wished Congress could have tied the departments closely to the Senate or the House. But the first Congress was packed with staunch nationalists intent on enhancing the authority of the executive. Their decision was to create discrete executive departments each under the direction of a single head who would be responsible to the president. Something of an exception, however, was made of the Secretary of the Treasury, who was ambiguously linked to Congress which could require him to 'digest and prepare plans' on the national finances.[4] While this administrative system could never become a form of ministerial government in the British sense – since the Secretaries could not sit in Congress – nonetheless a form of government was being created in which the directive power would apparently reside in a group of ministers acting under the authority of a strong chief executive. The Secretaries were even frequently referred to as 'ministers' in these early days.

A potential rival to the authority of the Secretaries was the Senate, which had to consent to their appointment. The Constitution also decreed that the president could only make treaties and appoint Supreme Court judges and other major officers 'by and with the advise and consent' of the Senate. Some had seen the Senate as a sort of privy council, assisting the president in the performance of his duties. One blow to its pretensions was early administered by James Madison and other nationalists in Congress, who protected the president's prerogative by establishing that he could remove officials without first consulting the upper house. George Washington also initially tried to consult the Senate before making treaties, even turning up in person and taking the presiding officer's chair, but senators were clearly uncomfortable in his presence and the relationship between them soon cooled. Thereafter treaties were only submitted for ratification after they had been made, and the Senate never evolved into a privy council. To that degree it approximated more to the British House of Lords than to the upper houses of the colonial assemblies.

The failure of the Senate to develop consultative and quasi-executive functions eased the emergence of the departmental heads. The Constitution itself does not recognize a cabinet, but the Secretaries of the Treasury, State, and War, together with the Attorney-General, were soon acting in that role. Washington, not a man to make decisions without conferring with others, adopted the practice of meeting regularly with the departmental heads. This added to the stature of the Secretaries, as it also in time meant that their posts became political. The Secretaries could have become – as may have been intended – senior civil servants, holding their offices permanently, but their cabinet status drew them into the policy-making sphere of government and they became the president's ministers, their political fortunes closely tied to his. The early emergence of the cabinet rather than the Senate as a directing organ of government again testified to the lure of British forms, although the supremacy of the president in the executive branch militated against the emergence of a separate prime minister. Not that powerful cabinet members did not fancy themselves in that role from time to time.

The United States, however, was not Britain, and Washington recognized this by maintaining a geographical balance in his selection of cabinet officers. The choice of Alexander Hamilton of New York as first Secretary of the Treasury was balanced by that of Thomas Jefferson of Virginia as Secretary of State. Washington's fat friend, Henry Knox of Massachusetts, continued as Secretary of War, a position he had held under the Confederation, and Edmund Randolph of Virginia became Attorney-General. If the composition of the new government seemed to lean a little in a southerly direction, this was compensated for by the election of John Adams as vice-president and by the appointment of New Yorker John Jay as Chief Justice. In addition, like most later presidents, Washington made some use of unofficial advisers, the most important of these in the opening years being James Madison, now a member of the House of Representatives. Most of these men had been working for a stronger central government for some years and they could now be expected to complete the work of 1787. Washington, Adams, Knox, Jay, Hamilton, and Madison were all identified with the nationalist or Federalist position, while Jefferson and Randolph were at least closer to that than they were to Anti-Federalism.

This nationalist unity did not long survive the first actions of the new government, or at least of its energetic Secretary of the Treasury, who seemed to see George Washington as a sort of constitutional monarch, himself as a prime minister, and the British governing and economic systems as worthy of imitation. In Britain it was the first Lord of the Treasury who had emerged as prime minister, a position currently held by the young William Pitt, who was also Chancellor of the Exchequer. Hamilton could hardly miss the parallel, which was made stronger by the provision apparently requiring the Secretary of the Treasury to report directly to Congress. Hamilton at first sought to develop this connection, hoping to be able to deal personally with Congress and perhaps to lead it from without, but early in 1790 Congress decided that he had to submit his reports in writing. Nonetheless in 1792 Hamilton was still able to speak of a congressional faction as 'hostile to me and my administration'.[5] But whether or not Hamilton wished to emulate Pitt's political position, he certainly admired his financial reforms and these he did use as a model for his own measures. And it was in this that Hamilton precipitated an ideological conflict that was to transform American politics.

Born on an obscure West Indian island, the illegitimate son of a vagrant if well-born Scotsman, Hamilton's prodigious talents had carried him far in his adopted land, where he had served as an *aide-de-camp* to Washington during the revolutionary war, led a storming party at Yorktown, married the daughter of a prominent New Yorker, and played a leading part in securing the new Constitution.

Well-versed in the writings of the classical and modern political theorists, Hamilton dreamed of being the supreme legislator of his nation, the disinterested and far-sighted statesman who laid the foundations of her future security, freedom, and greatness. A member of Congress he had written many years earlier, 'is to be regarded not only as a legislator, but as the founder of an empire'.[6] Whatever his personal ambitions, Hamilton's vision was of an America united, strong, and independent, capable of taking its place among the great nations of the world, and his measures as Secretary of the Treasury were designed to make the vision real. His critics accused him of raising up a moneyed aristocracy, but insofar as this was true it was but a means to a more patriotic end. Hamilton, like Madison and others of their rationalist generation, recognized the power of self-interest in human affairs, and he wanted to harness it for the benefit of the nation. It was fruitless 'to oppose the strong current of the selfish passions', he remarked in 1788. '*A wise legislator will gently divert the channel, and direct it, if possible, to the public good.*'[7]

In 1790 and 1791 Hamilton presented Congress with a series of proposals which were designed to divert the energies and passions of the people along constructive channels, at least in his own eyes. The Constitution, he believed, was but a half-finished document and much more had to be done to establish the supremacy of the national government and to assure the independence and survival of the nation. Britain's celebrated political stability was widely attributed to the support for the government of the propertied classes, and her strength in the world to her commerce, manufacturing, and sound financial system. If the United States was to have a strong central government, capable of enforcing its will on state governments and refractory individuals, then she too needed the services of the rich and the well-born, and if the United States was to maintain her dignity and independence before the depredations of foreign nations, then she too had to develop a strong and self-sufficient economy. Or so Alexander Hamilton reasoned. Like his mentor Robert Morris in the early 1780s, Hamilton wanted to use the financial instruments of the government to carry out an ambitious programme of social and political engineering.

Hamilton's first objective was to restore the nation's credit. The long-standing problem of the national debt had still to be resolved. Standing at over $50 million in 1789, nearly a quarter of the debt was owed to foreign governments and bankers, while the rest consisted of domestic securities which had depreciated in value and had largely been bought up by speculators. Hamilton proposed first that the national government should pay off the entire debt at the original face value, thus establishing its credit with domestic and foreign investors and, incidentally, earning the goodwill of the monied men who had bought up the depreciated certificates. Second, Hamilton recommended that the national government take over the debts of the state governments, thereby establishing the supremacy of the former and averting any resurgence in the power of the latter, and, as it happened, attaching the interests of speculators and other debtholders throughout the Union to the national government. Third and most important, Hamilton proposed that the domestic debt be funded, that is negotiable bonds would be issued to debtholders to be paid off at stated periods. These bonds, being underwritten by the government, would in effect serve as a form of specie. The economy would thus be injected with a much-needed supply of capital which would enable trade and commerce to expand. Furthermore, by replacing the tattered certificates of the war years with new stock, the funding scheme would maintain the army of investors throughout the country with a mercenary interest in an energetic and efficient central government. A national debt, noted a writer in the *Gazette of the United States*, 'attaches many citizens to the government, who, by their numbers, wealth, and influence contribute more perhaps to its preservation than a body of soldiers'.[8]

The funding scheme also meant that the government needed revenue, and Hamilton next called for the imposition of excise duties. At long last an American central government was to levy an internal tax. At the same time he recommended the creation of a national bank, modelled largely on the Bank of England. Designed to act as the fiscal agent of the government and to provide a supply of paper currency, the bank would be mainly in private hands, the government appointing only a fifth of its directors and possessing a fifth of its stock. The bulk of its stock – $8 million – would be sold to investors, who could buy it if they wished largely with government bonds. By this ingenious scheme, Hamilton secured a major financial institution, provided a circulating medium to invigorate the economy, enhanced the value of government bonds, and ensured that both the bank and its monied stockholders would have a vested interest in the welfare of the central government and its finances. Finally, in his ambitious Report on Manufactures, Hamilton proposed protective tariffs, subsidies for new industries, and awards for inventions. By thus diverting American resources into manufacturing he hoped to create a diversified and self-sufficient economy, in which the farming areas traded with the industrial areas and sectional divisions were submerged in a complex unity of interests. The cohesive political union that Hamilton dreamed of would thus be cemented by a prosperous commercial union and, as it happened, the interests of American businessmen would again be allied to those of the national government. This vision was a recurring one in American politics, having been anticipated by Robert Morris in the 1780s and beguiling conservative politicians again in the nineteenth century.

Some years after he had left office Hamilton remarked to Gouverneur Morris that the Constitution was a 'frail and worthless fabric' which he was 'still laboring' to prop up.[9] In a sense Hamilton's financial measures were designed to complete the work of the Philadelphia Convention. At Philadelphia Hamilton had offered the model of the British government and had urged the creation of a powerful executive, supported by a senate elected for life. 'All communities divide themselves into the few and the many. The first are the rich and well-born, the other the mass of the people', he had said. 'Give therefore to the first class a distinct, permanent share in the government.'[10] In this way a stable political order would be created in which the turbulence of the people would be restrained. Hamilton looked more to the government than to the governed to sustain the republic. He had failed to get what he wanted at Philadelphia, but as Secretary of the Treasury he could try again. His audacious programme was intended to enhance the authority of the central government (so that unlike the Confederation it could resist the encroachments of both state and foreign governments), to promote national integration, to create an expansive industrial and commercial economy, and to harness the weighty influence of the monied classes to these desirable ends. Hamilton had no particular affection for the wealthy as such, but reasoned that they could be of service to the Union. The bank, he once remarked, was a device for uniting 'the interest and credit of rich individuals with those of the State'.[11] By recreating something like the British sociopolitical system public strength and individual security would also be obtained in the United States.

If Hamilton's political views had been unacceptable to most members of the Philadelphia Convention, they were little more palatable when presented in this elaborate financial guise. Inevitably his proposals reawakened the old fears inherited from the English radicals, whose warnings against the degeneration of balanced constitutions had been so thoroughly absorbed by the American revolutionaries. In particular, the Bolingbrokean spectre of a corrupt alliance between government and the monied interest, originally invoked by Robert Morris's schemes in the 1780s, now began to haunt some Americans. If Walpole had used banks, funding schemes, excise taxes and corporate interests to give the British ministry despotic power, as his Country critics charged, was Hamilton about to embark on a similar subversive course? The Virginia legislature submitted a memorial to Congress in December 1790 in which it noted 'a striking resemblance between this system and that which was introduced into England at the Revolution – a system which has . . . insinuated into the hands of the executive an unbounded influence which . . . daily threatens the destruction of every thing that appertains to English liberty. . . . '[12] Such fears at first surfaced in an isolated and sporadic way, but they underlay much of the resistance to the Hamiltonian system.

As Hamilton's reports were placed before Congress the ranks of the nationalists, hitherto so dominant, began slowly to give away. Madison was the most prominent defector, now emerging as the principal leader of the inchoate congressional opposition. He admitted the need for some kind of funding scheme, but Hamilton's measures seemed both unjust and dangerous. The blessings of a national debt were no longer so evident now that a revolution had broken out in France, brought about in part by the chronic indebtedness of her government. And a public debt seemed particularly undesirable in a republic, where all men were supposed to possess equal rights, because the government would have to raise revenue to pay its creditors, which is to say that the many would be taxed for the benefit of the wealthy few. Madison particularly disliked the way in which speculators would profit from Hamilton's scheme. Generating even more opposition was the proposal that the federal government assume the state debts, several southern states having already largely paid off their debts and seeing little reason to help relieve the northern states. The impasse was finally broken by an understanding that the new national capital be built in the South. The 'political deal' thus early found its way into American politics, and the funding-assumption scheme was approved by Congress.

The projected national bank aroused intense distrust. Banks were still novel phenomena to most Americans, and rural spokesmen in particular suspected that they were the snares of the commercial men of the cities. The Country opposition to the British governments had long inveighed against that 'engine of corruption', the Bank of England, and Hamilton's critics feared a similar self-serving alliance between the ministry and the monied interests.[13] The bank might be used by the national government to suppress state banks and state governments. But despite Madison's insistence that it was unconstitutional, Congress passed the measure and the real clash came in the cabinet. Jefferson too argued for a strict construction of the Constitution, which did not expressly grant Congress the power to create corporations, but Hamilton persuasively justified the bank under the clause permitting any laws 'necessary and proper' to the functioning of the government and prevailed on Washington to sign the bill. Hamilton's sweeping proposals in the Report on Manufactures required an even more elastic interpretation of the Constitution and Congress refused to implement them, in part because the southern states suspected that they would simply be supplying new materials to northern industry while sharing in the costs of the tariff and subsidies. Again farmers were apparently to be taxed for the benefit of businessmen. Nonetheless a modest tariff was agreed to as a separate measure in 1792. With the enactment of the greater part of his programme, Hamilton did succeed in bequeathing a fairly energetic federal government to his country and in laying some of the foundations for her remarkable commercial and industrial growth.

Taken together, a newspaper charged, Hamilton's measures threatened to introduce to America 'all the weaknesses, vices, and deformities of the decayed and expiring constitution of Britain'.[14] By further enriching the wealthy classes and attaching them to the national government, Hamilton seemed to be creating a financial aristocracy to support an increasingly centralized regime. By putting such financial machinery in the hands of the government, he seemed to be creating a powerful executive with the means of corrupting the legislature and riding roughshod over any opposition. Furthermore, his schemes seemed to be designed to draw money away from the great mass of farmers and planters of America and divert it towards the relatively few merchants, manufacturers, and financiers. In short, Hamilton was subverting the republic by creating an American monarchy and an American aristocracy and was denying equal rights by favouring businessmen over agriculturalists. Or so it was alleged. A little substance was lent to these charges when it was discovered that a number of congressmen were public stockholders or even Bank directors, or, in less friendly words, 'Treasury placemen'. This seemed to smack of the way English ministries maintained their majorities in the House of Commons. Many of the attacks on Hamilton were of course exaggerated for partisan reasons, but a number of moderate and serious-minded men undoubtedly felt that he was subverting the American experiment in republican government. Hamilton's system, Jefferson wrote to Washington, 'flowed from principles adverse to liberty and was calculated to undermine and demolish the republic by creating an influence of his department over the members of the legislature. . . .'[15]

The original split in the cabinet and in Congress was primarily ideological. Republicanism was a notoriously fragile form of government, as all agreed. To Hamilton the constitutional fabric itself was far too frail, and he believed that by his measures he was strengthening the republic. The people left to their own devices could not be relied on to preserve their liberty. Jefferson and Madison were equally convinced that Hamilton's measures were tending to destroy the republic, for a system in which the national executive could not be effectively checked by the legislature or by the states, and in which privileges were conferred on a few at the expense of the many, could not in their eyes be designated republican. A true republic rested ultimately on the good sense of the people, not on a forceful government which by its very nature could only imperil liberty. It was this ideological cleavage which rendered the political battles of the 1790s so intense. The survival of the republic itself was at stake. But there were other bases of opposition to the Hamiltonian programme. State governments were uneasy at the threatened erosion of their power. The southern states, with their economies tied closely to planting, were suspicious of the benefits Hamilton seemed to be trying to confer on merchants and manufacturers, with their centre of gravity in the Northeast. And farmers generally disliked the excise taxes and the tariff, which served to increase their costs with little discernible compensation. The excise on distilled liquor aroused the greatest popular resentment. A quarter of the nation's whisky stills were located in western Pennsylvania, since the grain from which it was distilled was too bulky to be transported easily over the mountains, and the farmers of that region protested vehemently that their livelihoods were threatened. Their protests failed to move Hamilton, who said that Americans drank too much anyway, and the farmers rose in revolt in 1794. Washington raised a massive army, larger than any he had commanded in the revolutionary war, and it marched off in a vain search for the rebels, who quickly melted away. Nonetheless the government had demonstrated to the world that it was capable of enforcing its laws.

Although Hamilton's measures had been resisted, there was no coherent opposition to the administration in the early 1790s. Every roll call in Congress produced a different voting pattern, reflecting a maze of sectional and interest group pressures. While Hamilton employed his friends in Congress to try to ease his programme through, and while Madison used his influence to increase the opposition to some parts of it, voting was not on party lines. But distinct political views were gradually being articulated, the one dubbed Federalist approving of Hamilton's programme and the centralizing tendencies of the Washington administration, the other dubbed Republican emphasizing states rights and equal rights and betraying an agrarian suspicion of commercial interests. If party organization as such barely existed, contemporaries were beginning to identify party positions. In 1794 Jefferson's friend, John Taylor of Caroline, published his *Definition of Parties*, in which he argued, echoing generations of English radicals, that the Constitution was failing to provide for the public good because the legislature was corrupt. The majority of congressmen, who should be promoting the interests of their constituents, had instead fallen prey to a 'paper interest', raised up by Hamilton's programme. The Secretary of the Treasury, the Bank, and the paper junto, argued Taylor, could be seen as 'a compact representation of king, lords, and commons'.[16]

Taylor's attack was a partisan one, but it exposed the weakness of the Hamiltonian position. Hamilton, it was said, was re-creating the despised British form of government in America, with a powerful executive in place of a king, a monied aristocracy in place of a hereditary aristocracy, and even, according to some, a lower house packed with obedient placemen. To Hamilton, toiling long hours to create an enduring republic, these charges were preposterous, but any attempt to put meat on the bones of the new Constitution would have met with resistance. A fundamental axiom learned from classical and English political theorists was that balanced constitutions were almost inherently subject to decay, for the liberty-preserving equilibrium was in perennial danger of being upset by the expansion of one of the component parts. The English constitution had degenerated in the classical manner in the course of the eighteenth century, or so it was believed, and only eternal vigilance would save the American

Constitution from the same ignominious fate. Given this widely-held assumption, any active statesman in American government in its early years could expect to be charged with subverting the Constitution. And when Alexander Hamilton seemed to be fashioning the political order after the notoriously corrupt forms of England, the prophesy seemed fulfilled. His proto-British philosophy of government, together with his economic strategy, irretrievably divided the national elite. The Federalists had taken command of the government in 1789 united and confident; by 1793 they were in complete disarray.

Chapter 7

The spectre of party

One characteristic of the American style of politics which has served to distinguish it from that of most other countries has been the two-party system. Particular parties have come and gone, but a vigorous competition for popular electoral support between two major party structures, each bent on winning possession of the national government, has been the norm in the United States. Even in Britain politicians were much slower to organize the electorate in this way, and the two-party form itself was a somewhat intermittent phenomenon there in the hundred years preceding the Second World War.

It was in the 1790s that Americans generally first witnessed this distinctive political creature. Something approximating party competition at the polls had sometimes been experienced in certain colonies and states, most notably New York and Pennsylvania, but not until the closing years of Washington's administration did the first national party system begin to emerge. Its appearance, however, did not imply a welcome to this novel way of ordering politics. Not for another generation or more was the legitimacy of party activity widely accepted, even the architects of the first parties regarding them as temporary expedients in a time of crisis. The crisis that they perceived was a political one, public men of different persuasions having convinced themselves that republican government faced imminent destruction. Hamilton's economic and financial measures in the early 1790s had been sustained by a determination to save the republic from the perils before it, and so were the subsequent domestic and foreign policies of the Federalist administrations. Similarly, the Republicans too believed that the end of the American experiment was all but nigh, seeing in Federalism an elitism, authoritarianism, and an obsession with English forms which together represented the very negation of republicanism. Eventually the Republicans were to persuade a majority of the people to reject the Federalist vision for America.

Jefferson's resignation from Washington's cabinet in December 1793 might be said to mark the advent of the new political era. Actually, Jefferson had never intended to serve for more than four years and it was now his resolve to retire to Monticello, but his departure seemed to underline the irrevocable nature of the split between the members of the nation's political elite. Further, it served to identify dissent with opposition to the government. Hitherto the discord which had so strained Washington's patience had been something of a family quarrel, being located within the government as much as outside it, but now the political lines were being redrawn. As Hamilton finally completed his ascendancy over the cabinet the Federalist viewpoint came to permeate the administration, while the growing distance between Washington on the one hand and Jefferson and Madison on the other enabled Republican ideas to be associated with an opposition.

This ideological cleavage was deepened by the work of the newspaper press, for partisans on both sides had found it necessary to express their views to the world. Even earlier, in 1791, Jefferson and Madison had been instrumental in bringing Philip Freneau to Philadelphia, then the seat of the federal government, to establish and edit the *National Gazette*. As its name implied, this newspaper was meant to be a national organ for broadcasting the opinions of those hostile to Hamiltonianism, which was already receiving a good enough press in John Fenno's *Gazette of the United States*. A newspaper war developed prior to the 1792 elections and further party presses appeared in subsequent years. The emergence of the political press was a new and important step in the republic's political evolution. Polemic pamphleteering had long been known, and political journalism had been a feature of Pennsylvania's contentious politics in the 1780s, but a journalistic continuum attuned to day-to-day practical politicking only developed on a national scale in the 1790s. Men throughout the Union thus became aware of the battle to save the republic being waged in Philadelphia, and the partisan press played a role in sucking the scattered local parties, factions, and interest groups into the mighty struggle. The appearance of such newspapers, of course, was a tacit recognition that politics was no longer exclusively the reserve of great men. Political journalism was to remain a major formative influence on American political culture.

It had been Hamilton's ambitious financial schemes that had originally destroyed the harmony in the nation's councils, the nascent Republicans espying in them monarchical and aristocratic implications. Into this atmosphere obtruded the war in Europe. The French Revolution had originally been welcomed by most Americans, who saw the French people as following the trail of liberty recently blazed by themselves. But the execution of Louis XVI, the Jacobin 'reign of terror', and the outbreak of war between France and Brtain caused some Americans to recoil in horror and alarm. Increasingly the issues raised by the French turmoil impinged on American politics, touching much the same ideological and emotional chords as Hamilton's prógramme and thus greatly exacerbating party divisions. Indeed, events in Europe seemed to involve the same issues that Americans had already been fighting over at home. If the Federalists had long been uneasy about democracy, the French terror served to vindicate their fears and convinced them that they must annihilate the Jacobins they perceived around them at home. Similarly, the Republicans saw their own struggle for liberty exemplified in the French Revolution, a liberty which the monarchies of Europe seemed to be ganging up on. If the British crushed republican liberty in France, perhaps they would next seek to suppress it in the United States with the aid of the cryptomonarchists around Hamilton.

The struggle over foreign policy, then, was a struggle for the destiny of America. To the Republicans, the pro-British sympathies of the Federalists were tantamount to a betrayal of the American Revolution, and to the Federalists the pro-French sympathies of the Republicans seemed designed to invite anarchy and subvert the Constitution. Each side identified itself with the true interests of the country and was tempted to see its opponents as traitors. A French request that the United States stand by her old ally of the revolutionary war was turned aside when George Washington issued his neutrality proclamation, which brought charges from the Republican press that the administration was deserting the cause of human liberty.

The administration's refusal to cooperate with France seemed all the more suspicious to the Republicans because while France was offering trade concessions Britain was interfering with American shipping. The British, trying to disrupt France economically, were seizing neutral shipping in the French West Indies, and some 250 American ships were carried off. Adding to American resentment was the British failure to withdraw from her forts in the Northwest, as promised in the Treaty of Paris. Chief Justice John Jay was sent to Britain to try to prevent this situation from escalating into war, but the treaty that he obtained merely confirmed Republican suspicions that the administration was succumbing to British influence. Britain did agree to evacuate the forts but conceded little else, while Jay had made financial concessions to the British and had failed to protect American shipping. The Senate ratified the treaty by the narrowest possible margin in June 1795, and Washington unhappily signed it in the face of mass protest meetings across the country. Public opinion was becoming a major fact of American political life.

Washington's decision not to seek a third term then unleashed a bitter struggle for the succession. Congressmen of both parties took a lead in preparing and distributing pamphlets and encouraging acquaintances at state and local levels to activate their friends. In a number of states separate Republican and Federalist tickets were drawn up, and party newspapers and pamphlets furiously sought to demonstrate the patriotism of their favoured candidates and the subversive tendencies of their rivals. Jefferson and Adams were the Republican and Federalist presidential candidates respectively, and they showed that the rise of party was still far from complete, for they both maintained a scrupulous silence in their respective country retreats, perfect models of the eighteenth-century gentleman awaiting the call of his country. A major issue was the Jay Treaty, which to the Federalists had been necessary to avoid war, and to the Republicans was but the latest step in a conspiracy to restore monarchy and aristocracy to the United States with the aid of the British. In a private letter to an Italian friend Jefferson presented his considered view of American politics: 'In place of that noble love of liberty and republican government which carried us triumphantly through the war, an Anglican, monarchical, and aristocratical party has sprung up, whose avowed object is to draw over us the substance, as they have already done the forms, of the British government.'[1] Many Americans still thought otherwise, however, and Adams won the election. Jefferson, as the runner-up in the electoral college, became vice-president, as the Constitution then prescribed.

To the participants of this first battle for control of the federal government the crucial issue was the shape of the American republic, not the success of a party as such. Jefferson himself believed this, writing to Madison soon after that 'If Mr. Adams can be induced to administer the government on its true principles, and to relinquish his bias to an English constitution', it might be 'for the public good' to let him be re-elected unopposed.[2] Better that than the election of Hamilton, he concluded, with his scheme to establish a British-style monarchy in the United States. The Adams administration did witness a growing gulf between Adams and Hamilton, but the Republicans were soon persuaded that the president had not renounced his unrepublican ideas.

The impact of foreign affairs on domestic politics continued to be deeply divisive. The French had interpreted the Jay Treaty as a *rapprochement* between the United States and Britain and had retaliated by attacking American shipping in the West Indies. If war with Britain had seemed possible in 1794, it was now war with France that loomed, much to the embarrassment of the Republicans. Adams dispatched three envoys to France to negotiate the differences, but in 1798 it was revealed that the French agents, known as X, Y, and Z, had demanded a large bribe to sweeten their dispositions, and public opinion became fiercely anti-French. Now the Federalists could plausibly pose as the patriot party, indignantly rebuffing foreign insults, and could cast the Francophile Republicans in the unpatriotic role. Republican editors were attacked by mobs and Federalist newspapers called for war. The president built up the navy and an unofficial shooting war did in fact develop on the Atlantic and in the Caribbean. The Federalists had for years regarded the Republicans as a dangerously disloyal element, working to reduce the republic to anarchy and mob rule, and now that the country was virtually at war such subversive activities seemed quite intolerable. The Federalists believed that the Republicans' servility to France had encouraged the French aggression, and they suspected that many Republicans would join the enemy. The conspicuous presence of a number of foreign immigrants among Republican leaders added to the party's un-American image. At the height of the patriotic frenzy in the summer of

1798 the Federalists pushed through the infamous Alien and Sedition Acts, designed to protect the United States from these enemies within. The Alien Act gave the president the authority to deport foreigners he considered dangerous and the Sedition Act made it a crime to publish or even to utter false or malicious criticisms against the government or its officers. Another measure increased the residence requirement for citizenship from five to fourteen years, a blow at the Republican party which had been the more successful in attracting the immigrant vote. The Federalists were perceiving the value in a free society of marshalling and exploiting public opinion against their opponents. The Alien Act was not in fact enforced, but a number of Republican editors were convicted under the Sedition Act, becoming martyrs to their cause. Faced with this assault, the Republican party closed ranks and improved their organization.

In Republican eyes, the Alien and Sedition Acts were the logical culmination of the long-standing Federalist conspiracy to destroy republican government. In addition to the repressive acts, Congress had also decided to levy new taxes and to enlarge the army, ominous measures, a standing army being a traditional weapon used against republics. The Federalist administration now seemed to some to be a greater enemy of the American people than the French Directory. Republican resistance was formally expressed in the Virginia and Kentucky Resolutions, drafted by Madison and Jefferson respectively. These projected an interpretation of the American Constitution as a compact between sovereign states, the states retaining the right to judge when it had been violated. The Kentucky Resolution in particular argued that the states had a right to nullify an unconstitutional federal law, although exactly how they could set it aside remained rather obscure. Nonetheless the Republicans were now fully committed to the doctrine that the best guarantee of the survival of liberty in America was in a strict (or states rights) construction of the Constitution. In a republic governments were less trustworthy than the people themselves and their functions should be kept at a minimum. The tendency of the federal government, said the Virginia Resolution, was 'to transform the present republican system of the United States into an absolute, or at best, a mixed monarchy'.[3] In an Address to the People the Virginia legislature reviewed the fateful progress of Federalism: Hamilton's sinister financial operations, enlarged armies and navies to suppress imaginary insurrections, restraints on the freedom of the press, a loose construction of the Constitution, and the growth in the power of the federal executive. Could it be doubted, asked the Address rhetorically, that the architect of such a system would finally avow 'that so extensive a territory as that of the United States can only be governed by the energies of monarchy, that it cannot be defended except by standing armies, and that it cannot be united except by consolidation'.[4]

The conviction that the republic was being subverted by the

Federalist government gave rise to some resistance. In Virginia the militia began to arm, ostensibly to resist a French and Indian invasion, but more probably to resist federal troops if need be. Virginian leaders like John Taylor began to contemplate disunion, but the more cautious Jefferson successfully counselled his fellows to avoid any show of force. As Jefferson had perceived, the new tax on houses, land, and slaves, falling as it did on most white men, would arouse enough opposition to spell the end of Federalism, and the so-called Fries Rebellion duly erupted in eastern Pennsylvania. Adams promptly dispatched the army, so confirming Republican suspicions that it had been enlarged for domestic use. Denounced as 'a ferocious wild beast let loose upon the nation to devour it', the army in fact could not find any rebels to devour, apart from three ringleaders who were later pardoned by Adams.[5] By this time the French threat had receded, and the measures that had seemed necessary for national security in the manic summer of 1798 could no longer clearly be justified on those grounds. Realizing the unpopularity that they were now bringing on themselves by appearing to use wartime expedients against American citizens, in 1800 the Federalists reduced the armed forces and allowed the Alien Act to expire. A year later, the Sedition Act also died.

But Federalist repentance came too late. The party was already deeply divided between the High Federalists around Hamilton and the president's more moderate following. Adams had continued to work for peace with France and eventually his policy was vindicated, much to the frustration of the more warlike Hamiltonians. The peace policy, unease over the disunionist implications of the Virginia and Kentucky Resolutions, and a spurt of commercial prosperity improved the fortunes of the Adams Federalists in the nation at large, but many Federalist leaders were Hamiltonians bent on ending Adams's political career. In this divided state the Federalists entered the campaign of 1800, during which Adams called Hamilton 'a bastard', which he was, and Hamilton wrote a pamphlet dwelling on the president's 'disgusting egotism' and 'ungovernable indiscretion'.[6] Such tactics were hardly calculated to win the election.

There had never been much doubt as to who the standard-bearers of the two parties would be in 1800, but in the spring congressional caucuses met to ensure party unity. The Federalist caucus chose John Adams and Charles C. Pinckney as presidential and vice-presidential candidates, and the Republican caucus nominated Thomas Jefferson and Aaron Burr. This was the first election in which the congressional caucuses were able to exert their authority, both agreeing on their candidates and having them accepted by their parties in the country at large. Party machines and party presses throughout the nation then swung into vituperative action, and the election was fought out with an acrimony which makes modern campaigns appear rather genteel. Jefferson was accused of being a 'howling atheist' and an 'intellectual voluptuary' and it was predicted that his victory would be won at the cost of 'dwellings in flames, hoary hairs bathed in blood, female chastity violated . . . children writhing on the pike and halberd'.[7] Adams escaped perhaps a little more lightly, though he was inevitably charged with being a monarchist and an Anglophile, and one diverting story had it that he wanted to marry his son off to the daughter of George III and thus ultimately reunite Britain and America under the Adams dynasty! The Federalists, genuinely alarmed by the course of events in France, pointed to the anarchy, bloodshed, and despotism which a Godless and demagogic political creed was capable of giving rise to, while the Republicans rang the changes on the iniquitous acts of the Federalist governments of the 1790s.

Thomas Jefferson again retreated discreetly to Monticello, but in contrast to 1796 he took an active if private part in the election, propelled by a determination 'to see this government brought back to its republican principles'.[8] It was not all plain sailing for the Republicans, but when they finally won control of South Carolina early in December, partly through promises of patronage, it was clear that John Adams would have to leave the unfinished White House into which he had finally moved the previous month.

The outcome was as sectional as the 1796 election had been. All of New England went Federalist, as did New Jersey and Delaware, while the Republicans took New York and made a clean sweep in the South and West, save for a third of South Carolina's electoral votes. Pennsylvania and Maryland divided their votes between the two parties. The effect of party discipline was clear. In 1796 there had been some scattering of votes, but in 1800 every elector (save one) voted either for the Jefferson-Burr or the Adams-Pinckney party ticket. Party competition had also apparently encouraged the voters to go to the polls, at least where they could, for in most states the presidential electors were chosen by the legislatures. In the five states in which a popular vote was allowed, the turnout (of adult white males) averaged about thirty-eight per cent, quite a high figure for the day, though less than was often achieved in elections for state offices. The Republican party at least could also be well-satisfied with its organization in the congressional elections, for the Republicans won control of both houses, and even took several seats in New England, where Federalist control was weakening.

But if the election of 1800 was a testimony to party discipline it was hardly a tribute to party management. To their embarrassment the party leaders discovered that Jefferson and Burr had received the same number of votes, each member of the electoral college at that time having two votes, so that the presidency could go to the man who came first and the vice-presidency to the runner-up. Although the party caucus had agreed to support both men equally, Jefferson at least had assumed that a vote or two would be withheld from Burr to ensure that he ended the race in second place. But a breakdown in communications had determined otherwise, and now the tied election was thrown into the lame-duck House of Representatives, where the Federalists were still strong. The Federalists seized the opportunity to try to block the election of Jefferson and secure that of Burr, despite Alexander Hamilton's conviction that the latter was the more dangerous of the two. By voting for Burr the Federalist members prevented Jefferson from winning the necessary majority of state delegations, and thirty-five ballots ended in deadlock. Jefferson was peppered with pleas to give certain undertakings on policy and appointments, and although there is no evidence that he did, his Republican associate Samuel Smith of Maryland privately offered some assurances to the Federalists. Finally, on the thirty-sixth ballot, Federalist unity cracked and Thomas Jefferson was elected president of the United States. A few years later an amendment to the Constitution obliged electoral college members to vote separately for president and vice-president, so that the same kind of distressing affair could never recur.

By 1800 the near unanimity in the national councils which had prevailed in the early days of George Washington's administration had given way to the most bitter of life-and-death struggles. Congress and the nation at large had been convulsed by parties, each perceiving the other as traitors to the republic. But important though ideological convictions were in separating the political nation into two mutually hostile armies, they did not arise in a vacuum and they did not constitute the only reasons for dividing Federalists from Republicans. Hamilton's conviction that the Union would benefit from an expansion in commerce and the establishment of sound credit arrangements with England was no doubt strengthened by his long association with the commercial classes of New York, and it proved naturally attractive to many of the merchants of New England. Equally, Jefferson's belief that Hamilton's financial policies were raising up a monied aristocracy was the product of a political outlook fashioned in no small part by the plantation society of Virginia. As the dissension in the cabinet and Congress rippled outwards across the nation, carried by newspapers, pamphleteers, and fence-mending congressmen, a host of local parties, factions, and interests erratically yet gradually aligned themselves with one persuasion or the other. The old Federalist and Anti-Federalist groupings of the 1780s had disappeared, most of the governmental leaders who divided into Federalists and Republicans in the 1790s having been Federalist supporters of the Constitution in 1787-89. Probably, however, the Republicans absorbed much of the old Anti-Federalist support in the country at large. The complexity of the country and the peculiarities of local conditions prevented any neat demarcation between Federalists and Republicans, but very broad differences can be noted. The Federalist vision of the republic tended to be most acceptable to the older, more stable communities, often – though not always – strongly commercial in orientation and relatively cosmopolitan in outlook, to conservative well-to-do classes, to the mercantile and legal professions, and to certain religious groups, most notably the Congregationalists, especially those on the conservative wing of the church. Often, of course, these several conditions, interests, and classes existed together, especially in New England where Federalism was strongest. The Republican persuasion tended to prove most alluring to new, expanding and mobile communities and frontier areas, to many backwoods farmers and southern planters, to the poorer classes including urban mechanics, and to various ethnic and religious groups, most conspicuously the French, Irish Catholics, and Baptists. The presence of several of these conditions, classes, and groups in the South and the West made Republicanism a powerful force in those regions. The sectional orientation of the two parties was reinforced by the presidential races of 1796 and 1800, the New Englander Adams being run for the Federalists and the Virginian Jefferson for the Republicans on both occasions. Many New Englanders voted Federalist because they associated Republicanism with southern arrogance, and many southerners voted Republican because they associated Federalism with Anglophile and commercial New England. Sectional jealousies were giving a sharp edge to party antagonism.

American political leaders in the 1790s thus rapidly gained valuable experience in the arts of party organization and competition. But most of them never accepted the legitimacy of party forms. As is often the case, their ideological world never quite caught up with their real world, although the two interacted in important ways. Parties, they stubbornly believed, had no place in the ideal political order that the United States aspired to. In his Farewell Address George Washington conceded that there might be some use for party in a monarchy, where it could keep a check on the administration, but that 'in Governments purely elective' party spirit was definitely 'not to be encouraged'.[9] In this view, party was incompatible with republicanism. The republican system of government had been established by the people as a whole and should express the will of the nation; party combinations were but partial interests and threatened to subvert the power of the people by bending government to their own selfish ends. This holistic conception of the political order, which assumed a single public good which it was the duty of the people's representatives to identify, was particularly strong among Federalists, but many Republicans too saw no place for partial interests in the good political society. John Taylor of Caroline, for example, who was to be remembered as the philosopher of Jeffersonian Republicanism, still clung to an organic view of politics. 'The situation of the public good, in the hands of two parties nearly poised as to numbers, must be extremely perilous', he warned. 'Truth is a thing, not of divisibility into conflicting parts, but of unity.'[10] If Taylor and others contributed to the creation of an opposition party, it was because the public good was being betrayed by the administration.

The origins of the unwanted political parties of the 1790s, then, lay in a conviction among members of the national political elite that the republic was being subverted by enemies within as well as without. The early parties, unlike modern parties, were not machines whose primary function was to win office; they were patriotic associations of minute-men springing to the defence of freedom, like the Sons of Liberty of the Revolution, and like the revolutionary associations too they could disband when the danger was passed. To Jefferson and Madison, Hamilton had to be resisted because he was recreating a monarchical form of government in America, abetted by the old enemy England. Jefferson's view in 1795 was clear:

Were parties here divided merely by a greediness for office, as in England, to take a part with either would be unworthy of a reasonable or moral man, but where the principle of difference is as substantial and as strongly pronounced as between the republicans and the Monocrats of our country, I hold it as honorable to take a firm and decided part, and as immoral to pursue a middle line, as between the parties of Honest men, and Rogues, into which every country is divided.[11]

Alexander Hamilton pronounced 'absurd' the idea that there was a monarchical party, but described the views of Madison and Jefferson as 'subversive of the principles of good government and dangerous to the union, peace, and happiness of the Country'.[12] The builders of the first political parties were of the generation which had rebelled against George III, men who had been propelled into revolutionary action by the conviction that the English ministers were conspiring to deprive Americans of their liberty. They remained as sensitive to the prospect of conspiracy and subversion under their own Constitution as they had been under the English constitution.

The paranoid tendencies inherent in the heritage of English opposition thought thus ironically paved the way for the coming of party. Men could denounce party while themselves engaged in party activity simply because they did not see themselves as party functionaries. They were servants of their country, dutifully trying to convert all their fellow citizens to the one true faith. Once that had been accomplished and their disloyal opponents had repented of their degenerate and un-American ways, party forms could be expected to wither away. In the end it was the Republicans who won this ideological battle, largely because they were able to show more trust in the good sense of the people. The Federalists' commitment to American republicanism was genuine, but their methods seemed often to imply a reliance on hierarchical forms more suited to the Old World than the New. With the 'Revolution of 1800', the Republicans hoped, the errors of Federalist ways had been exposed for all to see and an era of republican harmony was not far distant.

Chapter 8

Towards republican harmony

'The greatest good we can do our country is to heal its party divisions and make them one people', Jefferson wrote to a friend soon after assuming the presidency.[1] The constitutional settlement worked out in 1787-88 had only been in operation for a few brief and tempestuous years and the vitriol of the recent presidential campaign had done nothing to dispel the widespread belief that party warfare could destroy the republican system. It was to be the great goal of Jefferson and his Republican successors in the White House to win over the bulk of Federalist voters to their brand of republicanism without betraying their own principles. In their eyes this meant a policy of accommodation and conciliation; to some Republican ideologues it meant betrayal.

By about 1815 the Republican strategy had largely succeeded, though for reasons which were in some measure fortuitous. Nonetheless the Republican administrations did eventually win the allegiance of much the greater part of the political nation, hence putting the first American party system on the road to oblivion. The Republicans' success rested in part on their willingness to place their confidence in the good sense of the people. Many Federalists had tended to believe that the republic would only be safe under an energetic and consolidated central government, sustained by the rich and the well-born, but Republicans were more disposed to trust the capacity of the people to maintain republican government without such paternalistic surveillance. The Republicans were to show their contemporaries and their successors that a faith in the people was a *sine qua non* of any successful political movement in the United States. But they were also to demonstrate that a willingness to conciliate and to compromise was also a necessary attribute in the American political environment. Much more than their opponents, they were to bequeath a pragmatic spirit to the American political tradition. But there was a limit to their pragmatism, and perhaps even more than the Federalists too they were to bequeath the assumption that it was a politician's first duty to defend the republic from degeneration. They were thus to help transmit to a later generation something learned in particular from English oppositionist thought, that balanced constitutions were almost inherently subject to decay.

The Jeffersonian Republicans had won power in some measure by equating Federalism with monarchical and aristocratic principles, but their own political creed was not exclusively an American creation. Jefferson's celebrated Inaugural Address contained little that was novel and made no reference to democracy. It spoke of republicanism, liberty, and equal rights, but this was the language of an eighteenth-century Whig rather than of a levelling democrat. Jefferson had drawn up the Declaration of Independence a generation earlier in defence of freedom, and he was still engaged in the same libertarian cause. He once remarked that he had 'sworn . . . eternal hostility against every form of tyranny over the mind of man', and it was as a foe of arbitrary power rather than as a tribune of the people that he earned his place in history.[2] He remained a believer in the notion of balanced government, criticizing the Virginia constitution because both houses of the legislature were chosen in the same way. 'The purpose of establishing different houses of legislation is to introduce the influence of different interests or different principles', he wrote in a classical defence of the mixed constitution.[3] And despite occasional talk about the principle of universal suffrage, he never tried to implement it and in his own draft for the Virginia constitution he included property qualifications for voting. Like others of his generation on both sides of the Atlantic, he tended to think of the legitimate political nation as comprising those with a stake in society. Economic independence, after all, was the surest safeguard against tyranny.

Jefferson's ideal citizen was the small farmer, independent, self-sufficient, and proud of his own labour. The farmer in his freehold estate was dependent on no man. He could not be coerced by a landlord or bought by a corrupt official or swayed by a demagogue. Rather he would be an agent of stability, a supporter of those rights and freedoms which guaranteed his livelihood. The unfortunate city worker, by contrast, lacked the economic independence to resist the pressures and seductions of others and was a source of danger to the polity. This agrarian view of the good society was one which still seemed tenable at the time of Jefferson's election, when the great majority of men were farmers or engaged in rural pursuits and when there seemed abundant land for a long time to come, even 'to the hundredth and thousandth generation'.[4] Not that the Jeffersonians wanted to concentrate landed property into a few hands. In 1776 Jefferson advocated giving all white adult Virginians at least fifty acres apiece. 'Wealth', said his friend John Taylor, 'like suffrage, must be considerably distributed, to sustain a democratic republic; . . . As power follows property, the majority must have wealth or lose power.'[5] The creed of the Jeffersonian Republicans was a democratized version of English Whiggery, in which political rights tended to be linked to a landed stake in society, which, ideally, everyone should enjoy.

In a land of self-sufficient farmers – and increasingly of small and self-reliant businessmen – the functions of government would be kept to a minimum, and this too was necessary for the survival of freedom.

To Jefferson and others strong government was equated with the despotisms of Europe, and liberty could only exist where governmental power was limited, especially that of the central government. The republic was to rest on the virtue of the self-reliant people rather than on governmental control. This was the political philosophy that Jefferson outlined in his Inaugural Address. He reiterated his commitment to the freedoms guaranteed in the American bills of rights, promised 'equal and exact justice to all men', anticipated peace with all nations and 'entangling alliances with none', supported states rights as 'the surest bulwarks against anti-republican tendencies', called for economies in government and hinted at the reduction of the armed forces, and offered encouragement to agriculture and its 'handmaid', commerce. He also revealed his hope that his brand of politics might accommodate all Americans and put an end to the unwanted apparition of party. 'Let us restore to social intercourse that harmony and affection without which liberty and life are but dreary things,' he pleaded. 'We are all republicans – we are all Federalists.'[6] In part this was a conciliatory plea for the toleration of minority opinions, but it also implied that fundamental disagreements with the true republican system were temporary aberrations. Jefferson suspected that most Federalist voters had been misled by their leaders, who themselves had been the victims of the mania of 1798. In his mind, the election of 1800 had witnessed a peaceful revolution in which the eyes of the people had been opened to the destructive ways of the misguided Federalists. It remained for the Republicans to provide good government, and Federalism would dwindle away.

Eventually the Republicans were to succeed in winning the allegiance of the great mass of the electorate, though it was at the cost of modifying their agrarian philosophy and losing the support of a few radicals. Jefferson himself had a deep distaste for bitter political controversy, and was prepared on occasion to compromise rather than precipitate a mutually destructive battle. Even before his election he appears to have decided to acquiesce in Hamilton's financial institutions, writing to Elbridge Gerry that from the moment the funding system had been adopted by the proper authorities, 'I became religiously principled in the sacred discharge of it to the uttermost farthing. . . . '[7] In any case, the complex financial and institutional arrangements of the Federalists would now be difficult to dismantle, and any attempt to do so would risk economic depression and Republican desertions. He wrote rather sadly to Dupont de Nemours that when the government had first been established it might have been possible to maintain it on true principles but the 'contracted, English, half-lettered ideas of Hamilton', whose financial system was now irremovable, had destroyed that hope. 'It mortifies me to be strengthening principles which I deem radically vicious . . . ,' he mourned, but in other parts of the government 'I hope we shall be able by degrees to introduce sound principles and make them habitual.'[8]

The republic, it seemed, was to be nursed slowly back to health.

It was not an easy task to advance Republican principles without incurring Federalist hatred, as Jefferson soon found when considering appointments to public office. The government service was packed with Federalists: to oust them would alienate Federalists in the country at large while to retain them would outrage Republican partisans. Jefferson decided to move slowly, hoping that deaths and resignations would in time enable him to give 'Republicans their *proportion* of office', but such vacancies were slow to occur and the president was assailed by demands to remove the proven enemies of republican government.[9] On occasions, Jefferson bowed cautiously to this pressure only to be met with Federalist abuse, as when the replacement of the collector of the port of New Haven with a Republican moved the conservative Theodore Dwight to fear for 'every trace of civilization in the world'.[10] Some officials were dismissed for incompetence or misconduct and some were removed for transparently party reasons, but Jefferson refused to make wholesale dismissals. Many of the appointees of Washington and Adams were still undisturbed when Jefferson left the White House in 1809, and a number of prominent Federalists were conspicuously retained, including Rufus King for a time as minister to England, perhaps the most coveted office below cabinet level. By the end of his first term Jefferson had created what might be called a bipartisan civil service, in which Republicans and Federalists worked side by side, with the former in a slight majority. In this way Jefferson hoped to make it easy for Federalists to renounce their misbegotten cause without denying his own supporters their expected rewards.

In his financial and commercial policies Jefferson also attempted to fashion a brand of republicanism which would be acceptable to most Americans. His Secretary of the Treasury was the Swiss-born Pennsylvanian Albert Gallatin, a long-time foe of the Hamiltonian system, and together the two men set out to restore republican principles as best they could. The Bank of the United States and the sinking fund, they reluctantly decided, could not be safely tampered with, but the public debt could at least be reduced. The Republicans had inherited from English radicals the idea that a permanent public debt was a source of corruption and a potential instrument of tyranny, and Jefferson was determined to free the nation from this incubus, even to the point of 'making all other objects subordinate to this'.[11] In keeping with Republican philosophy, expenditures on the regular army and navy were reduced and other economies were made, and the debt had been almost halved by the time that Gallatin left the Treasury in 1814. Its eventual extinction was a central article of Republican faith, for only then would the American experiment be safe. If the debt were allowed to swell, warned Jefferson as he retired to Monticello, 'we shall be committed to the English career of debt, corruption, and rottenness, closing with revolution. The discharge of the debt, therefore, is vital to the destinies of our government. . . . '[12]

By thus reducing the sinister financial operations of the government Jefferson could hope to show his partisans that the United States was indeed rejecting the wicked ways of the Federalists and of the English government. But the commercial and financial interests themselves were not to be alienated. Nothing was done by the Republican administrations to discourage the growth of industry or of cities, save indirectly by encouraging western settlement, and such unrepublican activities as banking and land speculation continued unabated. Indeed, Jefferson and Madison increasingly tried to find a place for productive business ventures within Republican political economy. In 1805 Jefferson suggested a constitutional amendment to allow the central government to apply surplus revenue '*in time of peace* to rivers, canals, roads, arts, manufactures, education, and other great objects within each state'.[13] At state level the Republicans even aided the establishment of new banks themselves, in even larger numbers than the Federalists had once sought, and Jefferson himself advised his Secretary of the Treasury to try to win the mercantile community over to the Republicans by the judicious distribution of government deposits among the banks. Increasingly entrepreneurial elements found a receptive home in the Republican party, becoming an important faction in the commercial cities and in parts of the South and West. Even in New England, where the more old-fashioned Federalists found the avid pursuit of wealth subversive of public morality, many of the newer businessmen threw in their lot with the Republicans. The Republican creed attributed virtue to small producers of all kinds, whether agricultural or industrial, and in practice many Republicans turned a blind eye to the more questionable activities of financiers, speculators, and monopolists. But in embracing the merchant and the manufacturer the Republicans were not abandoning the farmer. They had no intention of taxing the landed classes for the benefit of the monied classes, as they believed Hamilton had done. Rather, they recognized that a diversified economy was fast becoming a fact of life and that the government's obligations extended beyond the farming community. As Jefferson remarked in 1816, 'We must now place the manufacturer by the side of the agriculturalist.'[14]

The Republicans' desire to accommodate both agricultural and commercial interests while giving a distinctively New-World stamp to their policies was well illustrated by their attempts to open up the West. When Jefferson became president American territory stopped at the Mississippi, but the vast lands beyond that river belonged to decrepit Spain, and it was possible to dream of peacefully acquiring a great 'empire of liberty' stretching across the continent. Such musings were rudely shattered in 1801 by the news that Spain was returning the so-called Louisiana territory to France, for with France in the interior and the British navy in the Atlantic the United States would be wedged between two energetic – and mutually hostile – European powers. Further, American commercial interests were immediately threatened, for their Mississippi trade accounted for the greater part of the goods passing through the port of New Orleans, which France might be disposed to close. A few Federalists began calling for war, but Jefferson decided to try to buy New Orleans, only to find, to his astonished gratification, that Napoleon had tired of his trans-Atlantic diversions and was willing to sell all his American claims to the United States. The administration could only accept, so that in one spectacular move, and for a mere $15 million, American territory was doubled and the United States became – in area – the second largest country in the world. Having spent much of his life arguing that liberty could only survive where governmental power was strictly limited, Jefferson had his qualms about this measure for which the Constitution gave no explicit sanction, but his friends prevailed upon him to keep them to himself. So Louisiana was bought, the Mississippi trade was saved, boundless virgin acres were procured for American farmers, and Americans began to perceive a future for themselves in the West, where they might carve out a great republic of freedom that would put the decadent tyrannies of Europe to shame.

Jefferson's strategy, then, was to try to bring together Federalist and Republican, manufacturer and farmer, easterner and westerner. His attempts to reduce the public debt and the armed forces and to encourage agriculture, and his sensitivity to states rights, testified to his continuing commitment to the Republican faith, with its stress on the capacity of the people for self-government, but he wanted to make it possible for all Americans to embrace that faith. Where this accommodationist policy was subjected to greatest strain was in the Republicans' dealings with the federal judiciary, but even there moderation finally prevailed. In the exhilarating days of the Revolution some of the more radical state constitutions had made judges elective (sometimes by the legislature), and some Republicans still hankered after a 'democratized' judiciary, seeing in Jefferson's election an opportunity to give Congress the power to appoint and remove federal judges. Even the most moderate Republicans were unhappy at the fact that the courts were monopolized by Federalists, and they were certainly incensed by the Judiciary Act, pushed through in the last days of the old Congress in 1801, which had enabled John Adams to appoint several more Federalist judges, staying up till midnight on his last day in office feverishly signing their commissions, or so it was said. The Republicans, it seemed, might be denied the fruits of their victory by a judiciary which was bent on subverting their measures, ample reason, some felt, for extending the representative principle more fully into that branch of government. In the event the obnoxious Judiciary Act was repealed and the Federalist monopoly in the courts was ended, but Jefferson and Madison counselled against a more radical solution, reaffirming their attachment to the conception of a balanced constitution, though in this instance moving away from the strictly Whiggish notion of legislative supremacy.

But to the Federalists, less trustful of the people than the Republicans, the rule of law was central to the preservation of a republican polity, and even the repeal of the Judiciary Act seemed like 'the death wound of our glorious Constitution'.[15] Given this faith in constitutionalism, further clashes between the administration and the judiciary could only confirm Federalist suspicions that the Republicans were ruthlessly demolishing all restraints on popular tyranny. Yet the administration was not really bent on war with the courts. Both sides judiciously avoided a direct confrontation in the celebrated case of *Marbury v. Madison*, when Chief Justice Marshall took the opportunity to promulgate the doctrine of judicial review, whereby the Supreme Court was held to be the final arbiter of the constitutionality of a law, but issued no judgement against the administration. Jefferson was later to complain that judicial review made the Constitution 'a mere thing of wax in the hands of the judiciary', but he made no public objection in this case and again it seemed that the Republican administration and the Federalist judiciary might learn to live with one another.[16] What finally disturbed the rather cool peace between the two was the administration's decision to remove a district judge by the only means open to it, impeachment before the Senate, but although the judge was a drunken lunatic he was also a Federalist, and the proceedings became highly partisan. His conviction was followed by the impeachment of Supreme Court Justice Samuel Chase, another partisan Federalist. The assault on Chase in fact owed more to the initiative of the radical John Randolph than to any action of the temporizing president, and Randolph's failure to carry several moderate Republicans with him resulted in Chase's acquittal. Jefferson and other leading Republicans were probably not unhappy with this outcome, for as one Republican congressman noted, it 'would have a tendency to mitigate the irritation of party spirit'.[17]

The administration, then, never fully abandoned its accommodationist strategy, though nor was the strategy as successful as it would have wished. The High Federalists remained adamantly hostile to every administration measure, regarding the restrained redistribution of public offices as instituting a government 'by blockheads and knaves', the swingeing cuts in the army and navy as dangerously irresponsible, the clashes with the courts as an invitation to mob rule, and the Louisiana Purchase as a disaster which 'must result in the disunion of these States'.[18] The acquisition of Louisiana did indeed provoke some Federalists to secessionist thoughts, for it seemed to threaten permanent Republican rule, and a few Massachusetts and Connecticut irreconcilables hatched a plan for a separate Northern Confederacy embracing New England and New York. They even hoped for the cooperation of the vice-president of the United States, Aaron Burr, who in 1804 was running for the governorship of New

York with some Federalist support. Burr made no promises, but his heavy defeat in the election exploded the conspirators' fanciful dreams. The affair also cost the life of Alexander Hamilton, who had opposed both the Northern Confederacy and Aaron Burr, and his incautious remarks about the latter ensnared him in his fatal duel. By the autumn of 1804 the Federalist party was in hopeless disarray, its more extreme members having been contaminated by near-treasonable activity and its greatest leader dead. In the presidential election Jefferson's strategy of accommodation was finally vindicated. Many old Federalist supporters did desert their discredited chieftains and Jefferson carried every state in the Union save Connecticut and Delaware.

But there was a price to pay for conciliation and moderation. Accommodation towards the centre in American politics would always isolate the fringes. Such Republican purists as John Taylor of Caroline, John Randolph of Roanoke, and plain Nathaniel Macon fretted at every seeming compromise of the principles of '98. The administration 'favors federal principles, and, with the exception of a few great rival characters, federal men . . . ', wrote a disgusted John Randolph in 1806, 'The old republican party is already ruined, past redemption.'[19] The reasons behind the rebellion of the Tertium Quids, as these unhappy men came to be known, were complex, but their principal spokesmen generally shared an agrarian viewpoint and a commitment to a strict construction of the Constitution. They were too few to have much of an impact on the administration, but they did help to carry forward to a later day some of the hallmarks of eighteenth-century opposition thought: a fervent belief in legislative supremacy, a distrust of an active central government, a distaste for commerce and entrepreneurial capitalism, an assumption that the landed gentry should rule, and a conviction that individual liberty was the central political value. 'I am an aristocrat,' remarked John Randolph. 'I love liberty, I hate equality.'[20] In breaking with the Quids, the Jeffersonian Republicans were also in some measure freeing themselves from the Country tradition of Old England and addressing themselves to American realities.

Jefferson's tolerant brand of Republicanism, then, succeeded in winning the allegiance of many ex-Federalists, merchants, and manufacturers at the cost of losing a few agrarian ideologues. Yet there were limits even to Jefferson's tolerance. His amiability did not extend to Aaron Burr, who had misguidedly turned to the Southwest to recoup his political fortunes after his infamous duel with Hamilton. Many had believed that the Louisiana territory recently acquired from Napoleon would not long be content to remain with the United States, and when Burr sought to interest a number of prominent westerners in an attack on Mexico it seemed that he might be conspiring to bring about a western secession. But whatever Burr's murky scheme was, it went awry and Jefferson ordered his arrest. Jefferson was convinced that Burr had committed treason and he used all the resources at his disposal to secure a conviction, publicly declaring Burr's guilt 'beyond all question' before the trial was even begun.[21] In the event Chief Justice Marshall required proof that treason had actually been committed before permitting a charge of conspiracy for treason, an impossible task for the prosecution, and Burr was acquitted. The verdict moved the outraged Jefferson finally to abandon his belief in an independent judiciary and to propose – vainly – that judges be removable by the president at the request of Congress.

Jefferson's defence of the republic against foreign aggressors also revealed a limit to his libertarianism. War between Britain and France had been resumed in 1803, and neutral shipping again suffered as the belligerent powers swung clumsily at one another with a series of economic blockades. Since Britain was largely in command of the seas it was her actions which antagonized Americans most, and the British added insult to injury by stopping and searching American ships for deserters and pressganging sailors and passengers into the Royal Navy. When H.M.S. *Leopard* opened fire on the frigate *Chesapeake* in June 1807 American newspapers and mass meetings called for vengeance and war seemed imminent. Jefferson, however, hung back. The United States was badly prepared militarily, but perhaps even more important to Jefferson was his conviction that republicanism and war went ill together. Wars meant crippling taxes, public debts, speculation and military establishments, all of which the Whig libertarian tradition had taught could be fatal to liberty itself. The only proper recourse open to a republic, decided the president, was economic sanctions against the aggressors, and he persuaded Congress to adopt a series of embargo acts, designed to stop all American exports.

The embargo, then, was begun in an attempt to protect America's rights without endangering the experiment in republican liberty, but so committed was Jefferson to this solution that he tolerated little opposition. The embargo was highly unpopular in large parts of the country, for it deprived planters and other commercial farmers of their foreign markets, it seriously disrupted shipping, and it produced acute distress in seaports. Widespread evasion led the libertarian president into ever more stringent measures of enforcement, so that by the end of his second term he seemed to be almost at war with some of his own people. Customs collectors were given extensive powers to search out smuggled goods, prohibitive penalties were prescribed for violations, and civil liberties were threatened as the administration attempted to close every loophole. The Massachusetts legislature called the other states to join together in mutual protection against 'the oppressive measures under which they now suffer'.[22] Resistance continued. Defiant citizens of Vermont and New York ferried beef, flour, and lumber across Lake Champlain to Canada, provoking Jefferson to issue a proclamation declaring the region in a state of insurrection. He testily described the obstreperous New York citizenry as being 'arrayed in a war-like manner', he encouraged his subordinates to press charges of treason against a group of Vermonters who had taken the law into their own hands, and he employed the navy and even the regular army to enforce his policy.[23] The Republicans had once denounced the Federalist administrations for over-reacting to the Whisky and Fries rebellions, but now it was their turn to use a standing army against American citizens in time of peace. As Gallatin had warned the president when he had counselled against an embargo, 'Governmental prohibitions do always more mischief than had been calculated. . . .'[24] But to Jefferson the embargo was necessary to save the republic and in his eyes the resistance to it 'in one quarter amounted almost to rebellion and treason'.[25]

But for men of Jefferson's generation it was not unusual to identify resistance with treason. Jefferson, in his own opinion, was not infringing the liberties of loyal American citizens; he was taking necessary measures against subversive elements who were practically in league with America's enemies. Jefferson, like other patricians, had not quite shed the eighteenth-century conception of a holistic political order in which there was no room for a legitimate opposition. In his American republic, as in Hamilton's, opposition all too easily became subversion and resistance became rebellion.

Eventually the Republican party was to succeed in its goal of virtually eliminating the Federalist opposition and restoring a degree of harmony to American politics. Ironically, it was the area of foreign affairs, which had done so much to create the party divisions of the 1790s, which was largely responsible for bringing an end to the first party system. Throughout the 1800s the Federalists suffered from repeated defections because their pro-British stance made their patriotism seem questionable. The embargo had not succeeded in subduing the British, and the milder economic sanctions that the United States resorted to during Madison's presidency proved no more effective in protecting her maritime rights. In areas where these measures bit hard the Federalists gained in popular support, but the gulf separating them from the Republican administrations widened so much that again partisans on each side accused the other of subverting the republic. Many Federalists still held a Hamiltonian conception of economic progress, looking to an expansive commercial connection with Britain and her empire to enrich and strengthen the United States. From this perspective, the diplomatic and economic policies of the administration seemed suicidal, for while the British were being held strictly accountable French depredations on American shipping often seemed to be excused. Some Federalists began darkly to suspect that the Republicans were in league with France, seemingly the only beneficiary of American policy, and if so they were guilty of betraying the American cause, for since 1793 successive French governments had proved themselves the bloody enemies of liberty, not least that of the Emperor Napoleon. The tendency of the Republicans' foreign policy, complained one incensed Federalist in Congress, was 'to throw this people into the embraces of that monster, at whose perfidy and corruption Lucifer blushes and Hell itself stands astonished'.[26] So ruinous seemed the administration's course to some Federalists that resistance of almost any kind was justified. What was the virtue, asked Robert Troup, in supporting a government 'apparently bent on a system of policy that is likely to ruin, not only our commerce, our agriculture, and, I fear, our constitution and our liberties? . . . If such be Americanism, may God in his infinite mercy deliver me from it!'[27] In the eyes of such men 'Americanism' could come to mean seceding from the Union or even dealing secretly with the British. Federalist patriotism, genuine as it was, was capable of becoming scarcely distinguishable from treason.

Where the Federalists saw themselves as defending the republic from its powerful enemies within, the Republicans were battling to save it from its external foes. A variety of motives and impulses, both noble and ignoble, governed the behaviour of Federalists and Republicans alike during these years of crisis, but men of all persuasions were united by the belief that the fate of the republic itself was at stake, although they disagreed profoundly as to who or what were the real enemies of American liberty. While the Federalists excoriated the Republican administrations for perverting the republican experiment, the Republicans were becoming convinced that British actions were imperilling the nation's existence. The French may have illegally seized their share of American shipping, but the British were going beyond mere search and seizure, for they were demanding that all neutral ships call at a British port, pay British dues, and be given a British licence before trading with a port from which the British were excluded. In short, Britain was seeking to regulate international maritime trade for her own benefit, which to the United States meant that she was being reduced once more to the status of a colonial dependency. For four-and-a-half years American administrations fought Britain's arrogant pretensions by diplomacy and economic sanctions, but by 1812 it was becoming clear to the Republicans in government and in Congress that only war would secure respect for the United States as a sovereign independent power. 'Nothing would satisfy the present ministry of England, short of unconditional submission, which it was impossible to make,' wrote Secretary of State James Monroe. 'This fact being completely ascertained, the only remaining alternative, was to get ready for fighting, and to begin as soon as we were ready.'[28]

In June 1812 the United States declared war on Britain, unaware that Parliament had finally suspended the obnoxious orders-in-council. War had come for a variety of reasons. Many Americans attributed the distressed state of southern agriculture and of northern commerce to the British blockade and hoped that war would restore American markets. Some westerners, weary of bloody battles with the

Indian tribes of the Mississippi Valley, blamed the British in Canada
for inciting the Indians and looked to war as a means of ending this
suspected British-Indian connection and facilitating western expansion. Patriotic Americans were incensed at the British government's
apparent disregard for American sovereignty. 'Our ancestors of the
Revolution resisted the first encroachments of British tyranny,' Henry
Clay reminded Congress, arguing that submission to British dictates
was an abandonment of American independence and American
honour.[29] And, as Roger H. Brown has persuasively argued, the very
survival of republicanism was felt by many to be at stake. For one
thing, a failure to solve the crisis in foreign relations could result in the
government being recaptured by the Federalists, who might then
march the country down the dread road to monarchism. But more than
that, if republican government wanted to gain the respect of the world
it had to demonstrate a capacity to defend itself. If the United States
were humiliated now, the reasoning went, few other peoples would be
tempted to join the cause of liberty and America's own free institutions
might not survive. 'Being the only republick,' wrote Richard Rush, 'the
destinies of that sort of government are in our keeping. Should we
stand by and see it longer debased by submission, or sordid avarice, its
cause is gone forever.'[30]

The Republicans, then, went to war – and the Federalists resisted
war – in the name of republican government. The War of 1812 was to
be more than a quarrel with Britain, for it was also in a sense the
occasion of the last battle between the Republicans and the Federalists
for control of American destiny. So wicked and unnecessary was the
war, and so incompetent were the Republicans to fight it, the
Federalists told themselves, that an indignant people might finally see
the Republicans in their true criminal colours and banish them forever
from the councils of the nation. The Republicans for their part could
hope that the treacherous designs of their opponents would now be
fully exposed and Federalism rapidly consigned to a deserved oblivion.
The Federalists occupied the most vulnerable position on this
ideological battleground since their ties with Britain could earn them
the odium of being in league with America's enemy, and, indeed, some
Federalists even believed that this was the Republican objective in
calling for war. But the war was unpopular in large sections of the
country, particularly in New England and New York, where
Federalism enjoyed a revival. Many Republicans in this region too
were far from convinced that war was the best policy, most notably the
powerful DeWitt Clinton of New York, who agreed to stand against
Madison in the presidential election of 1812. Many Federalists
decided to throw in their lot with the peace Republicans, and with the
aid and organizational flair of the younger Federalists Clinton carried
most of the New England and Middle Atlantic states. But this was not
enough to displace Madison, whose narrow victory enabled the

administration Republicans to feel that the country had accepted theirs as the true patriot cause.

This final Republican victory, together with the resurgence of Federalism in New England, turned logical Federalist minds once more to secession. Christopher Gore wrote to Rufus King from Waltham, Massachusetts, in September 1813 to say that 'Some men talk here of making a Declaration, next Winter, that the Union is dissolved and that Massachusetts is willing to be at peace with G.B. . . . '[31] The war seemed all the more suicidal now that Napoleon had apparently been defeated and Britain was able to turn all her considerable resources against the United States. For twenty years some Federalists had believed that America's political and economic future would best be guaranteed by a close association with the British, and now the only hope for the future seemed to lie in the right-minded states severing their links with their incorrigible and reckless sisters. In December 1814 a number of New-England Federalists, harried by local pressures for secession, assembled at Hartford, Connecticut, though moderation finally prevailed and the convention restricted itself to demanding amendments to the American Constitution. Yet the Federalists had already gone too far, for even to talk of secession while the nation was at war could be held to be tantamount to treason. Two further events then sealed the Federalists' fate. One was the signing of a peace treaty with England. The other was the sensational American victory over a larger number of British troops at New Orleans, which General Andrew Jackson contrived so fortunately to win after the peace treaty had been agreed but before news of it had arrived. The Republicans thus ended their war with Britain vindicated, jubilant, and triumphant. Their twenty-year war with the Federalists was ended too, for the Republicans had successfully equated the Republican cause with the American cause and the Federalists with Anglophilia, toryism, and treason. Even earlier, one partisan complained, the word Federalist had come to mean 'every thing that is base and infamous . . . '.[32] By the end of the War of 1812 it had become irretrievably associated with un-American and unrepublican implications and the party that wore the name would not long survive in the American environment.

The first American party system did not die overnight, but its days were numbered. Federalism remained strong in a few states for a decade after 1815, but it became increasingly irrelevant to national politics as the Republican administrations maintained their accommodationist strategy, even to the point of chartering a new national bank and enacting a mildly protective tariff. The ending of the war in Europe removed one major source of discord, and Americans could reasonably hope that party distinctions and party battles were now a thing of the past, that the harmonious republic of which Federalists and Republicans alike had dreamed might finally be upon them. More pragmatic and less elitist than their opponents, the Republicans had won the mass of the people to their cause partly by compromise and conciliation, rewriting their political creed so as to find a place for commerce and industry, partly by their success in exploiting nationalist sentiments during the foreign policy crises and in thus identifying their opponents with subversion, and partly by their greater mastery of the arts of popular politics. Pragmatism and the popular touch were to remain invaluable attributes for the ambitious American politician. But the Republicans' very success in equating their cause with American republicanism also served to encourage their political heirs to maintain their vigilant scrutiny for enemies within as well as without. The Republicans had never entirely escaped the holistic confines of eighteenth-century Anglo-American political culture.

Chapter 9

The patrician order of
the early republic

'The war has renewed and reinstated the national feelings and
character which the Revolution had given . . . ', mused Albert Gallatin
in 1816; the people, he thought, 'are more American'.[1] No one could
plausibly accuse Thomas Jefferson and James Madison of not being
good Americans, but like the rest of their generation they had once
been loyal subjects of the English king, and, unlike some of their
successors, they recognized that the American polity owed something
to English traditions. Jefferson, for example, doubted whether there
had been any decisive break with the British past, perceiving the
American experiment in representative government as deriving from
the 'little specimen formerly existing in the English constitution (but
now lost)'.[2] The United States could never be mistaken for an English
colony during the era of the first American party system, but it could
not hope to conceal its British parentage.

Few members of that divided political elite which directed the
nation's affairs between 1789 and 1815 ever lost entirely their
attachment to traditional political values or even their fascination with
English forms. Men of all political persuasions still retained a
consensual ideal of the political world, though some like Jefferson
were now conceding that parties had reluctantly to be lived with as the
inevitable products of human nature. Most Federalists and Republicans also tended to assume that the political nation should be confined
to those with some sort of financial stake in society, however little, as is
illustrated by Jefferson's celebrated fears of the destructive potential
of the propertyless urban mob. The protection of liberty remained the
central purpose of constitutional structures, and liberty was not as yet
generally equated with democracy. These attitudes were deeply rooted
in Anglo-American political culture, and they were essentially those of
gentlemen in a world which still retained a role for gentlemen.
America's gentlemen had also not quite rid themselves of their old
habit of looking to England for models of political behaviour. At any
rate, as American politics became polarized in the 1790s the
Federalists found themselves admiring those English features which
seemed designed to preserve order, such as the hierarchical social
structure, the checks against democracy in the (not-quite-so) balanced
constitution, and those public and private financial institutions which

helped to promote sound government. Republicans too sometimes felt the pull of English influences, but they were attracted not so much by the example of aristocratic order as by the heritage of libertarian thought and by the accomplishments of parliamentary government.

Yet innovation was as much a fact of life in the early republic as was tradition. In some ways the period witnessed a remarkable modernization of the political process, most notably in the emergence of a competitive party system and the mobilization of an extensive electorate. Parties gave men extra-local attachments and served to weaken those community values, customs, and habits of deference which sustained the traditional political order. It was not easy to reconcile the ideological and institutional inheritance from the Anglo-American past, not to mention the continued respect for certain aspects of contemporary British political culture, with the political realities of republican America, but for a while the patrician elite retained both their political vision and their authority, particularly in national governmental councils. They did so in part because of the sheer durability of traditional political attitudes, such as the association of political rights with economic independence, but also because they made use of the very means that the constitution-makers had intended, the system of representation. At both state and national levels, political authority – as opposed to constitutional or legal authority – tended to become concentrated in the legislatures, where America's gentlemen could continue to seek to guide the republic's destiny. These representative assemblies had sound historical claims for exercising leadership, though at times they seemed close to subverting the constitutional principle of the separation of powers. At the national level the political authority of the president eventually declined as that of Congress increased, and by 1815 the United States seemed almost to be on the verge of a system of parliamentary government not unlike the one that was evolving in England.

The Federalists of course clung most faithfully to a hierarchical conception of the good political society. They barely concealed their distrust of the 'Mob', which Gouverneur Morris identified as the 'the vicious, hotheaded, and inconsiderate Part of the Community together with that numerous Host of Tools, which Knaves do work with, called fools', which, moreover, formed ' . . . the majority of all empires, kingdoms, and commonwealths . . . '.[3] The Federalists looked to religion, learning and the law to buttress the position of society's natural rulers, though they also placed an uncertain faith in the continued power of deference. Harrison Gray Otis upbraided a colleague for his disrespectful address to the president because 'where the Chief Magistrate is elective, and the dignity of his character is upheld . . . by the esteem of his constituents and the strength of public opinion, it is an incumbent duty to demonstrate, by all ordinary means, our respect for the character and the office'.[4] Federalism tended to be strongest among those social elites which were relatively insecure, such as the mercantile and professional classes of New England, who felt threatened by the constant rise of new men and whose wealth was not so exceptional as to mark them off clearly from the rest of society. Fearing the growth of democracy, many Federalists in the early nineteenth century actively encouraged the formation of benevolent societies devoted to distributing Bibles and religious tracts and preaching the virtues of temperance, hoping to teach the lower orders to be sober, industrious, and respectful to their betters.

The Republicans saw less need for artificially preserving a stratified sociopolitical order. Indeed, the Republicans survived in large part because they did put their faith in the people, although in so doing they also in some measure assumed that deferential attitudes themselves would survive. 'The cherishment of the people then was our principle,' wrote Jefferson in old age, 'the fear and distrust of them, that of the other party.'[5] It was the more secure elites, like the landed gentry of Virginia, which tended to support the Republican party, perhaps because they sensed that the people would continue to turn to them for political leadership.[6] Jefferson himself saw little merit in selecting political leaders from the wealthy and the high-born, preferring a natural aristocracy of 'virtue and talents', and arguing that 'that form of government is the best which provides the most effectually for a pure selection of these natural aristoi into the offices of government'.[7] Yet his party at large did little enough to search out men of wisdom and virtue among the ordinary people, and as long as patricians could display these qualities they had little to fear from Republicanism. The Jeffersonian Republicans were sincere champions of the common man, but they conducted no crusade against gentlemen of property and standing.

Nonetheless the transformation of the American political structure had already begun. The advent of party, however unwanted, pointed the way to a more modern system of politics in which traditional notions of hierarchy and deference would play little part. The two-party system invaded and divided communities which previously remained politically united, offered men new loyalties in place of those towards their traditional leaders, and provided voters with a choice. Even where the first party system soon disappeared, it had given men an experience with a system of politics characterized by competition and change. Old habits not easily lost were, by the same token, not easily regained. Also, more people were becoming involved in the political process than ever before. The repeated battles between the Federalists and the Republicans and between the different Republican factions unquestionably helped to stimulate popular interest in politics. The election statistics gathered by J.R. Pole and R.P. McCormick demonstrate a dramatic rise in voter activity in the late 1790s and more especially the 1800s, turnout reaching a high of seventy per cent of adult white males in New Jersey and Pennsylvania in 1808, and sixty-eight per cent in Massachusetts in 1812, and in 1814 New Hampshire reached an incredible eighty-one per cent.[8] By this time a younger generation of Federalists were constructing efficient party organizations and taking their cause to the people, and this electoral competition, together with such divisive issues as the embargo, served to attract men to the polls, particularly in elections for governor or for Congress.

Yet this arousal of the masses and the entry of new men into politics in these years does not appear to have represented any very significant revolt against 'the better sort'. Gentlemen planters like Jefferson and Randolph, distinguished political families like the Clintons and the Adamses, and successful lawyers like William Plumer and Josiah Quincy, still held commanding positions in politics. It may have been, however, that patrician leadership survived better at national level than at state level – the Constitution had after all been devised partly with this intention – though even within the states popular participation was not translated immediately into an aggressive egalitarianism. Most states remained content with the constitutions that they had inherited from the revolutionary period and generally made little or no attempt to revise them. There was some whittling away of suffrage requirements, though where this happened the Republicans did not show themselves to be markedly more egalitarian than the Federalists. In Maryland a campaign for universal white manhood suffrage was supported by liberals in both parties and resisted by conservative Republicans and Federalists in the state senate, and only succeeded in 1802 by a threat to make the senate elective. Some states moved over to a taxpaying qualification, notably Delaware in 1791 and New Jersey in 1807, and while this may have provided an approximation of universal suffrage it still assumed that the vote should be earned. Several Republican-dominated states, including Virginia and New York, left property qualifications untouched (despite the efforts of some New York Republicans), and in Rhode Island neither party showed much interest in suffrage reform, the freehold qualification surviving there until 1842. Tom Paine in 1805 was still able to denounce the Pennsylvania constitution as 'a copy in miniature of the Government of England, established at the conquest of that Country by William of Normandy'.[9] The charge was preposterous, but most state governments still in some measure represented property as well as persons.

The survival of such Whiggish relics helped to maintain some sort of relationship between social position and political influence, though equally the broad electorates and the remarkable activity at the polls meant that there were no firm constitutional barriers against reform. The disintegration of the first American party system did not restore a traditional or pre-party political order in many states, for the Republican party itself sometimes divided into antagonistic factions; elsewhere state parties battling over local issues emerged. American voters became used to being presented with alternatives at the polls, and came to expect a politics of controversy and change. Yet the patrician elites retained a high measure of political authority. In successive presidential and congressional campaigns, both Federalist and Republican political managers sought to build their parties by recruiting the support of local notables. John Beckley is often regarded as the Republicans' first party manager, and a recent study of his activities concludes that they were 'directed toward winning the support of important citizens who could be counted upon to have influence on their neighbors'.[10] The people were being invited to go to the polls to support the established political leaders.

The patricians in government protected themselves against the passions of the multitude in a variety of subtle – and often unconscious – ways. Both Federalist and Republican administrations tried conscientiously to recruit and to appoint to office candidates of some respectability. George Washington as president wanted to appoint 'the first characters' to his government, and John Adams was equally determined to apply the test of fitness, although in his eyes Federalists invariably seemed better qualified than Republicans.[11] The Republicans were perfectly happy to accept men of humble birth among the ranks of their leaders, but they liked to think that such positions must be earned by superior talents rather than party service. In 1808 Jefferson urged the lawyer William Wirt to enter Congress, assuring him that with 'your reputation, talents, and correct views . . . you will at once be placed at the head of the republican body in the House of Representatives . . .'.[12] But even Jefferson could not remain quite true to his ideal of an 'aristocracy of talent', as is betrayed by his description of the man he appointed as first civil governor of Louisiana: 'Sound judgment, standing in society, knolege of the world, wealth, liberality, familiarity with the French language, and having a French wife'.[13] The survival of such traditional public service ideals helped to perpetuate gentlemanly rule, even though gentlemen now needed to be of the right political persuasion. Under both the Federalists and the Republicans sons not infrequently succeeded their fathers in office and nepotism was not unknown. The best and the worst features of the politics of deference and patronage remained to be eliminated.

The politicians also restrained the multitude by gathering political authority into their own hands. This was particularly evident in presidential elections, in which the people were allowed a very limited role. If the Republicans claimed to be democrats, their methods of choosing presidential electors did not conspicuously validate that claim. Fewer states – absolutely and proportionately – allowed a popular vote in 1800 than in any other presidential election in American history. In ten of the sixteen states during the so-called 'Revolution of 1800' the electors were selected by the state legislatures, and in another, Tennessee, the legislature nominated thirty-three individuals to choose the electors. The proportion of states denying the people an opportunity to vote in presidential elections remained fairly high in the era of Republican ascendancy; in 1812 nine of the eighteen states were still using the legislative system. Other states used either the district system, whereby each district in the state could vote for one (or more) presidential elector, giving both parties a chance to win some electoral votes, or the general ticket system, in which the election was conducted on a statewide (or winner-take-all) basis. In both cases, of course, the people could vote. The district system was generally held to be the most democratic and Jefferson himself described it as the 'best', but he connived at the Virginia Republicans' decision to abandon it, for when most states were consolidating their votes by using the legislative or general ticket systems, it was 'folly and worse than folly' not to follow suit.[14] Both systems worked to the advantage of the dominant party in the legislature, its members meeting in caucus to compose the electoral ticket.

But even the role of the state caucuses was limited. Of increasing importance in presidential elections was the congressional caucus, consisting of all a party's members in the two houses of Congress, which took upon itself the task of choosing a presidential candidate. Both the Republicans and the Federalists had chosen their candidates by this method in 1800, though thereafter only the Republicans persisted with it. With the Republican party in the ascendancy in the nation at large, the Republican members of Congress were in effect determining the presidential succession, a point which was not lost on the caucus system's many critics. In 1808 seventeen members of Congress, including several Quids who were hostile to Madison's nomination, issued a protest against the intervention of the caucus in the election of president and vice-president, charging that the result was 'virtually to transfer the appointment of those officers from the people, to a majority of the two Houses of Congress'.[15] But the administration Republicans defended the practice as a necessary evil, without which the Republican vote might be split between several different candidates, and they did not abandon it until their party itself was dissolving in the 1820s.

This concentration of political authority into the hands of members of the national and state legislatures seemed to reflect the Federalist model of a representative republic, in which the people respectfully deferred to the judgement of their elected agents. The Federalists, conscious of their elitist image, were apparently more anxious to avoid the popular election of presidential electors than the Republicans, but the latter also resorted to the legislative method and they were more prepared than their rivals to use the congressional caucus. Both parties in some measure acted on the patrician assumption that elected representatives could take decisions on the people's behalf, even where the people could have been consulted more directly. In this sense, and probably unwittingly, American politics were evolving in a manner not unlike the politics of England, where power tended to centre on the party leadership in Parliament. The caucus system in particular tended to create something approximating parliamentary government, for it meant that the legislature was in effect naming the executive. As in England, too, the favoured candidates for the highest offices tended to be men with long experience in public affairs, men who had emerged at the top after faithful service in lesser capacities. Every president from John Adams in 1797 to his son John Quincy Adams in 1825 had graduated to that position either from the vice-presidency or from the secretaryship-of-state. When it seemed possible that the election of 1796 might result in a tied vote in the electoral college, a deferential Jefferson decided that he must yield to the stronger claims of Vice-President Adams, for 'He has always been my senior, from the commencement of our public life . . . '.[16] Presidents – like prime ministers – were not thrown up spontaneously by the sovereign people. They tended to be chosen by the nation's leading men from among themselves, and Congress played a major part in the process.

By thus claiming a role in the selection of the president, congress-men were resisting the principle of the separation of powers. The framers of the Constitution, determined to avoid anything like the English example whereby the independence of the House of Com-mons had been undermined by crown patronage, had tried to keep the legislature and the executive as far apart as possible, but now the United States seemed to be reverting to a system where the two were intermeshed. It was the Republicans more than the Federalists who abetted this trend towards a kind of parliamentary government. Thomas Jefferson as president early recognized a need for some organization of Congress if Republican measures were to succeed, and he quietly facilitated the appointment of his own partisans to important congressional posts. Nathaniel Macon became speaker of the House and John Randolph chairman of the powerful ways and means committee, and when the Quid schism estranged these men from the administration they were replaced by other loyal lieutenants of the president. One innovation was the establishment of a floor leader, whose function it was to act as the administration's spokesman and to steer its measures through Congress. William B. Giles of Virginia served in this capacity for a time and was predictably referred to on occasion as 'the premier, or prime minister'. 'Mr. Giles continues to be our *Director*', wrote Senator John Quincy Adams in 1805, 'and in general meets with little opposition to what he thinks beneficial to the public service.'[17] There were grumblings about presidential dictation, but, as Jefferson wrote to one prospective floor leader, if the executive kept to itself and allowed 'the House to plunge on in the dark, it becomes a government of chance and not of design'.[18]

Jefferson was able to maintain his ascendancy over Congress during most of his time as president, but his successors found that it was Congress that increasingly called the tune, insofar as anyone did in the nation's new and ill-organized capital. James Madison owed his elevation to the Republican caucus, and the king-makers in Congress were little disposed to bow to his will. Where Jefferson had been able to choose his own cabinet, Madison was obliged by a group of powerful senators to accept the incompetent Robert Smith of Maryland as his first Secretary of State, when he would much have preferred Albert Gallatin. President Monroe too found himself faced with an uncooperative Congress, led by a speaker who had no qualms about embarrassing the administration. Unlike Jefferson, Monroe had no congressional lieutenants to promote administration measures, 'except members who occasionally appear as volunteers, and generally even without any previous concert with the Executive'.[19] The Republican presidents had once been rebels against an over-powerful executive in the shape of George III, who, they believed, had corruptly subverted the celebrated English constitution by the improper use of the offices in his gift. Their continued respect for the old radical Whig doctrine of legislative supremacy, and their reluctance to use patronage to buy support, contributed to the decline of the presidency. In 1818 Justice Story was able to remark that 'the Executive has no longer a commanding influence. The House of Representatives has absorbed all the popular feeling and all the effective power of the country.'[20] The president, it seemed, was fast turning into a constitutional monarch.

As power slipped away from the presidency, developments within Congress itself served to enhance its political influence, if not its capacity to provide sound government. The emergence of specialist committees provided Congress with its own instruments for gathering information, acquiring expertise, and formulating policy, so that it became less dependent on the administration. The House of Representatives had begun to use standing committees in the mid-1790s, but whereas only four existed in 1800, by 1810 there were ten and by 1820 twenty-one. House committees were appointed by the speaker, and this office too grew in importance, especially after Henry Clay assumed it in 1811. Impulsive and charming, agile and eloquent, this young Kentuckian proved himself the best parliamentarian of his generation, and during and after the War of 1812 Clay made the speakership into a centre of power which rivalled or even overshadowed that of the presidency.

The president was only saved from total humiliation by the disorganized state of Congress itself. As James Sterling Young has shown, the Washington community in the early republic was hampered in its attempt to provide good government by its own lack of internal cohesion.[21] Party machinery in the Capitol was weak, particularly after Jefferson lost political control in 1808. The turnover of members of Congress was high, over 40 per cent on average being replaced biennially, and senators and congressmen tended to give their first loyalties to their states, their regions, and even to the boarding-house cronies with whom they messed during their short sojourns in Washington each year. Steeped in the libertarian tradition of Anglo-American political thought, they also tended to believe that centralized power was a danger to be sedulously guarded against and they were reluctant to exercise it themselves. Thus, many of these transient legislators were more interested in defending their con-stituents than in governing the nation. Actually, these weaknesses in the Washington community probably increased after 1815, for reasons which will be suggested in later chapters, but they were already apparent enough during Madison's presidency.

In the thirty years following the adoption of the Philadelphia constitution, then, political authority at both state and national levels tended to centre on the legislatures. These bodies were certainly responsive to public opinion, particularly the lower houses for which terms were short, though they also exercised considerable power on behalf of the people, formulating policies, selecting candidates for office, consenting to executive appointments. Legislators still tended to act on the eighteenth-century assumption that they were quasi-magistrates who could expect their constitutents to acquiesce in their decisions. The representative, said one Federalist editor, should cast his votes in the legislature 'according to the dictates of his own conscience, and in pursuance of a judgement maturely formed'.[22] Republican politicians might deny that they believed this but they often behaved as if they did, and their own continued suspicion of party betrayed an assumption that men in government should ideally be free to exercise their own judgements. Such attitudes served to strengthen the position of the gentlemen who continued to hold considerable sway in politics, and the much-respected doctrine of legislative supremacy helped to legitimize their exercise of power. The Republicans in particular had absorbed from English libertarian thought the idea that the legislature was the principal guardian of liberty and should be the crucible of public policy. They saw little danger in allowing political leadership to reside in Congress and the state assemblies.

At the national level in particular there were signs that American government was moving towards a parliamentary system, despite the intentions of the Constitution's framers. The principle of the separa-tion of powers was eroded as the executive became dependent on the legislature, and the eclipse of the presidency left Congress as the foremost branch of government. The constitutional balance set up in 1787 was being tilted towards the House of Representatives. Despite the disordered state of the Washington community, it was at least conceivable in 1815 that the presidency in time would become a largely honorific office, that the primary decisions respecting govern-ment policy would be taken in Congress, and that effective power would rest with whichever political leaders were able to command a majority in the lower house. The British political system was after all evolving in roughly this way, and many Americans continued to look across the Atlantic for surreptitious guidance. It was Jefferson himself, as vice-president, who compiled a *Manual of Parliamentary Practice* for American legislators, in the process acknowledging a debt to the Clerk of the House of Commons. That the United States might parallel British political development was perhaps made the more likely by the degree to which the patrician elites in the two countries shared the same beliefs and values, by their adherence to the Lockean conception of a liberal political order, by their assumption that the political nation was best confined to the propertied or at least to those who had earned their political rights, by their distaste for factions and parties, by their cherishing of the traditional constitutional constraints upon power, and by their conviction, implicit if not always explicit, that the political system should be leader-oriented, with enlightened statesmen in deliberative assemblies promulgating enlightened measures for the public good.

Yet America's gentlemen had already committed the republic to an increasingly ungentlemanly political future. An extensive electorate had been the legacy of the colonial and revolutionary eras, and as the patrician leaders had called upon this electorate for aid in their ideological and fratricidal battles with one another, they had been obliged to mobilize, organize, and politicize it. Their reluctant creation of political parties may have been designed to secure popular support for established leaders, but it made those leaders perilously dependent on public esteem and even public fashion. High-minded Federalist politicians increasingly found themselves obliged to bow to the wishes of their constituents rather than to the dictates of their prized consciences. The calling of the Hartford Convention in 1814, for example, was more the result of an attempt to contain the enraged passions of some of the citizens of Massachusetts and Connecticut than of a genuine conviction among Federalist leaders that secession was a realistic solution to their problems. The Republicans for their part owed their considerable political success in no small measure to their willingness to put their faith in the people, but the demotic edge to their rhetoric in itself constituted an invitation to the people to assume an ever more commanding role in government. 'The people may err mistakenly,' observed one Republican editor, 'but never intentionally.'[23] Through their legislative caucuses and other devices the Republican political leaders may have tried to gather authority into their own hands, but their public pronouncements committed them to the position that the people could safely be entrusted with the exercise of power. The focus of American politics was gradually shifting from the elected to the electors. 'I dare not look beyond my Nose into futurity . . .', wrote an ageing John Adams to an ageing Thomas Jefferson in 1814. 'Every thing is transmuted into an Instrument of

Electioneering. Election is the grand Brama, the immortal Lama, I had almost said, the Juggernaught, for Wives are almost ready to burn upon the Pile and Children to be thrown under the Wheel.'[24] Adams's metaphorical misgivings were not all that far-fetched, for the patrician political world of the Founding Fathers was already beginning to fall victim to such passions.

Part 4

The changing
political environment (1815-1830)

The disintegration of the patrician political world of the early republic
was a slow and gradual process. The erosion of the habits of custom
and deference which had helped to cement the traditional hierarchical
structure had begun before the Revolution and was not fully
completed even by the time of the Civil War. But in the 1810s and
1820s American politicians sensed a changing and uncertain world
about them. American republicanism was increasingly being equated
with an egalitarian democracy, and state constitutions were amended
to conform more fully to the majority principle. The people
themselves, ever more conscious of the power they wielded at the
polls, revealed a growing reluctance to accept the directions of the
traditional leadership. At the same time, sectional pressures further
undermined the authority of federal institutions and promoted a
greater degree of decentralization in American politics. Both trends
acted together to undermine the fragile order of the early republic.

These centrifugal and popular pressures in particular contributed to
the weakening of the presidency, the collapse of the caucus system, and
the decline in the political authority of the national and state
legislatures. The traditional forms of ordering American politics had
helped to sustain a system which had its roots in the eighteenth century
and which shared some characteristics with the British pattern of
government, but patrician and parliamentary styles were ill-equipped
to survive the assaults of the changing American environment. As in
the 1780s and 1790s, some politicians sought to combat these
disintegrative tendencies by either constitutional revision or economic
reform, responses which were essentially conservative in nature, their
political objective being the restoration (or creation) of that harmonious republic which had always been the ideal. But remedies based on
organic conceptions of the polity could hardly succeed in the highly
egalitarian, individualistic, and conflict-oriented political world that
America was fast becoming. Only a political response was capable of
restoring order, and politicians eventually turned to fashioning new
techniques to woo the voters, to finding candidates capable of
exploiting popular currents, and to developing new organizational
devices compatible with democratic imperatives. The election of
Andrew Jackson to the presidency in 1828 marked the advent of a new
political order.

Chapter 10

The old structure crumbles

The decay in the old political superstructure first became apparent in the failure of the first American party system to survive Monroe's presidency. The Federalists never again succeeded in fielding a presidential candidate after 1816 and within a few years the Republican party had ceased to exist as a coherent political movement. The disappearance of the first parties was widely welcomed as heralding a return to a healthier and less divisive state of affairs, but this celebratory view overlooked one important party function, the exercise of leadership at the nation's centre. And as the old national parties passed from the scene, so too did the first generation of national leaders. James Monroe was the last of the revolutionary heroes to occupy the White House, and the dramatic symmetry of the deaths of both Thomas Jefferson and John Adams on 4 July 1826, the fiftieth anniversary of Independence, again reminded the American people that their great experiment in republican government was now passing into the hands of men who had not known British rule.

The disappearance of the old national parties and of the men who led them hastened the dissolution of the old political order. In these years new currents emerged which seemed to be directed against the existing political establishments. Both at Washington and in the state capitals professional politicians found themselves defending the customs, institutions, and privileges they had inherited from the past. This widespread suspicion of the pretensions of political elites was cannily fanned by those who were seeking office, but it was to have far-reaching effects on the political structure. The rights and liberties of the people, it was often said, were being undermined by the self-interested machinations of powerful politicians and unscrupulous officeholders. There was more than a touch of partisan propaganda in such charges, but they also testified to a kind of populistic strain in American politics, a popular suspicion of and a hostility towards what appeared to be entrenched political interests. (Populist sentiments in this sense were to become a familiar feature of American politics, though only rarely did they fuse into a coherent political force like the Populist movement of the 1890s.) Reinforcing the corrosive effects of populism were the divisive effects of sectionalism. As the Northeast, the West, and the South became more conscious of themselves as distinct sections the federal government experienced greater difficulty in reconciling their varied demands. The nationalism associated with the War of 1812 defined itself – and survived – by a chauvinistic rejection of the affectations of European culture; it did little to create lasting bonds of sentiment within the American Union.

The popular democratic currents of the period together with the growing pressures of sectionalism combined to bring about a reduction in the authority of the national and state capitals. Neither the politicians in Washington nor the legislative caucuses in the several states were able to exert the influence over political events that they had once enjoyed. The erosion in the authority of the old leadership, the abandonment of traditional political practices, and the increasing decentralization of the American political system underlined the differences between the politics of the Old and the New World. In Britain, political leaders continued to be recruited from 'the well-born and the able', from those with long experience in public affairs, ministries continued to depend on Parliament for their support, and London continued to be the centre of political authority. Americans had long been developing their own political style; as the political superstructure of the early republic was dismantled after 1815, the remaining similarities vanished almost beyond recall.

The new political patterns were in large part a response to the changing nature of the American environment. Geographical expansion and economic growth created new political constituencies with interests of their own to protect. The ever broadening white suffrage and, perhaps more importantly, the heightened awareness of the voters of their own rights and power, enhanced both the popular and sectional pressures on politicians, whose ingenuity was remorselessly tested by the disparate demands of the large, critical, and increasingly divided electorate. At another level, politicians were sensitive both to the widespread unease for the future of the republic, generated by the erosion of the simple agrarian society of the past and by the departure of the revolutionary generation, and to the chauvinistic and belligerent nationalism triggered by the War of 1812, which asserted the superiority of the nation's own institutions and which identified the truly American as the non-European. Those bold enough and ambitious enough to venture into the unpredictable political arena of these years had to tread warily.

The increasing heterogeneity of the nation was underlined by the emergence of the West as a distinct and self-conscious section. The western states were the fastest-growing in the Union, representing under fifteen per cent of the whole population in 1810, about twenty-three per cent in 1820, and over twenty-eight per cent by 1830. 'Old America seems to be breaking up and moving westward,' observed an English traveller in 1817, a comment which could have been applied to the political structure as well as to the movement of people.[1] As the new states grew in size and number their political importance increased correspondingly. Thomas Jefferson as president had had to cope with but ten congressmen (out of a total of 142) from west of the mountains. The House of Representatives which elected John Quincy Adams to the presidency in 1825 contained forty-seven westerners (among its 213 members) and their vote was decisive. The West was never unified as a section and the slavery issue in particular drove a wedge between its northern and southern tiers, but by the 1820s a number of distinctively western demands were discomfiting eastern politicians. One of the most implacable was the call for the removal of the Indian tribes that obstructed white settlement, which accounted in part for the popularity of Andrew Jackson in the Southwest, for in 1814 he had won the admiration of his neighbours for the ruthless impartiality with which he drove both hostile and friendly Creeks alike out of what was shortly to become the state of Alabama.

Westerners also tended to favour federal aid for internal improvements, since better transportation connections with the East would enlarge their markets. A cheap land policy was another western demand. The federal government was offering for sale more public land than was being readily absorbed, and increasingly men settled on this land without purchasing it. The squatters wanted a reduction in the price of land, protection from speculators, and a pre-emptive right to purchase (or even to be given!) the land they had improved, and they soon found their spokesmen in Washington. Colonel Davy Crockett, for example, half frontiersman and half clown, was elected to Congress in 1827 as the champion of the squatters of western Tennessee.

Crockett became a well-known celebrity, but he was never taken seriously as a spokesman for the West. Of far greater stature was Henry Clay of Kentucky, whose frontier manners the Austrian traveller Francis Grund found graceful and dignified though distinctively American, for he 'chews tobacco, drinks whisky punch, gambles, puts his legs on the table or the chimney, and spits . . . "like a regular Kentucky hogdriver" '.[2] From his election as Speaker of the House in 1811, Clay wielded an inordinate power over Congress, which always remained the political arena in which he functioned best. He became an early exponent of the protective tariff, persuading western farmers that it was in their best interests to encourage industrialization in the eastern states, for it would provide them with a domestic market. As it happened Kentucky, although a slave state, tended to favour the tariff anyway, for her hemp-growers constituted an important and politically-influential group, and their calls for protection Clay never cared to ignore. Clay did resist the demand for cheap land, a cause which was taken up by the lumbering Senator from Missouri, Thomas Hart Benton, who spent a considerable part of his thirty belligerent years in the Senate haranguing his colleagues on the importance of the West and the virtues of democracy in long-winded and statistic-laden speeches, roaring and mumbling by turns. To men like Benton, the West *was* America. 'Every reflecting man is convinced, that the sceptre of empire in America is passing into western hands;' reported one observer, 'and whether for weal or for woe, will ultimately depend upon their fitness to wield it.'[3]

The surge of people across the mountains meant that the residents of New England and the Middle Atlantic states became a smaller proportion of the whole, but these areas remained the most densely populated. Northerners quarrelled among themselves as much as westerners, but they were developing identifiable economic interests of their own. The spread of textile mills and factories in Massachusetts, Rhode Island, and Connecticut, the growth of the iron industry in western Pennsylvania and New Jersey, and the emergence of a variety of small manufacturing interests throughout the Middle Atlantic and western states aligned a large part of the people of the North on the side of business enterprise. In 1828 a New York politician informed his chief in Washington of the 'manufacturing excitement' raging through most of the state, warning that unless strenuous efforts were made to secure a high protective tariff, 'we shall have a difficult and doubtful contest as the next election'.[4] The fact that the North also contained vociferous pockets of free traders made it no easier for the federal government to reconcile her interests with those of other sections. The religious and cultural traditions of New England's Yankees, who carried their piety and sobriety with them as they moved into western New York, Ohio, and other developing areas, also left a vivid mark on the political complexion of the region. During the campaign of 1824 a southerner complained with some feeling that the issue of slavery 'has become commingled with the politics and religion' of the people of the North.[5]

One of the most adroit of northern politicians was Martin Van Buren, who, according to one disrespectful critic, could laugh on one side of his face while crying on the other. As Senator for New York during the 1820s, Van Buren was said by some to be the best political manager in the United States. His attempts to create an understanding between the 'plain Republicans' of the North and the planters of the South blunted his effect as a sectional spokesman, but the same could not be said of Daniel Webster, whose passion for the presidency was destined to remain unrequited because of his inability to overcome his regional identification. In 1824, reflecting the views of the merchants and financiers of Boston whose fortunes were based on foreign commerce, Webster was still an eloquent spokesman for free trade, but a few years later 'the Godlike Daniel' was pushing a tariff bill through Congress, for more and more of his well-heeled constituents were switching their investments to manufacturing. Vain and a little venal, Webster was equally prepared to use his formidable presecne, piercing intellect, and superb oratory to line his own pocket, to defend the interests of New England, or to save the Union that he revered.

As a sectional spokesman, Webster more often crossed swords with southerners than with westerners, for the interests of South and North seemed to be growing increasingly apart. The most vital difference between the two was rendered yet more conspicuous in the early nineteenth century as slavery gradually disappeared from the North. In the South, on the other hand, the invention of the cotton gin in 1793 and the growing demand for cotton from the multiplying textile mills of Lancashire and Massachusetts greatly strengthened plantation agriculture and revitalized slavery. Tobacco had once been the main southern staple, but by 1830 cotton was both the section's principal crop and the country's biggest export. The insatiable demand for cotton accelerated the settlement of the Southwest, and in the 1830s Alabama and Mississippi overtook South Carolina and Georgia as the chief cotton-producing states. As the Cotton Kingdom expanded, the number of slaves grew and their price increased. The fall in the price of cotton in the 1820s encouraged many southerners to adopt a hostile attitude towards the tariff, which they blamed for increasing the costs of the manufactured goods that they were obliged to buy, while their increasing reliance on slavery, which shaped their social and cultural values as much as it brought them wealth, made them morbidly sensitive to any signs of slave unrest or to northern disfavour with their peculiar institution.

Perhaps the most distinctively southern figure of major stature during Monroe's administration was the Secretary of the Treasury, William H. Crawford of Georgia. A burly and genial man, Crawford was quicker than many southern politicians to shed the nationalistic doctrines that had made some inroads in the South during Madison's presidency, summoning his brethren to return to the strict constructionist and states rights doctrines of the early Republicans. A paralytic stroke in September 1823, however, blasted his ambitions, and the section's political mantle fell on John C. Calhoun of South Carolina, a more belated convert to strict constructionism. For many years a fervent nationalist, Calhoun fought the election of 1824 as a southern man with northern principles, but by 1828, harried by the increasingly virulent anti-tariff sentiments of his constituents and convinced that the North had won control of the federal government, he was constructing a formidable intellectual defence of the states rights position. Not all southerners followed Calhoun (indeed, surprisingly few were his committed partisans), but by about 1830 he had established himself as the most formidable champion of the section's interests.

The strains of sectionalism had always been a feature of American politics, but as the spread of population westwards reduced the influence of the Atlantic states, and as separate lines of economic development increasingly differentiated the various sections, the tensions became more acute. By about 1820 sectionalism was widely perceived to be a serious potential threat to the Union. The depression of 1819-22 increased demands for tariff protection, particularly by groups in the Middle Atlantic states, Ohio and Kentucky, much to the displeasure of many southerners, who were anxious both about their foreign markets and about any enhancement in the authority of the federal government, which might one day be turned against slavery. The spectre of disunion was more terrifyingly invoked by the Missouri Crisis of 1819-21. Missouri had been carved out of the Louisiana Purchase, and although most of it lay above the line separating freedom from slavery southern settlers had nonetheless taken their slaves there and now wanted the area to be admitted to the Union as a slave state. Many northerners, long resenting what they saw as the over-representation of the South in the nation's councils as a result of the infamous three-fifths clause, were determined to repel this northwesterly thrust of slavery. Attempts by northern congressmen to outlaw slavery in the proposed state seemed to southerners as at best evidence of a design to exclude the South from the colonization of the West and at worst evidence of a design to mobilize the North in a united assault on slavery. If this wicked interference continued, raged one southern congressman, 'the Union will be dissolved'.[6] Frightened by such talk, Henry Clay and others eventually fashioned a compromise by which Missouri entered as a slave state and Maine as a free state, and which guaranteed that in future slavery would be barred from the Louisiana territory north of the latitude 36°30′. As had happened before and was to happen again, the perilous issue of slavery had been removed from the national agenda by the politics of compromise and conciliation.

But the Missouri Crisis had awakened deep sectional fears which were never to be entirely quieted. The South in particular became more conscious of itself as a distinct section, whose interests seemed increasingly vulnerable as the North and West continued to outpace the slave states in population and influence. No geographical section was homogeneous and alignments in Congress varied from issue to issue, but throughout the 1820s there was a nagging unease among political leaders over the ability of the American political system to meet the disparate demands now made upon it. 'We are led forward by a heedless enthusiasm for sectional men and sectional measures,' complained one political commentator in 1828, identifying 'an indulgence in *sectional pressures*' as the most dangerous threat to the system.[7] 'Mr. Clay spoke to me with great concern of the prospects of the country,' noted a weary John Quincy Adams just before he left the presidency, ' – the threats of disunion from the South, and the graspings after all the public lands, which are disclosing themselves in the Western States'.[8] He reflected with gloomy self-satisfaction that such intractable problems would soon no longer be his responsibility.

The diverse sectional and particularistic interests exerted a kind of centrifugal pressure on the American political system. If there had been some tendency to enhance the authority of the federal government, or at least of Congress, in the fifteen years prior to the crisis year of 1819, in the fifteen years thereafter the trend was reversed. William H. Crawford as Secretary of the Treasury (until

1825), and Andrew Jackson as president (from 1829), made at least partially successful efforts to reduce federal expenditures, while the ambitious proposals of the more nationalistically-minded John Quincy Adams were frustrated by his political and sectional enemies in Congress. The disintegration of the Republican party removed another source of central authority, and made more apparent the essentially decentralized nature of the American political system. The fragmentation of the Washington community became greater than ever, as politicians found themselves increasingly obliged to bow to local pressures and even less able to provide national leadership. Their reluctance to defy their constituents was all the more natural in a political environment which was becoming increasingly democratic. The populistic currents of the period were also to leave a distinctive mark on the American style of politics.

American electoral methods always had been liberal compared to those of Europe, but it was only after 1815 that the idea of democracy came to rival the idea of liberty as a central element in the American creed. The first generation of Americans had tended to define republicanism as a government of free men; by the 1820s it was being argued that to be free, men had also to be equal, or should at least enjoy equal rights. The strengthening of egalitarian doctrines was partly the result of a greater awareness of the democratic practices which had already been widely established. The extensive franchise, the wide recognition that the majority principle should operate at least for the lower houses of the legislature, the competition by parties and factions for the popular vote, and the growing pride in America's political institutions all combined to encourage Americans to push majoritarian ideas to their logical conclusions. By the 1820s an aggressive egalitarianism was lacing political rhetoric. If the preservation of republican liberty depended on resting ultimate political authority in the people at large, it was being argued, then all people should have an equal voice in the polity – provided they were white, adult, and male. The idea of universal suffrage was now being debated more widely than ever before, and was embodied, for example, in the new constitution adopted by the state of New York in 1826, when the taxpaying qualification was abolished in favour of a measure giving the vote to all adult white male citizens. In thus specifically linking the franchise to persons rather than to property, New Yorkers were enunciating a democratic principle which was not to be formally accepted in Britain for another century. In other ways, too, the rules of the political game underwent subtle modifications in the majoritarian direction in the fifteen years after the War of 1812. Several states revised their constitutions, and the majority principle was recognized in the attempts to make electoral districts more equal in terms of population, while the right of the people to representatives of their own choosing was acknowledged in the measures to reduce or eliminate property and religious qualifications for office-holding.

The electorate was not greatly extended by such constitutional changes, for most men already had the vote, but the debates gave reformers the opportunity to redefine American republicanism and to celebrate the peculiarly American nature of democracy. Man's rights to life, liberty, property, and the pursuit of happiness, argued one egalitarian Virginian, invoking the language of the Declaration of Independence, were sustained by the suffrage, 'the paramount right upon which all these rest for protection, preservation, and safety'.[9] Democracy, after all, was not the enemy of liberty. Conservatives gamely resisted such levelling doctrines, fearing for the social order, but they were fighting a losing battle, in part because the egalitarian doctrines had become intertwined with the rather chauvinistic patriotism of the period. If the fight for the liberties of the citizen could be traced, at least in part, to the English constitutional struggles of the seventeenth century, democracy was an indigenously American creation. Englishmen and others might enjoy certain specific 'freedoms', such as the right to free speech, but no other political system could be called democratic, as Americans proudly pointed out. Only in the United States were men really free, for only there did they determine their affairs in a democratic way. When the conservative Daniel Webster drew some ideas from the English political theorist James Harrington, he was upbraided for not having thrown off Old-World authority: 'A free people will adopt that form of government which please the majority, without regard to what might have pleased nations in other times and in other conditions.'[10] The Americans, it seemed, had now broken with the British past and were set on a unique political path of their own.

The conscious celebration of democracy hastened the demise of the patrician style of politics. The politician who lauded the rights of the common man was helping to erode the deferential attitudes which had survived in much of the electorate. The old conception of the elected representative as a sort of quasi-magistrate, already unmercifully savaged by the democratic doctrines of the revolutionary and Jeffersonian eras, was finally put to rout by the idea that the representative was the servant of the people and owed humble obedience to them. Members of the House of Representatives were rudely reminded of their servile status in 1816, when, having passed a bill to raise their own stipend to $1,500 per year, two-thirds of them were swept away by their indignant masters at the general election. Popular interest in political affairs was further heightened by the unnerving Panic of 1819, which threatened the homes and livelihoods of many ordinary farmers, merchants, and working people throughout the country, though particularly in the West. Sudden and serious contractions in both British markets and British credit produced a collapse in the prices of agricultural products, and when the Bank of the United States sought to save itself by reducing loans and moving funds from its interior branches to the East many rural communities were left almost without a circulating medium. Several state banks failed, penniless debtors were subjected to intense pressure by their hard-pressed creditors, and some state governments were severely shaken by popular demands for 'relief' laws. The depression eventually eased but bitter memories remained, serving to intensify the populistic suspicion of the old political elites (and of the national bank), not least in such states as Kentucky, Tennessee, and Ohio.

If the growing sectional pressures tended to undermine the attempts by the federal government and the Washington politicians to give a central direction to the nation's affairs, the populistic currents tended to undermine the authority of leadership groups at all levels. Both the congressional caucus at Washington and the party caucuses in the various state legislatures seemed increasingly anachronistic in a political system in which the people were meant to choose their own leaders. The loss of political authority suffered by legislative bodies was also seen in the trend towards the popular election of presidents. Formally, of course, presidents were elected by the electoral college, but the members of the electoral college had themselves to be chosen, and by the 1820s the state legislatures were being forced to vest their election in the people at large. Politicians who resisted this trend did so at the risk of losing their own offices.

The reasons for this erosion in the authority of the established politicians are far from clear, although it can be partly explained by the strengthening of the democratic ideology to which they themselves were contributing in their bid for votes. There was a fear, too, that the republic had degenerated since the days of the Founding Fathers. The powerful sway of commercial and acquisitive values, the intermittent hard times, the extraordinary increase in wealth in general and the temptations it offered, the factional squabbles of the politicians and the self-interested demands of particular sections and regions, all contributed to a sense that the republic was not what it had been. Mahlon Dickerson warned his fellow senators in 1819 that the time would come when 'luxury and extravagance' would banish 'republican virtue' from the country.[11] The passing of the heroes of the Revolution strengthened these fears for the republic and focused attention on the second generation of political leaders, who seemed to be men of lesser stature. The respect accorded to the revolutionary worthies and the general acceptance of their leadership, it was sometimes suggested, had muted internal strife, but with their departure, 'personal and local partialities, with a whole train of interests and feelings, are largely and perhaps unreasonably indulged'.[12] Another political commentator put it more bluntly when he spat that 'interest and ambition multiplies candidates for office like maggets [sic] in the hot sun'.[13]

The distrust of politicians seemed to be focused particularly on those in the nation's capital. The popular response to the 'salary grab' bill of 1816 had suggested a certain wariness of self-serving office-holders, and the manoeuvrings for the presidency in 1824, when several prominent men threw their hats in the ring, further confirmed that Washington was the centre of intrigue and corruption. The suspicion that the Washington political establishment was a kind of self-perpetuating oligarchy was not without some foundation. In a sense, every president from Thomas Jefferson to John Quincy Adams owed his position to Congress, in that he had either been nominated by a congressional caucus or had been elected by the House of Representatives. The strident patriotism of the period also served to weaken the authority of the Washington politicians, who were suspected of behaving too much like a European aristocracy. 'The Western people', reported one correspondent, ' . . . have an entire aversion to exchange the plain, dignified, American simplicity of manners for those wanton formalities, generating extravagance, luxury, and idleness, which have been imposed on them and introduced from Europe into the heart of their country at Washington city, corrupting both men and meas-ures.'[14] Any practice which seemed to smack too much of Old-World politics was subjected to merciless criticism.

One practice which seemed to many to be unacceptably elitist was the procedure whereby presidential candidates were chosen by Washington politicians. There had always been doubts about the propriety of the caucus system, and these could only increase as the heroes of the Revolution ceased to be available for the succession. In 1816 only fifty-eight out of 141 Republicans responded to the first call for a caucus meeting and a second had to be held, which most members attended, although some of them, led by Henry Clay, protested at the proceedings. With the disappearance of the Federalist party the Republican caucus was in a position to determine who should be president (as long as its nomination continued to be generally accepted), rendering yet more conspicuous the undemocratic nature of the system. Actually, the collapse of the Federalists as a national party accelerated the disintegration of the Republicans. When several of their leading men entered the presidential race of 1824, the partisans of those candidates not likely to be favoured by the caucus turned their considerable political ingenuity to discrediting it. Jackson's supporters in Tennessee pushed anti-caucus resolutions through the state legislature, pointing out that since congressmen were expressly disqualified by the Constitution from serving as presidential electors, their interference in the election was an unconstitutional usurpation of power. The public reaction to an incautious remark by Nathaniel Macon (who himself disliked the caucus for the electioneering and intrigue associated with it) again revealed the widespread distrust of congressional management. 'The people with us are astonished at Nat. Macon for saying that "Congress always have elected the President and always *will* elect him . . . ",' wrote one North Carolina politician to another, 'If it be so and there is balm in Gilead all good republicans must admit that 'tis time to apply it to this breach in our constitution'.[15]

In the event only sixty-six congressmen attended the caucus meeting of February 1824. They nominated William H. Crawford for president, but it is doubtful whether their blessing did him much good. The controversy continued to rage, and when Crawford, who had been further incapacitated by a paralytic stroke, won fewer popular votes than any other candidate, the reign of King Caucus was at an end. 'The aristocratic league', crowed one editor, ' . . . which sought to usurp the privileges of the people . . . has been dismembered, broken up, and every where put to rout.'[16]

The congressional caucus was not the only aristocratic device that hostile observers perceived in Washington. Presidents and cabinet members were also darkly suspected of manipulating elections. Since the retirement of George Washington the succession had always fallen on a senior member of the government, and since 1808 the palm had invariably gone to the Secretary of State, who had after all been given this appointment by the retiring president. This Secretary was sometimes colloquially referred to as the 'prime minister' or even as the 'heir apparent', terms which invoked Old-World models of government. Monroe's decision to appoint the New Englander John Quincy Adams to the State department and the southerner Crawford to the Treasury muddied the situation somewhat, for Crawford could claim the succession as the natural heir of the Virginia Dynasty and the favoured candidate of the caucus, and critics broadened their attack to embrace the whole cabinet. The partisans of Clay and Jackson, who in 1824 were the only aspirants who were not heads of government departments, were particularly scathing in their denunciations of the claims of the 'merely cabinet men' to the presidency. 'The practice of the government has been calculated to flatter the expectations of Secretaries, thus paving the way for the President to appoint his successor, an usage at war with the genius of our government, founded on free suffrage.'[17] Clay's partisans did not remain hostile to 'the secretary succession' for long, however, for when he became Adams' Secretary of State in 1825 they soon found much to commend in 'the line of safe precedents', as their candidate himself felicitously put it. The Jacksonians redoubled their attacks on the practice. According to one western editor, republicanism itself was at stake in the election of 1828, for every president since Jefferson had appointed his own successor. 'If defeated now, the struggles of the people to break the succession will become more faint hereafter, and we shall have grim monarchy fixed on us, more horrible than those of Europe, because each succession will be secured by widespread corruption.'[18] The election of Andrew Jackson finally broke the pattern.

The pervasive suspicion of self-serving political elites also unsettled established political leaders at state level. One bizarre manifestation of a populist hostility towards privilege was the Antimasonic movement, which first erupted in the rural communities of western New York when the authorities seemed reluctant to act on the case of a turncoat mason who had mysteriously disappeared after promising to expose the secrets of freemasonry. A popular grassroots crusade against the order was propelled by a growing conviction that masons in government were conspiring to obstruct the course of justice and to advance their own selfish interests, and opposition politicians moved swiftly to take up this egalitarian cause. The emergence of a number of Workingmen's parties in the major cities in the late 1820s, pressing for free school systems and better working conditions among other egalitarian demands, was evidence that some urban citizens were also dissatisfied with the existing political leadership. These local outbreaks of popular unrest warned the state politicians that they too had to accommodate to a new style of politics.

The state capitals indeed were suffering from a serious erosion of their political authority. The new constitutions adopted by several states in these years had tended to make the conditions of survival more difficult for the old leadership. The disestablishment of the Congregational Church in Connecticut, for example, and the abolition of the powerful Council of Appointment in New York, a body composed of a group of senior state senators (plus the governor) which controlled the disposal of 15,000 offices, indicated an unwillingness to accept the *dictats* of unrepresentative bodies. Legislative caucuses were also falling into disfavour. Prompted to reflect on the matter by the decision of the congressional caucus of 1820 not to make a nomination, William Plumer of New Hampshire observed that caucuses in general were 'at a low ebb', having discovered 'too much regard for *private*, and too little respect for the *public interest*'.[19] But politicians had to find some way of nominating one another to office, and various methods were experimented with – newspaper nominations, public meetings and, increasingly, state conventions. Many, of course, attempted to keep alive the legislative caucus as a convenient instrument for making nominations to state offices, but found themselves vulnerable to the criticisms of rival factions who made a show of using more democratic methods.

The abandonment of the legislative caucus was a sign of the declining political influence of the state legislature. Legislatures might pass bills, but they were not expected to usurp their functions by trying to control appointments and elections which were properly the concern of the people. Their declining political role was also reflected in the trend towards the popular election of presidential electors, for the method whereby the legislatures chose the electors was becoming increasingly difficult to defend. If one faction sought popularity by promising to vest the election in the people, rival factions were usually obliged to follow suit. In 1824 the lower house of the New York legislature passed by a huge majority a bill providing for the popular election of presidential electors, something that had been promised in the 1823 campaign, but seventeen partisans of Crawford in the Senate defeated the bill, knowing that the only hope for their candidate lay in the legislature. The 'Immortal Seventeen' were quickly obliged to retire from politics by the wave of protest that swept the state, and by the time of the next presidential election the state's political leaders had judiciously decided to give the election to the people. The same trend was apparent in other states. In 1820 nine states used the legislative method of electing presidential electors; in 1824 six still used the system, but by 1828 only Delaware and South Carolina persisted with it. The political power of the legislatures had reached a new low.

The American people had emerged from the War of 1812 with renewed confidence in their ability to sustain their remarkable experiment in republicanism and democracy. In the years following the Peace of Ghent they turned their backs on a decadent Europe in more senses than one. The expansion of population into the American interior accelerated, and helped to identify the nation's destiny with the moving frontier. In 1823 the Monroe administration rejected the opportunity for an Anglo-American diplomatic entente and warned the European powers against interfering in the affairs of the emerging nations of the New World. In 1825 a new American president, John Quincy Adams, brought down on his head a storm of chauvinistic abuse for having dared to imply that foreign nations were making giant strides in the cause of public improvement, while the American government was in danger of being 'palsied by the will of our constituents'.[20] In the same years Americans subjected to a suspicious scrutiny the political institutions and customs that they had inherited from the past, and sought to purge from them any relics of the aristocratic and unrepublican practices of the Old World.

The expansive and defiant patriotism of these years was not a fundamental cause of the refashioning of the American political order, but it helped to give the changes a certain legitimacy. The collapse of the old national parties, and with them the loss of a central political direction, the unmourned death of King Caucus, the reluctance to accept the leadership pretensions of cabinet members, the amendments to the state constitutions and the weakening in the political authority of local caucuses and state legislatures, were the products of a countless variety of complex, interdependent, and subtle processes. An exuberant celebration of democracy and a populistic suspicion of entrenched political elites played a part in breaking down those political practices which could not be readily accommodated to the principle of popular sovereignty, while the centrifugal forces of sectionalism further undermined the unity and authority of the Washington community. The old forms of political organization and decision-making were crumbling, rendering the political environment a highly uncertain one.

The erosion of legislative authority at both national and state levels, the loss of effective direction from Washington and the growing decentralization of American politics, and the destruction of the procedures whereby chief executives emerged from an experienced leadership group at the nation's capital, all served to arrest any tendency for the American political system to evolve in much the same direction as British government. But the course on which the American nation was set was not yet clear. The old political superstructure had been pulled down; a new one remained to be built.

Chapter 11

The politicians respond

The Baltimore editor Hezekiah Niles sardonically reported in 1823 that the word 'politician' had been redefined, for it was now being applied to 'persons who have little if any regard for the welfare of the republic unless as immediately connected with . . . their own private pursuits'.[1] But it is unlikely that the politicians of this period were any less principled or more self-interested than those of any other period. The frequency with which they shifted their positions and revised their views was more the result of the unsettling and unpredictable changes in the political environment than of any exceptional depravity on their part. The disappearance of the old institutions left them momentarily fumbling for guidance on the political stage, like under-rehearsed actors deprived of their cues. Martin Van Buren remarked on one occasion that he really did not mind very much whether his party nominated its presidential candidate by a congressional caucus or a national convention, provided 'that we have either'.[2] Both for the sake of the republic and for their own survival, the professional politicians began to explore ways of restoring some stability to American politics. They needed to find and to fashion new institutions, techniques, and candidates capable of winning the confidence of the people, withstanding the strains of sectionalism, and giving the politicians a degree of control over their environment. In the process they helped to create a political culture which was undeniably American.

The politicians' search for order proceeded along three main fronts. First, there were the attempts to accommodate the political system to the new pressures being exerted upon it by constitutional revision. The federal and state constitutions laid down the fundamental rules of American politics. If some of those rules could be changed, it was thought, a more stable and tranquil political environment might be secured. Second, some politicians favoured a form of social engineering, arguing that under government direction the economy could be developed in such a way as to secure the better integration of American society and greater harmony in American politics. And there was a third solution too. Increasingly politicians sought to come to terms with the egalitarian doctrines and populistic currents, with the sectional jealousies and xenophobic patriotism of the period by the promotion of candidates who would appeal to or placate these emotions, and by the creation of new forms of organization which would bring a degree of coherence to American politics. These three approaches, the constitutional, the economic, and the political, were not necessarily mutually exclusive and they did not follow one another in any coherent chronological order. In a sense, they parallelled the earlier search for stability of the 1780s and 1790s, when the first generation of political leaders had sought to combat the anarchic tendencies of the Confederation period with a similar range of responses.

With the disintegration of the old national parties and the repudiation of the political devices that they had employed, it was natural for Americans to look once more at the constitutions they had inherited. The first party system had developed in part because the Constitution of 1787 had not by itself done enough to create a stable and workable political structure; with its demise the weaknesses in the Constitution were exposed once more. And there were other reasons too for a reappraisal of the state and federal constitutions. With only occasional exceptions, the constitutions were still what they had been in the late eighteenth century. For nearly half a century the country had been growing rapidly, new interest groups had been created, and more egalitarian ideas had emerged. After the return of peace in 1815 many Americans felt that it was time to revise their instruments of government to take account of those new conditions, and the movement for constitutional reform gained strength. Several states called constitutional conventions and Congress debated at length the wisdom of recommending further amendments to the federal Con-stitution. The responsibility assumed by the would-be constitution-makers was an awesome one. Aware that they were treading in the sacred footsteps of the Founding Fathers, they explored the sources and ends of government and the nature of the republic with all the self-consciousness of their predecessors. To some their activities bordered on sacrilege. The tall and emaciated figure of John Randolph of Roanoke, for example, shrilly warned the members of the Virginia convention that they were 'undoing what the wiser heads of our ancestors did more than half a century ago'.[3]

The revisions of the state constitutions have been alluded to earlier as a symptom of the democratic pressures of the period. They also provided the politicians with an opportunity to accommodate them-selves to the new political currents. Many protected themselves by making some concessions to the notion that the people should rule, but they were often reluctant to endorse far-reaching changes. In New York, for example, Martin Van Buren and the Bucktails, as his faction were known, took up the cause of reform in their war against their rivals, the Clintonians. At the convention they supported the abolition of the Council of Appointments, with its enormous powers of patronage, but fought shy of the popular election of magistrates, who comprised a part of the patronage network that they were loathe to abandon. Similarly, the Bucktails helped to extend the franchise substantially, those eligible to vote for governor and senator rising from about thirty-four to eighty-three per cent of the adult white male population, but they resisted universal suffrage and even conspired to take the vote away from many black men. The Bucktails won a temporary popularity as the champions of responsible reform, but in 1826 they were obliged to join the Clintonians in amending the constitution again to provide for white universal suffrage and the popular election of magistrates.

Politicians in other states also tried to find a middle way between the surrender to popular sovereignty and the retention of their own power and privileges. The reformers had some success in Connecticut in 1818, providing for the annual election of the governor and overthrowing the established Congregational church, thus administering the *coup de grace* to the state's Federalist party. In Massachusetts the debate of 1820-21 turned largely on the issue of the separation of church and state and the anomalies in the representation in the legislature, but the conservatives frustrated all but the mildest changes. Five western states were also admitted to the Union in these years, with constitutions at least as democratic as those of the more liberal eastern states. In the conventions reformers demonstrated their commitment to American republicanism by assailing those aspects of the constitutions which seemed to survive from the un-American past. Erastus Root reminded the New York delegates that the framers of their constitution 'had received their education under the system of British government' and complained that 'indubitable traces of the British constitution (are found) throughout the whole of our own'.[4] He cited in particular the veto power of the executive. Suspicions of an energetic executive branch died hard. In Illinois, too, supporters of the secret ballot denounced the practice of open voting as a survival of British tyranny, for it exposed voters to pressure from candidates. So the politicians, or at least many of them, safeguarded their own survival by affirming their belief in the political capacity of the people.

Perhaps the most important political consequence of the cautious surrenders to the principle of popular sovereignty was the increased number of elections allowed for in the new constitutions, since more officials had been made elective and the lengths of political terms had often been made shorter. The resulting frequency of elections worried European visitors, who felt that representatives became too dependent on the whims of their constituents and that the people were kept in a state of perpetual excitement. Constant elections also made for frequent changes in government policy. 'In short', concluded one observer, 'it is an inherent and monstrous evil, that American statesmen must legislate for the *present*, not for the *future*. . . . Immediate and temporary expediency is, and must be, the moving and efficient impulse of American legislation.'[5]

As such comments implied, the new and amended constitutions of the 1810s and 1820s did not succeed in bringing much stability to

American politics. As conservatives had warned, there was no natural limit to the reform process once it had begun, and the greater political power entrusted to the people made it more difficult to resist later public pressure for constitutional revision. Thus while the state constitutions of the 1770s and 1780s had for the most part survived forty or fifty years without significant amendment, those adopted after the War of 1812 were soon being tampered with. The New York constitution of 1821 was amended in 1826 and a new one was adopted in 1846, and many other states also revised or replaced their constitutions in these years. The temporary nature of the new constitutions would not perhaps have been apparent in the 1820s, but their lack of uniformity was. Where Connecticut broke the connection between church and state, Massachusetts upheld it. Where New York abandoned the freehold qualification for voting, Virginia retained it. The debates in the conventions drew attention to the idiosyncrasies of each state, and the constitutional revisions did little to remove them. The new constitutions on the whole enlarged the role of the electorate and obliged politicians to accommodate themselves to democratic demands, but they brought neither permanency nor uniformity to the American political scene.

If a stable environment could not be secured by constitutional amendment at state level, perhaps the federal constitution might be revised to that end. Presidential elections in particular tended to expose the ills to which the American body politic was subject, and in themselves seemed to place the republic in jeopardy. 'To choose a chief magistrate for ten millions of people, jealous of their rights, and impatient of control, even in the best regulated system, must be attended with with no small degree of danger:' observed Senator Mahlon Dickerson of New Jersey in 1819, and 'this danger increases with the increasing extent of our territory, and the increase of our population.'[6] If that part of the Constitution relating to the election of the president could be amended, thought Dickerson and others, the American political system might be so restructured as to enable it to survive the threats of sectionalism, corruption, and party strife.

Between the War of 1812 and the election of Andrew Jackson literally dozens of proposed constitutional amendments were put to Congress, particularly by those who were disturbed by the variety of methods used in the different states to appoint presidential electors. The lack of uniformity in the mode of electing the president had been the subject of complaint for many years, the more so since states often changed from one system to another. The most flagrant offender in this respect was Massachusetts, which did not use the same method in two successive elections until 1828. The dominant factions in state legislatures regularly rewrote the election laws in order to procure a system best suited to their own interests, thus increasing the disfavour with which the public regarded self-appointed caucuses and political factions. The only way to secure uniformity seemed to be by constitutional amendment, and the pressure for reform increased in the 1820s with the demise of the caucus, the multiplication of presidential candidates, and the growing strains of sectionalism. Most states used either the legislative or the general ticket system to appoint electors, but the former was patently undemocratic, since it gave the people little voice in the election of their own chief magistrates and placed power in the hands of legislative caucuses, while the latter was said to promote the emergence of parties or factions which put their own interests before those of the nation. The need to organize a slate of electors on a statewide basis, for example, was thought to put power into the hands of political managers and to encourage manipulation and corruption. Both methods were blamed for their divisive effects, and most reformers called for the uniform adoption of the district system throughout the Union. 'The States, when voting for President by general tickets or by their Legislatures, are a string of beads;' argued James Madison, 'when they make their elections by districts, some of these differing in sentiment from others, and sympathizing with that of districts in other States, they are so knit together as to break the force of those geographical and other noxious parties which might render the repulsive too strong for the cohesive tendencies within the political system.'[7]

By 'other noxious parties' Madison may have been referring to the partisan political groupings that many felt had no place in a true republic. Certainly it was hoped that a district system would do away with the need for political managers, parties, and caucuses. The districts would be small enough for a large proportion of the constituents to know their electors personally and numerous enough to frustrate the designs of would-be managers at the state capitals. By the uniform adoption of the district system, it was argued, the interests of democracy would be advanced, the centrifugal forces of sectionalism would be countered, the intrigues and manipulations of self-appointed caucuses would be confounded, and republican virtue would be restored to the American body politic. 'It is thus only that the rights of the majority can be properly secured:' argued one editor, 'it is thus only that our elective franchise can ever be safe from the machinations of intrigue, and the influence of designing, unprincipled demagogues.'[8]

The debate on amending the Constitution reached its peak in 1826, having been further inflamed by the events of 1824-25, when the election had been thrown into the House of Representatives which had proceeded to give the prize to John Quincy Adams, despite the fact that Andrew Jackson had won more popular votes. Perhaps the partisan turn that the debate took prevented a resolution. At any rate, Congress was unable to agree on any of the several proposals before it, and ultimately decided to recommend none to the states. In any case, proposals to amend the Constitution which emanated from Congress or the state legislatures, according to one advocate of reform, were 'viewed with much circumspection and jealousy by the people'.[9] By the summer of 1826 the attempt to re-order American politics by constitutional amendment was effectively at an end.

The failure to secure a closer political union by revamping the Constitution meant that the specific problem of how to select presidential electors was returned to the separate states and their politicians, who for the most part adopted the same strategy that they had employed in the state constitutional conventions – that of finding a middle way between the demands of popular sovereignty and the exigencies of political expediency. Election by state legislature was no longer considered acceptable. The district system was widely admitted to conform to democratic ideology most successfully, but since its use almost always divided a state's electoral votes between the various candidates, and thus reduced that state's impact in the election, most states refused to adopt it unless all other states did so also. So the general ticket system prevailed. By 1828 only two states retained the legislative mode of election and only four states retained the district system, and by 1836 only South Carolina had refused to adopt the general ticket system. As it happened, the triumph of the general ticket did meet one of the demands of the reformers, a uniform and permanent system throughout the Union. But it also carried other implications for American politics. It put a premium on political techniques capable of organizing politics on a statewide level, and thus probably strengthened the positions of party machines. In presidential elections, the general ticket system created the need for a strategy which would carry as many *states* as possible, and this was to have a profound effect on the evolution of American politics. And in emphasizing the primacy of the state it rendered even more difficult the restoration of cohesion in national politics.

Constitutional revision was one possible route to a more stable political order. Economic reform was another. The nationalists of the 1780s and 1790s had worked for a more perfect union by a combination of constitutional and economic reform, and so too in the years after 1815 a new generation of nationalists turned to economic and financial measures as a means of providing a stronger and healthier political union. There were major differences between the new economic nationalism and the old, but both were in some degree sustained by a corporatist view of the Union. 'The great object of the institution of civil government', wrote John Quincy Adams, 'is the improvement of the condition of those who are parties to the social compact . . . '.[10] It was the function of government to identify the common good and actively to promote it, using its powers to encourage economic, scientific, and educational enterprises, and to reconcile conflicting interests. Like the Federalists before them, the new nationalists believed that political and social benefits for the whole people would flow from the better integration of the economy and its component parts, and they looked to government for some sort of coherent guidance. Mercantilist economic ideas fitted naturally with the concept of society as an organism and with the idea of the Union as a corporation.

The leading exponent of economic nationalism was now Henry Clay, who unveiled his revealingly-named 'American System' in a series of eloquent speeches. Clay saw the need for a *system*, for a methodical interweaving of the different elements in the American economy, as he also saw the political need to distinguish it from Hamiltonianism, with its despised English connotations. Less dependent on the British connection, Clay's programme looked to the interests of the farmer as well as the merchant and the industrialist and aimed at a high degree of economic self-sufficiency. One proposal was for a protective tariff, which would encourage manufacturing industry and the growth of cities in the Northeast, thus making the country less dependent on foreign suppliers and giving American farmers a domestic market. The American farming community would sell to the industrial community and *vice versa*. To facilitate this, better roads and canals would be needed, and Clay advocated the vigorous use of federal funds for a programme of internal improvements. Better transportation would enlarge the markets of farmers and manufacturers alike and would promote the interdependence of the different sections. Without such measures looking to 'great national objects', Clay warned, 'the Union . . . of these now happy and promising States, may, at some distant (I trust a far, far, distant) day, be endangered and shaken at its centre.'[11] Finally, Clay believed that the whole system needed to be underpinned by a national bank, which would provide the sound currency so urgently needed by an expansive commercial economy. The American System, then, was designed to make the United States economically independent of Europe, to encourage economic growth, and to bind American farmers, planters, merchants, and industrialists together in a fruitful unity of interests.

The full articulation of Clay's economic philosophy did not come until the 1820s, by which time some of the measures he was calling for had already been introduced in a piecemeal and incomplete fashion. The Republican administrations, in accommodating themselves to commercial interests, had begun to see some virtue in Hamilton's national bank even before the War of 1812, though Congress frustrated the attempt by the Secretary of the Treasury to have the charter renewed when it expired in 1811. But the war then demonstrated the difficulty of managing the nation's finances without such an institution, and in April 1816 that fierce foe of Hamilton's bank bill of 1791, James Madison, signed into law a bill creating the second Bank of the United States. In the same year a modest tariff was enacted, in order to protect the manufacturing interests which had grown up in the years of embargo and war from British dumping. The War of 1812 had also revealed the inadequacy of the nation's road and canal network, and John C. Calhoun was among those to take up the cause of internal improvements. 'Let it not be forgotten, let it be forever kept in mind, that the extent of the republic exposes us to the greatest of calamities – *disunion* . . . ', warned Calhoun in his most nationalistic phase in 1817. 'Whatever impedes the intercourse of the extremes with this, the centre of the republic, weakens the union. . . . Let us, then, bind the republic together with a perfect system of roads and canals. Let us conquer space.'[12]

But Calhoun's bid to establish a permanent fund for internal improvements was frustrated by Madison, who on his last day in office reminded Congress of his Jeffersonian principles by vetoing the so-called 'bonus bill'. But Madison would probably have been happy with the scheme if a constitutional amendment had sanctioned it, and Monroe too spoke of the desirability of 'one system' to 'promote the welfare of the whole',[13] although he also felt constrained to veto an internal improvements bill in case it upset the balance of the Constitution and led to tyranny. The proponents of the American System must have been vastly irritated by this early example of 'Catch 22': a federally-sponsored transportation system was needed to knit the union together and promote a healthy national spirit, but it could only be legitimized by a constitutional amendment and such an amendment would only be secured if there were a stronger national spirit. In fact the federal government did aid several internal improvement schemes in a piecemeal way, and state governments too embarked on schemes of their own, the most ambitious being New York's great Erie Canal, cut from the Hudson River to Lake Erie and hence linking New York City with the interior.

Like Hamilton a generation earlier, the champions of protective tariffs and internal improvements hoped for more than economic advantages. A well-balanced and prosperous economy, they suggested, would overcome the hideous danger of sectional conflict by making the sections interdependent and by encouraging a national feeling, and would make possible educational, scientific, and artistic progress. The principal advocate of the Erie Canal, De Witt Clinton, predicted that to avert the negation of the republican experiment 'all local prejudices and geographical distinctions should be discarded, the people should be habituated to frequent intercourse and beneficial intercommunication, and the whole republic ought to be bound together by the golden ties of commerce and the adamantine chains of interest'.[14] To John Quincy Adams such measures were needed to advance civilization itself, for 'moral, political, intellectual improvement are duties assigned . . . to social no less than to individual man', and it was the task of government to bring about 'the progressive improvement of the condition of the governed'.[15]

The American System, then, was designed to promote a healthier society and a more united political order. In this it was similar to Hamiltonianism, with which it shared a holistic view of the American polity, though it cannot be seen as a crude recrudescence of Hamilton's programme. While economic nationalism implied an expansion in the functions of the federal government, there was no special intent to increase executive power as such, and such measures as were adopted were more the work of Congress than of the president. Nor was there any obvious attempt to recruit the rich and well-born to the support of national institutions. 'The National Bank ought not to be regarded simply as a commercial bank', argued Secretary of the Treasury Alexander J. Dallas. 'It will not operate upon the funds of the stockholders alone, but much more upon the funds of the nation.'[16] Similarly, the American System did not imply a reliance on British markets or British investment, and indeed, a principal object was to divorce the United States from foreign economic partners. Henry Clay made a much greater issue of the home market than Alexander Hamilton had done and stressed the benefits to the American farmer. If the American System was a revised version of Hamilton's programme, it was Hamiltonianism divested of its unrepublican implications.

But while Henry Clay and his colleagues succeeded in producing a positive economic system which was compatible with American republicanism, at least in the eyes of many Republicans, they did not succeed in having it adopted. Henry Clay identified himself strongly with this programme during his race for the presidency in 1824, and the humiliating 13 per cent of the popular vote that he won could be seen as representing a repudiation of the American System. John Quincy Adams as president did encourage federal expenditure on internal improvements, but the Jacksonian opposition in Congress frustrated any attempt at a systematic development, as did Jackson himself when he reached the White House. A moderate protective tariff was adopted in 1824, but the so-called 'tariff of abominations' of 1828 made a nonsense of economic planning. Cobbled together by Jacksonians in Congress for electoral purposes, its duties were designed to attract certain interest groups in New York, Pennsylvania, and the western states and they generally worked to the disadvantage of New England manufacturers and southern planters. This did nothing to foster economic integration, and, indeed, it served greatly to increase those sectional tensions that the American System was meant to overcome.

By the late 1820s, then, the attempt to secure political stability through the orderly development and management of the nation's economic resources was effectively at an end. Federal aid to internal improvements was only to be allowed in a piecemeal way and the protection that the tariff offered was decidedly perverse. The national bank itself survived for a time, but the Panic of 1819 had made it unpopular in large parts of the country and the Jacksonians were soon making ominous noises about it. Politicians were increasingly surrendering to local pressures, prejudices, and interests, allowing a transport scheme here and a tariff duty there with an eye to harvesting more votes. The forces of particularism and populism were already too strong to permit the economic nationalists to unite and to elevate the American people by systematic government action.

What was needed after all was a political response to the forces which were pulling apart the old structure, which is to say a recognition that a new political world was coming into being. If the politicians could not restore order by imposing constitutional and economic remedies on a refractory people, they would have to surrender to popular demands where possible, or at least to construct a system of politics which took cognizance of the democratic and pluralistic nature of the American social order. In a polity increasingly characterized by incessant elections, political leaders would have to devote even more attention to courting the people, to promoting candidates capable of attracting votes, and to fashioning new kinds of organization designed to accommodate both popular and sectional pressures.

There was nothing very novel in the practice of campaigning for votes, but now political managers were raising it to the level of a popular art. In 'every quarter' of the country, complained a British visitor, 'the spirit of electioneering . . . seems to enter as an essential ingredient into the composition of every thing'.[17] The frenetic wooing of the voters often imparted a carnival atmosphere to campaigns. Exuberant electioneering methods had long been practised in the Southwest, and were soon spreading to other areas. In Kentucky, for example, political barbecues or 'bergoos' were held, day-long festive picnics attended by men, women, and children and punctuated by music, dancing, and stump speeches, often delivered quite literally from the stump of a recently-felled tree. In much of the North more formal dinners were common, at which political aspirants were toasted in ringing and flattering phrases. One campaign dinner in New York City in 1828 created a local record by consuming 400 bottles of champagne. Fourth of July celebrations, militia exercises, and even grand jury meetings were sometimes turned into political rallies, as their participants passed resolutions supporting their favourite candidates. The national contest between Jackson and Adams in 1828 demonstrated that such techniques were now being employed in presidential as well as local campaigns. Jackson's partisans in particular whipped up popular excitement by the use of rallies, barbecues, and parades, often enlivened with songs and cannon fire, and erected hickory poles in towns and villages across the country as a symbol of their hero, who had once been known to his soldiers as 'Old Hickory'.

Few such demonstrations were spontaneous, for they were normally staged by the professional politicians, though the enthusiasm generated at them was no doubt often genuine. Politicians also used the written word to rally support behind their candidates. By the 1820s virtually every important faction maintained its own newspaper, which became a major weapon in public political warfare. The newspaper was used to communicate with groups in other states, to send signals to the party faithful, and to lacerate the opposition. 'Without a paper thus edited at Albany', wrote Martin Van Buren to a fellow Bucktail, 'we may hang our harps on the willows.'[18] During election campaigns voters were bombarded with handbills, pamphlets, printed speeches, and addresses, and even songsheets. The impact of popular voting on presidential elections was seen as early as 1824, when there appeared the first campaign biographies of the candidates, who even then were concerned about their 'images'. William H. Crawford's biographer testified to the robust constitution of his sick hero, Jackson's stressed the general's heroic revolutionary services as a doughty teenager, while Calhoun apparently wrote his own political eulogy.

Haphazardly and largely unconsciously, political leaders were thus beginning to fashion a new political culture. Faced with a large electorate with little patience for aristocratic pretensions, the professional politicians gradually developed a wide array of popular techniques for the marshalling of political support. But even more important than the parades and the gimmicks were the candidates themselves. Men were needed who could attract votes. In Tennessee in the 1820s the flamboyant Davy Crockett clowned his way first to the state legislature and then to Congress, where more conservative politicians were soon hiding behind his homespun appeal. A popular image was not necessarily an uncouth image, however, for among the serious-minded citizens of Massachusetts the young professor Edward Everett found that his polished rhetoric and clerical past were invaluable political attributes. But it was easier for political managers to answer the needs of a democratic electorate at the local level than at the national level. How were they to find a candidate whose popular appeal stretched considerably beyond his own state and sectional boundaries? Yet such a figure was needed in the 1820s to counter the localistic and centrifugal pressures which plagued American politics.

Textbook writers have traditionally invoked Andrew Jackson as the symbol of the new political style which was emerging in the 1820s, although more specialized studies have occasionally cautioned against this, pointing to the wealthy Jackson's lack of sympathy for debtors and strikers and to the conservative temperaments and self-interested motives of many of the men around him. But the Jacksonian movement was a complex phenomenon, in which conservatism and liberalism, nationalism and strict constructionism, altruism and personal ambition jostled uneasily together, and which, in any case, changed in nature as time went on. However thin Jackson's sympathies for the common people had been during his early forays into the rumbustious politics of Tennessee, there is little doubt that he was the chief beneficiary of the populistic political currents of the 1820s and that the movement which took his name helped to reshape the American political landscape.

By traditional standards, Jackson was an unlikely candidate for president. He was, of course, a nationally-acclaimed hero by virtue of his dramatic victory over the British at New Orleans in 1815. But he was no statesman. He had served only briefly and rather unhappily in the Senate of the 1790s, whose presiding officer, Thomas Jefferson, later confided to Daniel Webster that Jackson could never make an effective speech there because of his tendency to 'choke with rage'.[19] Jackson never held high civil office in any national administration, and, as his enemies were quick to point out, he had usually soon resigned the few state offices he had occupied, though whether through a virtuous lack of ambition or through incapacity and boredom was a moot point. He was the author of no thoughtful papers on political philosophy, he had given his name to no major pieces of legislation, he was associated with no great principles of public policy. Unlike earlier presidents, too, Jackson was not a highly educated man, he came from the parvenu frontier state of Tennessee, and his family and political connections were unimpressive. 'I know what I am fit for. I can command a body of men in a rough way, but I am not fit to be President', commented Jackson in 1821, an opinion which was probably shared by most of the professional politicians in Washington.[20] He had been occasionally spoken of for president before that date, but, as the *Richmond Enquirer* said, 'we never supposed by any one, seriously'.[21]

But the very attributes which seemed to disqualify Jackson for the presidency formed the basis of his appeal to many people. He was not a cabinet member who had misused his public position to forward his own interest. He was not a spokesman for the narrow parochial interest of any single section. And he was an authentic American hero, self-made and self-taught, who had proved his patriotism by routing the British at New Orleans, and whose simple republicanism had never been tainted by a stay at any European court. The Jackson boom had first been launched in Tennessee by a group of men with local objectives of their own who did not really expect to elect him president. 'There are too many great men in other States to suffer a man from the young and small State of Tennessee at the present day to be made President of the United States', wrote an early supporter to a friend in Virginia.[22] But the great men were no longer fully in control. For one thing, the popular resentments generated in several western and southern states by the Panic of 1819 had served to weaken their authority. To the discomfort of several of his original backers and to the surprise of professional politicians throughout the Union, a surge of popular support for Jackson swept through Alabama, Mississippi, North Carolina, and Pennsylvania. Shrewd local newspaper editors and politicians looking for a cause no doubt scrambled aboard the bandwagon for less than selfless reasons, but that there was a genuine grassroots movement for Jackson seems beyond dispute. In February 1824 George M. Dallas, a Calhoun leader in Pennsylvania, was forced to lead the Keystone State into the camp of Andrew Jackson, who was enthusiastically endorsed at a convention at Harrisburg in the following month. 'The truth is that the movement in Pennsylvania was made by the people altogether and not by the politicians', wrote William Plumer Jr. to his father. 'The truth is', echoed Daniel Webster, 'he is the people's candidate in a great part of the southern and western country.'[23]

The remarkable accomplishment of the Jackson campaign of 1824 was to popularize presidential politics at local level. Established leaders like Clay and Calhoun were now finding themselves rebuffed by communities they had expected loyally to follow them. In a very real sense Jackson was the candidate of the people, or at least of some of them, not because of his views on government policy or his democratic convictions, but because he was the Hero of New Orleans and because he was a political outsider. His partisans were not slow to capitalize on his attractions, arguing that he should be supported because 'in contra-distinction to all the other candidates he is unconnected with party politics, local feelings or sectional jealousies, and of course the only one among them who can go into the Presidential chair, unpledged to any thing but the interests of his country.'[24] The astonishing excitement that his candidature aroused gave Jackson 153,544 popular votes in the general election, over forty per cent more than the runner-up, John Quincy Adams.

But presidential elections are not determined by the popular vote. The electoral vote was divided between four candidates, and although Jackson headed the list he had not obtained the necessary overall majority. The events of the winter of 1824-25 confirmed in the minds of many, if confirmation were needed, that the real enemies of the republic were the professional politicians in Washington. The Constitution required that an indecisive election be resolved by the House of Representatives, which now had to choose between Jackson, Adams, and the semi-paralysed Crawford. The key figure in the situation was Henry Clay, who had carried only three western states and had been knocked out of the race, but who still wielded an unrivalled influence in the House of Representatives. Cautiously the friends of the various candidates put out feelers to one another. On the 9 January Clay and Adams spent the evening in private conversation. A month later the fateful vote took place, and Adams won on the first ballot with the aid of Clay and his western allies. Once again, it seemed, Congress had defied the will of the people.

Two days after his election Adams offered the State Department to Clay, who, in accepting, sealed the fate of the administration. It was useless and, indeed, rather disingenuous for Clay and Adams to deny that there had been a 'corrupt bargain', for although they probably had not made any explicit deal, they were experienced public men who had worked together for years and their signals to one another had been unmistakable. At any rate, at a time when the country had been hearing endlessly about the machinations of the congressional caucus, the manoeuvrings of cabinet Secretaries, and the undemocratic intrigues of Washington politicians, to appear to conclude a bargain which frustrated the popular will was to play right into the hands of their opponents. The Washington political establishment, it could be said, had closed ranks to exclude the uncouth outsider from Tennessee. This impression was heightened when Adams asked all the remaining members of Monroe's cabinet to retain their posts. After having been repudiated at the polls, the old guard had survived by means which seemed to come naturally to them – by bargain and corruption. As one old friend observed to Jackson, 'the rascals at Washington cheated you out of it'.[25]

If Jackson had been popular before the election, he was perhaps twice as popular after it. Politicians and newspaper men throughout the country hastened to hitch their wagons to his ascending star, bringing to the Jacksonian movement a considerable degree of professional expertise. The campaign of 1828 began as soon as John Quincy Adams was installed as president. Western congressmen who had voted in the House for Adams despite instructions from their states to vote for Jackson found themselves turned out of office in the mid-term elections. Although party lines were never clear, unstable anti-administration majorities emerged in both houses of Congress. Prominent political leaders whose fortunes were not tied to the Adams administration found it expedient to associate themselves with the Jacksonians. John C. Calhoun, now vice-president, indulged the administration's critics in the Senate over which he presided, much to the fury of the president. Martin Van Buren brought New York's powerful Albany Regency over to the Jackson cause, together with his old allies in Virginia, the Richmond Junto. By 1827 a new set of political alignments had emerged, with Adams, Clay, and Webster speaking for the administration, and Jackson, Van Buren, Calhoun, and Benton leading the opposition.

The peculiar political circumstances surrounding and following the election of 1824-25 thus reduced the election of 1828 to a two-man contest. Andrew Jackson 'who could fight' was pitted against John Quincy Adams 'who could write'.[26] Historians have sometimes complained that there was little discussion of issues in the campaign, but this is to misunderstand the nature of politics in that leader-oriented period. That there was relatively little discussion of *policies* was not in itself particularly unusual. Party platforms did not become an established feature of American politics until the 1840s, before which candidates formally stood on the basis of their characters and reputation as public men. But there was certainly discussion of *issues* in 1828, the dominant one being the corrupt bargain charge. As an emotive symbol, the charge was capable of invoking many of the populistic fears and allegations of the 1820s – the hostility towards the Washington establishment, the suspicion that the popular will was being frustrated by scheming politicians, the distaste for 'the line of safe precedents' (since the assumption of the State Department by Clay seemed to make him heir-apparent), and the unease over the aristocratic and unrepublican pretensions of the office-holding elite. The corrupt bargain charge was used unscrupulously, but to many the machinations of Adams and Clay represented a serious threat to the liberties of the people. 'A power founded in such gross usurpation, and I add confidently, corruption, cannot stand', George McDuffie had written in a private letter soon after Adams's election. 'I shall support the measures of Mr. Adams's administration, if they are judicious; but if he acts with the wisdom of Solomon, I shall feel solemnly bound to oppose his re-election. An example must be made of the offenders: a solemn offering to purify the Constitution from this pollution.'[27]

The Jackson movement was also in part the work of professional politicians who had seen the advantage of allying themselves to this remarkable figure. As in the constitutional conventions, they were moving to accommodate themselves to the popular currents of the period. The most important political manager to join Jackson was Martin Van Buren, who had perceived in the Hero an opportunity not merely to advance his own fortune but also to refashion the political environment. Worried by the disintegration of the old political order, Van Buren argued in 1827 that 'we can only get rid of the present, and restore a better state of things, by combining Genl. Jackson's personal popularity with the portion of old party feeling yet remaining.' Ideally, Van Buren wanted to revive the party structure of the early republic, or something like it. The answer to the Union's ills, he believed, was national political parties. 'If the old ones are suppressed, Geographical divisions founded on local interests or, what is worse prejudices between free and slave-holding states will inevitably take their place.' If national party attachments could be restored, they would function as a 'counteracting' force to sectional feelings. Van Buren proposed to achieve this goal by harnessing Jackson's popularity to the cause and by revising the political machinery so that it was 'fresher and perhaps more in unison with the spirit of the times. . . .'.[28]

What Van Buren was talking about was the need for efficient party organization, particularly in the form of political institutions which would meet the test of democracy. State politicians had been grappling with this problem for some years, for the popular distrust of legislative caucuses had forced them to look for other ways of nominating candidates and resolving disputes. The triumph of the general ticket system, which obliged political groups to draw up statewide slates of candidates, accentuated the need for a centralized nominating process which nonetheless commanded the confidence of the party's rank-and-file. The answer was the nominating convention, composed of party members elected from lower bodies. The convention system proved to be a highly efficient organizational device which had the incomparable merit of being democratic in form. Nominating conventions increasingly came to replace state legislative caucuses in the mid-1820s, and as Van Buren addressed himself to the task of electing Andrew Jackson, he began to wonder whether a national convention could replace the congressional caucus.

As it happened, national conventions were not to become established until a slightly later period, and in 1828 Van Buren and his fellow politicians had to fashion a national movement without their aid. Jacksonians throughout the country busied themselves with the creation of machinery for the purpose of fighting the election. Central committees were formed in Nashville (Jackson's home town) and in Washington to coordinate the campaign. Local, county, and state committees sprang up to carry on the battle in their own areas. A nationwide chain of newspapers was established, with the encouragement and sometimes financial support of Jacksonians in Washington. In the capital itself, the Missouri newspaper man Duff Green was brought in to edit the *United States Telegraph*, which became the Jacksonians' central organ, insofar as they had one. In some ways, the decentralized nature of the political machinery of the Jacksonians was an advantage, for the local committees and newspapers were able to present the Hero in the guise that best suited their particular audience. In Pennsylvania Jackson favoured a high tariff and in Virginia a low one, a strategy which helped him carry both states with large majorities in the election. The partisans of John Quincy Adams did their best to imitate the organizational techniques of the Jacksonians, but generally with less success. The political philosophy of the Adams-Clay group was clearer than that of their opponents, for Clay was the champion of the American System, with which Adams was also thought to sympathize. But in 1828 the political principles of the administration proved a poor match for the superior organization of the Jacksonians and the popular appeal of Old Hickory.

By about 1830 the politicians were beginning to acquire a degree of control over the new political environment. They had made cautious concessions to demands for constitutional reform at state level, bowing to the principle of popular sovereignty where necessary while resisting radical change. Some politicians had also vainly tried to construct a more resilient and cohesive system of federal politics through constitutional amendment, and some had sought the same goal by means of economic integration. Their failure confirmed the strength of particularism, the political primacy of the states and the political weakness of Washington. In the states, obliged to abandon the legislative caucus as a political instrument, the politicians had steered an adroit course between the Scylla of popular sovereignty and the Charybdis of central dictation. Both the convention system for nominating candidates and the general ticket system for electing

presidential electors represented attempts to make political procedures meet the test of democracy while retaining a managerial role for
the politician. The politicians further affirmed their faith in the people
by wooing them with stump speeches, liquor-laced barbecues, partisan
newspapers, and scurrilous broadsheets, and by the promotion of
attractive candidates capable of mobilizing a mass electorate. Pushed
out of the legislatures by the growth of egalitarian democracy and the
populistic suspicion of political elites, the political managers used
popular elections, state conventions, party newspapers, and campaign
hullabaloo to fashion a new political culture which both enchanted and
horrified European visitors.

In the course of the 1820s, too, the chaos and confusion which had
characterized national politics gradually gave way to a degree of order.
The disappearance of the old national parties, the collapse of the
congressional caucus, and the diminishing political authority of
Washington politicians had exposed the American political system to
the disruptive pressures of sectionalism and particularism. An
unsuspecting saviour had appeared in the figure of Andrew Jackson.
As a military hero who had humiliated the British, as an outsider who
had been wickedly rejected by the Washington political establishment
in the House election of 1825, and as a self-made and self-taught son of
the American backwoods, Jackson seemed the perfect embodiment of
the populistic currents of the period. Unlike most of his rivals, Jackson
was able to attract popular support in most parts of the Union, and this
made him an invaluable political commodity. Experienced politicians
like Martin Van Buren and John C. Calhoun moved to create a new
political movement around him, one that would unite 'the planters of
the South and the plain Republicans of the North', a combination
which Van Buren thought 'the most natural and beneficial to the
country.'[29]

When Jackson entered the White House the organization of the new
party was far from complete. But its foundations were being laid by the
professional politicians, and their attempt to harness the popularity of
Jackson to their organizational cause pointed the way to the future. At
the national level, the new political superstructure which was being
erected focused primarily on the office of the president. The popular
distrust of Washington politicians and the jealousies generated by
sectionalism had rendered Congress a poor agency for the provision of
political leadership, but the advent of the popular presidential election
shifted the initiative away from the legislature and towards the
executive. Unlike most of his predecessors, Jackson did not owe his
elevation to Congress. Rather, his power base was in the electorate and
he was able to draw his authority directly from the people. He saw
himself as a popular tribune whose duty it was to protect the people's
republic from designing aristocrats and corrupt Washington legislators. This new distribution of power restored to the federal
government a measure of unity and energy.

The uncertain trend towards a form of parliamentary government was thus at an end. So too was the patrician style of politics. No longer was the Chief Magistracy a reward for a distinguished career in government service. Now that the primary qualification was the ability to win votes rather than execute policy, political leaders would be recruited from a wide sector of public life. The first office of the nation had finally become the gift of the sovereign people. It remained to construct national political parties directed towards the winning of democracy's most glittering prize.

Part 5

The triumph of party (1825-1850)

In the second quarter of the nineteenth century the young republic finally evolved a system of politics appropriate to American conditions. The holistic images of the Anglo-American political tradition gradually gave way to pluralistic and atomistic conceptions of the political world, and Americans came to accept the inevitability of conflict in their highly variegated, extensive, and mobile nation of political equals. One way of reconciling conflict with order, some Americans now perceived, was through the device of party. Far from being unrepublican, they argued, popular political parties could actually advance the cause of liberty and democracy. Ideologically, parties were compatible with the egalitarian doctrines and practices of Jacksonian America, for they were seen as democratic structures which translated the will of the majority into governmental decisions. They realized the American ideal of rule by the people, rather than rule by gentlemen. Sociologically, too, they seemed to fit American circumstances, functioning as mechanisms to accommodate the varied demands of an extensive electorate. At any rate, Americans finally began to accept the legitimacy of party forms, and a two-party system established itself as the normal way of ordering American politics.

The nature of the electoral system immeasurably contributed to this polarization, but it is almost as if the two-party situation satisfied some need in the American political psyche. Perhaps because of the sense of destiny, which requires Americans to see in the future the completion of a mission begun in the past, American political parties have characteristically combined backward- with forward-looking features, and large parts of American history have been marked by a conflict between a party representing political conservatism and economic progress on the one hand and a party representing political (or democratic) advance and economic conservatism on the other. Between them the two parties have often seemed to maintain the political order by reconciling the contradictions in American political culture. In the Jacksonian era the Democrats combined a faith in the forward progress of liberty and democracy with an attachment to the simple agrarian society that was fast vanishing. Conversely, their Whig opponents tended to champion entrepreneurial and corporate capitalism even while nursing a nostalgia for the days of patrician and clerical authority. Both parties saw themselves as protecting the

republic, the Democrats giving themselves a *raison d'être* by resisting
the subversive tendencies of an aristocratic Money Power, and the
Whigs appointing themselves as the guardians of a liberty jeopardized
by an overbearing executive and political corruption. But while they
identified themselves with an American mission, they also recognized
that expediency and compromise were part of the art of American
politics. They knew, too, that a voter-oriented party system was highly
vulnerable to popular pressures, and the major parties eventually
began to disintegrate again. This disruption itself was partly owing to
differences over the republic's fate, some Americans wishing to extend
their great empire of democracy to new lands and new peoples, and
others fearing that the admission of alien elements would lead to the
subversion of their free institutions. Yet the two-party system soon
reasserted itself, and the general structure of American politics long
retained the imprint of the age of Jackson.

Chapter 12

The new American party system

It was as a pioneer of party politics that the United States was to make a distinctive contribution to practical political science. In the 1830s and 1840s American politicians demonstrated how the affairs of a populous democracy could be regulated by a system of party competition. Parties in themselves, of course, were not new, but what was fairly novel was the idea that parties should be disciplined and permanent structures encompassing the mass of the electorate, and the even more striking idea that the political system itself should be organized on the principle of competition between two such structures. Government by popular parties, it was now suggested, provided an alternative to government by gentlemen, and as such was peculiarly suitable for a democracy.

The first national parties, the Federalists and the Republicans, had never really been regarded as legitimate. To their architects, the first parties were temporary, patriotic alliances which would willingly disband when the danger was over, that is when their misguided political opponents had been vanquished forever. And the first American party system had indeed withered away as predicted, partly because of the strength of these traditional antiparty attitudes, which in themselves had inhibited party politicians from building lasting institutional structures. But by the Jacksonian era some Americans were beginning to glimpse some virtues in political parties. They could see the advantages of a disciplined organization for the purposes of electoral victory. They began to grasp the concept of a loyal opposition. And some men were able to appreciate the value of a party *system*, that is a political world ordered by regular competition between permanent party organizations. At any rate, whether Americans liked or disliked parties they now had to learn to live with them. In the Jacksonian era the so-called 'second American party system' was invented, which was characterized by competition between two new national political parties, each sustained by elaborate political machinery. Long before it happened in Britain, American politics became party politics and the deferential world of eighteenth-century Anglo-American political culture was left far behind.

The Founding Fathers, like most eighteenth-century gentlemen, had subscribed to the ideal of a cohesive political order in which impartial statesmen governed in the interests of all. This holistic view of politics, with its promise of an organic society, had been reinforced by a religious tradition which stressed the importance of the community and of covenant theology, and by the mercantilist philosophy of the political economists which presented the nation-state as a kind of corporation. But by the early nineteenth century such organic images were losing their force. Adam Smith's *Wealth of Nations* had been published in the same year as the Declaration of Independence, and over the next two generations the popularizers of *laissez-faire* broadcast the message that the key to economic progress lay in free competition between individuals. In the English-speaking world, too, the Protestant religion became increasingly evangelical in tone, and in the United States a series of explosive religious revivals was made possible in part by the growing belief that salvation was not predestined by God but lay largely within the capacity of the lone individual. In the romantic world of the nineteenth century, whether in the *laissez-faire* theories of the economists, the free-will doctrines of the revivalists, or the literary imagination of Sir Walter Scott or James Fenimore Cooper, each man's destiny lay largely in his own hands. The view of society as an organism was being replaced by an atomistic conception of society as an aggregation of distinct individuals. The national interest became the sum total of men's individual interests, not something which in some indefinably way transcended the collected parts. These shifting intellectual perspectives made possible a pluralistic conception of politics, in which the political nation consisted of a host of separate groups and interests in perfectly natural and healthy competition with one another.

Of course, the hard facts of American politics contributed immeasurably to the acceptance of the idea of a pluralistic political world. The American Constitution itself had been so constructed as to make it possible for a mass of different interest groups to live together, as James Madison had so lucidly explained. The continued arrival of new immigrant groups, the proliferation of religious sects, the emergence of new economic interests, and the creation of new states had all served to underline the increasingly heterogeneous nature of American society. For years, of course, American politicians had nonetheless pursued the quixotic quest for the harmonious republic and the common good, but by the 1820s their goal seemed more distant than ever. The terrifying confrontation of the Missouri Crisis, the revival of the contest for the presidency in 1824, the spectacular political battle between the friends of Jackson and the friends of Adams in 1828, and the implacable competition between increasingly solid sections, all told the lesson that conflict was an inherent part of the American system of politics. It made little sense to see the political nation as an organism with but a single public good; more plausible was the view of the nation as an aggregation of competing individuals, groups, and sections. And in such a polity parties could have a useful role to play. They made it possible to arbitrate the conflicts, to collect together the individual interests of the people, and to translate them into government action. Party competition, and particularly the alternation of parties in government, was a positive good in such a heterogeneous society, since each set of interests in turn would have access to government. In the pluralistic universe that the Jacksonians glimpsed around them, parties were safe, legitimate, and even valuable.

The acceptance of party forms was, of course, slow and grudging, and in the 1820s most Americans continued to look upon them with suspicion and disdain. But parties were now also beginning to find their defenders, particularly among the members of what were perhaps the two most notorious state political machines in the United States, New York's Albany Regency and Virginia's Richmond Junto. 'It is the vainest thing in the world to deny the existence of parties . . .', insisted the *Albany Argus*. 'They have accompanied the progress of all nations; and they are necessary to the just exercise of the powers of free governments.'[1] Parties were justified on a number of grounds. Far from being unrepublican, it was said, they actually sustained the republic by channelling and making known the will of the people. Party devices like the caucus, pointed out Andrew Stevenson of the Richmond Junto, 'enable the views and wishes of the People to be carried into effect; and not scattered and broken'.[2] Further, parties were said to bring a degree of order to the political system, while party competition dispelled apathy, encouraged the people to take an interest in public affairs, and acted as a spur to honest and efficient government.

The central feature of the new creed of party was the emphasis on loyalty and discipline. 'Nothing can give a party the command even of its own strength but *discipline*', wrote one Jacksonian to another.[3] A party could not function effectively without the regular support of its members and total loyalty to 'regular nominations' was held to be a fundamental principle. Parties, it was said, were democratically-structured organizations which operated by majority decision. At the grassroots level candidates for local offices were chosen by meetings of all the party faithful in that locality. These meetings might also elect delegates to county conventions, which in turn sent delegates to state conventions. It was the conventions – local, county, and state – which nominated candidates for office and (sometimes) articulated policies and adopted platforms, each such decision being made by the majority vote of all those present. The party structure, then, provided an opportunity for the rank-and-file to participate in political decision-making, and, most important, it provided a means whereby the will of the majority could be made known. Party activity was thus sanctioned by the democratic principle of majority rule. Party was the device whereby the popular will was transmitted into the inner reaches of government. To those who elaborated this defence of party, the greatest sin that a member could commit was to defy the party's decision. If the losing delegates at a nominating convention walked out and organized a rival electoral ticket, as happened all too often in the early nineteenth century, they were not merely splitting the party and jeopardizing its chances. Worse, they were treating with contempt the will of the majority, they were putting their own selfish interests and sordid ambitions above the democratic wishes of the people. Or so the argument went. Where the patrician leaders had told the people that they must subordinate their private interests to the good of the country, the party leaders told them that they must subordinate themselves to the party. The good party member was guided not so much by his own conscience or judgement as by the judgement of the party. Party discipline was equated with party loyalty and party loyalty was equated with democracy.

Martin Van Buren and his colleagues in the Albany Regency, as Michael Wallace and Richard Hofstadter have shown, fashioned this defence of party in a state in which politics in the past had tended to revolve around a number of great families.[4] Since the revolutionary war the Clintons had been a powerful family in New York, as first George Clinton and later his nephew De Witt Clinton claimed the leadership of the Republican party. It was against Clinton that Van Buren and his so-called Bucktails revolted in 1819, charging that the supercilious governor was treating the party as his own personal property. De Witt Clinton personified the patrician style of politics, assuming command by virtue of his family connections and high social standing and using the party machine to advance his own interests and reward his own friends. He did not defer to the party; he expected the party to defer to him. To the rebellious Van Burenites this form of politics was aristocratic and hence unrepublican, and they advanced the creed of party as a means of ending patrician rule. If political office was not to be monopolized by gentlemen of standing, they argued, the people had to be mobilized into an efficient fighting force capable of raising up its own leaders. Conservative New Yorkers were not slow to perceive the anti-aristocratic implications of party organization, Silas Wood complaining in Congress of political combinations which stirred up ignoble passions and misrepresented motives in order 'to weaken the confidence of the People in the integrity and patriotism of those in power'.[5] But the Bucktails were unabashed in their celebration of party, which they insisted offered a means of replacing the old patrician leaders with a class of men who had worked their way up the party ranks, men who, moreover, were the democratically-chosen agents of the majority of the people.

In excoriating personal parties the Bucktails were also advocating a form of party organization which would not collapse with the death of the leader. Parties were to be permanent devices for channelling the will of the people and carrying democracy into effect, and those who did not display proper devotion to the party cause would be banished to the wilderness, forever denied political preferment. Only such discipline, it was argued, could ensure that government did not fall into the hands of great families or of ambitious individuals but was fully responsive to the democratic will. By the adoption of such techniques and the propagation of such values, the Albany Regency succeeded in winning control of New York state in the 1820s. Their success did not go unnoticed elsewhere. Politicians of the old school thundered against such degenerate practices, but since they tended to bring victory the more supple political managers were soon imitating them, and the new party forms gradually spread from state to state, particularly in the North. In 1834 one southern gentleman complained that 'The discipline of the Albany school now holds in chains, Maine, N. Hampshire, N. York, Ohio and Penna. and is rapidly seizing after the other northern states.'[6]

As such comments implied, the new party organizations were not as democratic in practice as they were in theory. The doctrine of party discipline afforded substantial power to the leaders. Party machinery was almost as old as the republic, but the new ideas and devices strengthened it considerably and eased the emergence of new machines. Power remained divided between city, county, and state organizations, though in this period the state bodies tended to gain in authority. There were a number of reasons for this. Improvements in transportation speeded communications between the outlying localities and the centre, facilitating the transfer of decisions to the latter, and made the regular calling of state conventions a practicable process. Changes in the electoral environment also tended to put a premium on central organization. By the 1830s elections for governor and president were almost everywhere conducted on a popular statewide basis, and elections for these and other offices were increasingly held at the same time, and organizations were needed capable of composing party tickets centrally and of mobilizing the mass of voters. Actually, the strength of the state parties varied considerably from state to state (and from time to time). In Pennsylvania, for example, the state leaders exerted relatively little authority and had often to bow to the demands of the powerful county oligarchies. But in almost all states there were attempts to fashion workable statewide alliances, and these in turn could see some advantage in becoming part of a national coalition.

It was the desire for effective influence in Congress, but more particularly the renewed competition for the presidency, which encouraged the state parties to form links with one another. No one could be elected president without carrying several states in different parts of the Union, so state and local politicians who wanted access to the White House were obliged to make common cause with others of their own kind. Reinforcing this was a desire for influence in Congress, where new states were admitted to the Union, public lands disposed of, tariff schedules drawn up, and internal improvement schemes approved. Congress also played a role in facilitating the development of national parties by providing an arena in which state leaders could meet regularly with one another and explore their areas of mutual concern. It was in Congress that the disparate elements of the Jacksonian coalition first drew together, uniting in obstreperous opposition to the administration of John Quincy Adams.

But it was the races for the presidency which stimulated the most determined attempts to forge national alliances and which gave rise to the first formal national structures, as Richard McCormick has persuasively argued.[7] Unlike the first party system, the new national parties did not originate in ideological divisions in cabinet and Congress. Rather, they are better seen as an attempt by state and local politicians to come to terms with the intertwined phenomena of mass democracy and sectionalism. Presidential campaigns now had to be carried to the people, and politicians needed to mobilize this mass electorate behind a single candidate. They also needed to abate sectional tensions if they were to succeed in this objective, and this provided a highly patriotic justification for their coalitional activities.

Just as individuals were expected to defer to the decisions of state conventions, so the state parties might be expected to defer to the decision of a national convention. A spirit of compromise was essential to this system of politics and, like party regularity, was soon deified as a fundamental political principle. 'Concession and forbearance lie at the very foundation of the political fabric', said the New York Democrats in 1832, 'and it is only through concession and forbearance that the structure can be upheld.'[8] The new national parties represented the final accommodation of American politicians to the sectional and popular pressures which had so effectively broken apart the old political order in the 1810s and 1820s. In 1835 Andrew Stevenson reminded the public that the attempts to put presidential elections in the hands of the people by constitutional amendment had failed, leaving a national convention as 'the best means of concentrating the popular will'.[9]

The first national conventions assembled for the 1832 election. The Antimasonic party, a vehicle for the popular crusade against freemasonry which had ignited in a number of northern states, won the honour of holding the first national nominating convention in American history, assembling at Baltimore in September 1831. The party which had originated with the Adams-Clay coalition and had been ousted so rudely from office in 1828 was now dignifying itself with the name National Republican, and this held its convention at Baltimore in December 1831, nominating Henry Clay for president. Some months later the Jacksonians, increasingly known as the Democrats, held their first national gathering in the same conveniently-located city. Henceforth presidential and vice-presidential candidates were normally chosen by national conventions, which consisted of delegates sent by the state parties. In these arenas the state parties battled for their sectional favourites and party managers arranged deals between contending interests. The professional politicos, conscious of the precarious nature of their coalitions, repeatedly invoked the spirit of concession and preached the need to submit to the decision of the national body. 'Adherence to regular nominations, under all circumstances, and at whatever sacrifices', one party paper strictly instructed its readers, 'is the duty of every republican.'[10]

While the convention system was ostensibly democratic, enabling the party rank-and-file to participate in the nominating process, it also contributed to the emergence of the professional politician and the party manager. Permanent party structures provided men with an opportunity to make a career of party service, and the talented individual could hope to rise through the ranks and hold his share of dignified offices whenever his party was in power. The political leaders of the first party system had tended to see themselves as public-spirited gentlemen, amateurs who held public office temporarily before retiring once more to their private pursuits on the plantation, at the bar or in the counting-house. Planters, lawyers, and merchants continued to enter politics in large numbers in the Jacksonian era, but the party-oriented political system could now provide an alternative lifetime career to men-on-the-make. The more successful professional politicians were often those who were skilled in the arts of manipulation, communication, and conciliation. The breed of politician which best survived the new political environment was the broker, the publicist, and the regular party man, rather than the educated gentleman or philosophical statesman of yesteryear. The ability to orchestrate a campaign, to effect compromises between rival factions, to manage an efficient organization were skills which helped to raise many an obscure figure to power, from the tavern-keeper's son, Martin Van Buren, to the shiftless frontiersman's son, Abraham Lincoln. Lawyers and editors fared particularly well in this political world, lawyers perhaps because they were used to adapting their arguments to their brief, and because they were better equipped than others to comprehend legislative procedures, editors perhaps because they knew how to communicate with the public.

Editors played a particularly crucial role in the new system of party politics. Skilled in the techniques of mass communication, they found themselves drawn into politics at every level. Some newsmen reached the highest councils of their parties. The cadaverous Francis P. Blair, editor of the Washington *Globe*, became an intimate friend of President Jackson and a confidential adviser on all manner of political matters. The cigar-chewing Thurlow Weed, editor of the *Albany Evening News*, became the effective boss of the Whig party of New York state. Since major newspaper offices received copies of other newspapers from all over the country, they became centres in which political information could be gathered, which in turn could be sifted and passed on to the relevant party chief. Conversely, the party hierarchies used newspapers to convey information, advice, and instructions to the party rank-and-file and to the people at large. Each party maintained a number of newspapers as their semi-official organs, from which they broadcast the party line and coordinated national campaigns. These papers were frequently subsidized from public funds, for a party in power would see that its favourite organs were provided with lucrative government printing contracts. In this new party system, newsmen and elected officials sustained one another in a kind of political symbiosis.

If newspapers were used to coordinate party activity, patronage was used to inculcate party discipline. In the Jacksonian era the spoils system came to serve an important role in holding party organizations together – although the ruthless scramble for spoils could break them apart. Once a party was elected to office it could reward its supporters by giving them government jobs and contracts. Already well-entrenched in such states as New York and Pennsylvania, the Jacksonians systematized the partisan distribution of government offices at the national level. To Andrew Jackson himself the system represented a democratic reform. Invoking the principle of rotation in office, he argued that officeholders should be periodically replaced by other men, for this would ensure that offices were not regarded as a species of personal property, capable of being transferred from father to son, it would keep the incumbents alive to the public interest, and it would enable more people to participate in the affairs of government. In this light rotation was, as he said, 'a leading principle in the republican creed'. Some of Jackson's lieutenants, like the New York Senator William L. Marcy, were more forthright in admitting that they saw 'nothing wrong in the rule that to the VICTOR belongs the spoils of the ENEMY'.[11]

In fact Jackson only replaced about a fifth of federal officeholders in his eight years of office, but although there was no wholesale massacre of incumbents, the replacements were almost all loyal party men. The spoils system was an indispensable part of the new party system, for it became a means of paying for the organization and increasing party discipline. Loyal partisans were rewarded for their services with government jobs, and they in turn subscribed to the party newspaper and returned part of their public salary to the party funds. It has been argued that in this way the use of spoils advanced democracy in America: the spoils system paid for the competitive party system which gave voters a choice. The spoils system, like the nominating convention and the cigar-smoking boss, was destined to become a major symbol of that unique invention, the American political party.

The rise of the party professional, of the media men, of the convention system, and of the spoils system did not go unresisted.

Indeed, there was considerable opposition to these new political forms, which to many were sinister signs of an ominous degeneration in American public life. The phenomenon of party gave rise to another phenomenon which some historians have labelled 'antipartyism'. To many anxious and agonized Americans, that freedom for which their fathers had fought at the Revolution and the preservation of which was the nation's *raison d'etre*, now seemed in mortal peril.

Antipartyism took a variety of forms, but the basic conviction which sustained them was that party endangered the great American experiment in liberty and self-government. Many men in public life naturally retained the consensual ideal of the patrician leaders of the early republic, and bitterly condemned party for dividing the community and putting its own selfish interests before the public good. 'We have had no real quiet or tranquility [sic] in this Country for many years', complained one conservative in 1839. 'Party politics control everything – for an ascendance in power, the real good of the nation is constantly lost sight of.'[12] Such traditional views came readily to the older generation who had been raised on the conventional wisdom of the eighteenth century, to those of high social status whose political authority was threatened by the new creed of party, and to conservatives of all ranks and ages who for whatever reason yearned for an orderly political world. But antipartyism also received nourishment from a less likely source, that is from the evangelical crusades which scorched large parts of the North and Midwest in the 1820s and 1830s. Although evangelical theology now emphasized the capacity of the individual in his search for salvation, it also emphasized the primacy of religious and moral values. The religious missions of this period were fired by a millenial urgency, and there was no place for the compromises of politics in this last great battle against sin. Hundreds of thousands of people were touched in some measure by the evangelical crusades, the moral absolutism of which helped to perpetuate the holistic view of the good society, with its contempt for self-serving interests.

The critics of party tirelessly trotted out all the traditional arguments against it, but they also sounded some newer notes in their medley. Republics, it had always been said, survived for only as long as the virtue of the people, and distressing evidence of the degeneration of American public life was now seen in the ceaseless party machinations and in the election of the most undeserving men to office. Party apparatus was capable of raising up the obscure and incompetent to positions of great power. Party nominations went to good party men, it was said, men who had risen through the ranks by virtue of loyal party service and little else. Martin Van Buren in particular was denounced as a mere party man, and probably no other political figure of the period was abused as bitterly, for to the old school he personified everything that was going wrong with American politics. When the Democrats nominated Van Buren for the presidency in 1836, his enemies were quick to point out that he was identified with no great acts of statesmanship, with no major pieces of legislation, with no great political principles, not even with distinguished military service. He was a pure creation of party, the son of a tavern-keeper raised up not by virtue of his own public services but by party organization and government patronage. 'Van Buren has the sympathy of the people no where', complained one North Carolina politician. 'Twenty years ago he could not have got up at all. It is one of the alarming signs of the decay of public virtue, that a man may hope to attain that office without public service, high talent or any thing strongly to sustain him, except simply the patronage of the Ex: Govt.'[13] Seen from one perspective, then, the rise of men like Martin Van Buren represented the replacement of statesmen by self-serving party hacks. Seen from another, it represented the replacement of patrician gentlemen by ordinary men who had climbed up from the social depths. Either way, the election of Martin Van Buren in 1836 represented the final triumph of party in American politics.

But there were even more sinister implications in the loss of public virtue than the election of unprincipled intriguers to office. In traditional libertarian thought, the degeneration in the virtue of the people was equated with the loss of liberty, for as the people became politically indifferent or corrupt, so an unchecked power became concentrated in the hands of the rulers. The rise of party seemed to vindicate this critique, for it served to transfer power from the people to non-accountable party bosses, or so it was said. The doctrine of party regularity, in denying the individual a right to his own judgement, was creating a nation of slaves. 'A thorough-going party-man has nothing to do but to follow his leader', charged the *National Intelligencer* in 1827. Unless some reform takes place, complained a Virginian some years later, '*the People* will soon be suppressed by *the Party*'.[14] A party was all the more dangerous when it was in command of government, for then it could use public patronage to enforce obedience. Officeholders carried out the dictates of their chief under the threat of dismissal. Hence, when the Jacksonian Democrats called a national convention in 1835, their opponents charged that the convention was packed with officeholders who dutifully nominated Van Buren on President Jackson's instructions. The spoils system and the convention together enabled Jackson 'to dictate to the people' his successor, and to subvert that 'freedom of elections' on which republican government was based.[15] Just as the celebrated Whig constitution of 1688 had been subverted by the king's ministers in the eighteenth century, so now party devices were doing the same to the American Constitution, or so it was said. The convention system, complained the Illinois senate in 1836, is 'destructive of the freedom of the elective franchise, opposed to republican institutions, and dangerous to the liberties of the people'.[16]

The new system of party, in this view, was not merely unrepublican but antirepublican.

But although resisted, the rise of party was irresistible, if somewhat erratic at the national level. Historians speak of the 'second American party system' as that which was in operation between about 1828 and 1854, but few Americans before about 1840 would have perceived any coherent *system* around them. The presidential election of 1828 was rather abnormal in that there were only two candidates, resulting largely from the peculiar circumstances surrounding the disputed House election of 1825, and many Americans expected that elections would revert to being multi-sided contests thereafter. Indeed, the elections of the 1830s in some measure bore out this view. In 1832 there were three presidential candidates, Democratic, National Republican, and Antimasonic. In 1836 there were as many as five, the Democratic candidate being opposed by four other candidates running under different party designations in different parts of the country. By this time the main opposition party was known as the Whig party, but not until 1840 were the Whigs sufficiently united to be able to agree on a single candidate for president. This marked the full maturation of the second party system. Between 1840 and 1852 presidential elections were contested by two major candidates – Democrat and Whig – accompanied by the candidate of a smaller third party, an antislavery party which never succeeded in winning any electoral votes.

The rise of party had begun long before the Jacksonian era, but it was that era which witnessed its final triumph in the United States. The politics of deference, custom, and gentlemanly patronage had at last been wholly rejected in favour of the politics of party. Parties had been known in the eighteenth century and much of the partisan activity of the Jacksonian era was hardly unfamiliar, but parties were now widely accepted as legitimate and useful political devices. Some Americans certainly continued to damn them as unrepublican excrescences, but a growing number saw them as indispensable to a democratic polity. And the parties themselves differed in significant ways from the parties of the early republic. The old Republican-Federalist excitements had not infrequently drawn large numbers to the polls, especially in state elections, but high turnouts were more consistently achieved in the Jacksonian era, and from the 1840s a higher proportion of Americans were voting in presidential elections than ever before. The major parties had become mass parties and their constituencies were nationwide. Further, they were designed as lasting structures, organizations which transcended the personal interests of their leaders and the ephemeral issues of the day. Thus, party conventions began to adopt platforms as well as candidates, inviting voters to vote for the party rather than the man. They also slowly acquired a bureaucratic permanence, creating officials and machinery for more than immediate campaign purposes. The Democratic party in 1848 became the first to create a national central committee, under a party chairman appointed by the national convention, to remain in existence until the next presidential election. As in other areas of American life in the mid-nineteenth century, anarchic tendencies were being contained by the use of complex and specialized institutions managed by skilled professionals.

While parties evolved their own hierarchies, the ties in this political order were horizontal rather than vertical. Where the eighteenth-century voter might acknowledge an allegiance to a local notable, the nineteenth-century voter was asked to give his loyalty to a great political association of equals, one which united like-minded men across the country. Wealth remained a useful attribute for an aspiring politician, but high social standing of itself now conferred relatively little political influence and diligent party service provided an alternative route to the top. The parties were raising up their own elites to replace the old patrician class, though some of the well-born themselves proved highly skilled in the techniques of party politics. But however powerful the new managers became, their orientation was to the mass electorate, which they had to mobilize and organize and to which they had in large measure to defer. Leader-oriented politics was fast becoming a thing of the past; the mass political party, it could be said, was an administrative system for carrying into practical effect the will of the majority. The two-party structure, as Americans were beginning to appreciate, also provided a means whereby majority tyranny could be averted and orderly politics maintained in a pluralistic society. The checks and balances of the Constitution were to be supplemented by a party equipoise. 'Two parties exist now, as two have always existed, and always will', the New York Whig William H. Seward somewhat inaccurately declared in 1844. 'Each of them as a majority, by turns, controls the administration of government, and, as a minority, exercises a salutary restraint upon the controlling party.'[17] Yet despite such tributes to the two-party system, most committed party men still seemed to assume that the republic could never be entirely safe in the hands of their misguided opponents, a belief which vindicated the continued existence of their own patriotic party.

Chapter 13

The Democratic strategy

The Democrat and Whig parties together gave expression to the greater part of the influences shaping American political life, and of the two the Democrats were the more successful in accommodating themselves to the egalitarian, individualistic, and particularistic pressures of the America of Jackson and Clay. The Democrats' experiences as a national party and their search for an identity revealed much about the American way of politics.

The Jacksonians had unleashed their imaginative assault on the presidential citadel in 1828 in the name of the republic. They had been taught to believe that a recourse to party forms was only justified when republican institutions were in peril, and the essence of the 'corrupt bargain' charge was that the Constitution had been subverted by the machinations of Adams and Clay. A republican government was one whose officers were chosen from and by the people in free elections, the Jacksonians insisted, and once this choice was denied to the people the republic's days were numbered. Thus in a sense the Jacksonians' mission was largely accomplished with the successful election of their hero, who was committed to little more than a promise 'to cleanse the Augean stables'.[1] But it was also his patriotic duty to maintain a vigil for further threats to republican liberty, and espy them he did. In the course of defending the republic the coalition of party and factional chieftains which had taken command in 1829 was imperceptibly transformed into the Democratic party, arguably the first mass political party in history. By the time that Martin Van Buren was flushed out of the White House by the cresting Whig tide, the Democrats were associated with a recognizable constituency following, a philosophy of government, and a new political mission. The party had defined itself in its long years in office.

The political stance adopted by the Democratic party in the 1830s was in some ways new. Its limited government doctrines were in large part inherited from the Jeffersonians, but the Jacksonians went further than the Jeffersonians in denying a directing role for those in federal public office. Government officers, they seemed increasingly to believe, were not so much representatives formulating policies and taking decisions on the people's behalf; rather they were but lowly civil servants executing the will of the people within the constraints of the Constitution. In this sense, good government consisted in the absence of system, that is it left 'individuals and States as much as possible to themselves . . . leaving each to move unobstructed in its proper orbit'.[2] In such a polity the president was not so much a lofty statesman as a tribune of the people, striking down measures which might impinge on their freedom but not himself promulgating plans for the republic's development.

This permissive philosophy was only imperfectly articulated, but the Democratic party came to embrace it for a variety of reasons. For one thing, it accorded well with the Old Republicanism that several early Jacksonians subscribed to, that political tradition which distrusted governmental power and which thought that liberty might be best protected by a strict construction of the Constitution and by the fostering of states rights. Further, a negative government stance offered a good formula for winning national elections. Positive measures were liable to repel prospective voters, but by avoiding contentious legislation and by bowing discreetly to sectional and local pressures when necessary the Jacksonians could hope to maintain an electoral majority. In a sense it could draw support from local interests by allowing them to go their own way. Finally, the *laissez-faire* attitudes of the Democrats proved ideal for a party which was increasingly voter-oriented and which espoused a belief in majority rule. The federal government, in this view, was little more than an umpire, impartially policing the competition between the individuals, interest groups, and communities of which the Union was composed, and the Democratic party was little more than a passive instrument in the hands of the people for channelling their wishes to that government. This is not to suggest that the Democratic party itself stood for nothing. On the contrary, in the course of the 1830s it did acquire a mission, and that mission too was one which was able to combine the traditional values of Old Republicanism with the egalitarian imperatives of the new political order.

Martin Van Buren, Jackson's first Secretary of State, had early perceived the advantages of committing the party to a negative government stance. Throughout the 1820s he had sought to re-establish the old New York-Virginia alliance on the basis of a common commitment to states rights, for since New York had paid for her own internal improvements her politicians could afford to adopt a strict construction of the Constitution. On such old-fashioned principles, Van Buren hoped to forge a powerful electoral alliance between the planters of the South and the farmers and labourers of the Middle Atlantic and western states, and President Jackson proved admirably responsive to this strategy. It was 'understood between us', according to Van Buren, that he would alert Jackson when a bill appeared before Congress which could be used to make the administration's constitutional principles clear. An opportunity came with the Maysville Road bill in 1830, proposing that federal assistance be used to build a road in Kentucky, and Jackson determined that he must make a stand against financial extravagance in government: 'The Federal Constitution must be obeyed, State-rights preserved, our national debt must be paid, direct taxes and loans avoided and the Federal Union preserved.'[3] Apart from the repeated use of the ambiguous word 'federal', this was the language of Old Republicanism and was evocative of even older libertarian suspicions of government debts and taxes. The Maysville Veto, in insisting that the federal government had no powers to aid works of a local character, was warmly applauded in New York and throughout the South. The Jackson administration continued to provide federal support for internal improvements, particularly to improve rivers and harbours used for foreign commerce, but it had renounced any interest in a systematic use of government powers in this way. Jackson, like Jefferson in 1801, wanted a return to republican simplicity.

This strategy was one to which the Democrats would continue to hold, though in the early 1830s it was threatened by the Nullification movement. Driven almost to despair by exhausted soil, plummeting cotton prices, and occasional (and much magnified) disturbances among their vast slave population, many South Carolinians had developed a pathological hatred of the principle and practice of tariff protection. The tariff in fact had had little to do with their plight, but they complained that it robbed southern planters by raising the price of manufactured goods and reducing the European demand for cotton. If the federal government could enact a protective tariff at the behest of northern industrialists, moreover, it might also be swayed by the demands of the growing antislavery movement. The harrowed South Carolina politicians took refuge in the doctrine of Nullification, promulgated anonymously by Calhoun in his *South Carolina Exposition* of 1828, which held that a state had a right to declare null and void any federal legislation it considered unconstitutional. For a time the South Carolina radicals held off putting this disruptive doctrine to the test, hoping that an administration headed by two slaveholders would prove sympathetic to southern grievances, but when the new tariff law of 1832 retained protective duties their resentment drove them to furious action. A popularly-elected convention pronounced the tariffs of 1828 and 1832 inoperative within the boundaries of the state, which, it was indicated, would secede from the Union if force were used against it.

Such an act of defiance Jackson could not tolerate. 'In all Republics', he wrote to one South Carolinian, 'the voice of a Majority must prevail.'[4] To Jackson the Union itself was as vital to the preservation of liberty as a strict construction of the Constitution. The Union had brought happiness and prosperity as well as liberty and would effectively be at an end if a state could choose which laws to obey. The Confederation period had shown that states could not stand alone and Jackson warned South Carolina that her dream of independence would be 'interrupted by bloody conflicts with your neighbors and a vile dependence on a foreign power'. Besides South Carolina had no right to secede in his eyes since the Constitution had been formed by 'the people' collectively and could not be broken up by the unilateral action of one state.[5] Jackson's reaction was to extend the olive branch in one hand, asking Congress for a lower tariff, and to raise the sword in the other, proposing a force bill to enable him to collect duties in South Carolina by military means if necessary. The stratagem worked, though the tariff bill that was eventually signed by the president had been one introduced by Henry Clay, and the promised reduction in duties enabled South Carolina to abandon her lonely and vulnerable stance. The Nullification crisis allowed Jackson to demonstrate his commitment not to a strong central government but to the Union. States rights and the Union had both to be cherished if Americans were to remain a free people. This view of the American political system was to be widely shared by others.

By the end of Jackson's first term the sectional pressures which had threatened to tear the Union apart had been successfully contained. The Democratic party, with its machinery extending now into most states, provided a national institution within which different demands might be accommodated. The process of filtering and refining popular passions which the Founding Fathers had intended should be effected by the representative system was now being undertaken by a political party. By making concessions to regional interests and by adopting a negative government stance, the administration retained wide support. It pleased many westerners by adopting measures to promote Indian removal, dispatching the unfortunate tribes to unwanted lands in the heart of the continent, and also by proving increasingly receptive to the call for lower land prices. Jackson retained his popularity in Georgia by implicitly condoning the unconstitutional measures that state was taking against the Cherokee nation which occupied part of its territory. The internal improvement vetoes offered comfort to New Yorkers and southerners and pleased those Americans throughout the Union who had been brought up on strict constructionist principles, and the acceptance of a lower tariff also relieved many southerners and enabled South Carolina to save face. By the tactics of compromise, concession, and salutary neglect, within the broad strategy of maintaining the Union and reducing government to a minimum, the administration was able to quiet the most ominous threats to the American political system.

Once sectional issues had been contained or neutralized, issues related to commercial and industrial development came to the forefront of American politics. For the greater part of Jackson's tempestuous presidency the American economy was booming. In large measure, Jackson could feel that his decision not to lavish government money indiscriminately on internal improvements was vindicated by the frenetic activity around him, for new roads, canals and railroads were sprouting out in all directions, some exclusively the work of private enterprise and some aided by state governments, though some strategic schemes were discreetly assisted from federal funds. Improved communications meant more speed, provided not only by the locomotive but also by the steamboat, which came into its explosive own in this era and enabled goods to be moved swiftly upstream as well as down. The advocates of the American System were now witnessing that transportation revolution of which they had long dreamed, but it was being carried out with little direction from the federal government.

The breathtaking improvements in communications helped the industrialists of the Northeast by extending their markets, but the great beneficiaries in this period were the merchants and farmers. As freight charges plummeted American rivers, ports, canals, and railroads became thronged with traders of all descriptions. The vast hinterlands of the Great Lakes and the Mississippi Valley poured forth their riches, the dollar value of commerce reaching New Orleans from the interior more than doubling in the 1830s. One telling index of this exhilarating commercial expansion lay in the extraordinary multiplication of those handmaids of commerce, the banks. The number of state banks increased from 307 in 1820, to 330 in 1830, to 704 in 1835, and to 901 in 1840. The banker, perhaps, even more than the merchant, should stand as the personification of American business in this period. At any rate, the heady expansion of commercial activity and the ready availability of cash and credit provided unprecedented opportunities for the entrepreneur, and by the mid-1830s a speculative fever was gripping business circles. 'Business is the very soul of an American;' observed an Austrian settler in the United States, 'he pursues it, not as a means of procuring for himself and his family the necessary comforts of life, but as the foundation of all human felicity.'[6]

In the Jacksonian era, then, economic expansion was the dynamic element in American life. The agrarian society of Jefferson's day, with its small and in some measure self-sufficient communities, its farms, villages, plantations, and prim New England towns, was fast being replaced by an expansive commercial society, with its highly mobile population, its cotton-mills and counting-houses, its steamboats and railroads, its prosperous ports and its rapidly-growing cities. To many it seemed as if the old republic of virtue, the simple Jeffersonian arcadia which was said to be so essential to the nurturing of liberty, was being destroyed by the growth of commerce and of an exploitative, entrepreneurial ethos. The Jacksonian generation was the first to experience on a substantial scale the transforming and often terrifying influences of commercialization, urbanization, and industrialization.

Both the hopes and ambitions and the strains and fears generated by the irresistible forces of commerce inevitably invaded American political life. The Jacksonians may have taken power uncommitted to any specific measures, but they had to respond to the issues thrust upon them, many of them necessarily connected with the changing economy, and in so doing they acquired a political identity. Yet their response to the economic issues was not an arbitrary one. They were sensitive to demands from their own constituents, and, perhaps even more crucially, they were in some measure conditioned by their earlier response to the political issues of Jackson's first term. They had adopted a negative government stance as the best means of accommodating the disparate sectional and particularistic pressures, keeping their uneasy party coalition together, and giving expression to resurgent Old Republican sentiments, and that strategy now served to incline them against the government encouragement of business enterprise. In thus finally coming out against the measures of Clay's American System, the Jacksonians were able to harness the considerable disquiet over the way in which the old America was being destroyed by commercialization, materialism, and speculation. Or so it appeared to one Bostonian in 1835, who rejoiced that President Jackson was resisting 'that *commercial* spirit, which pervades everything in our Country, and which I heartily despise'.[7] American businessmen, the Jacksonians came to conclude, had to be taught to conduct themselves in accordance with republican principles.

It was Andrew Jackson's spectacular war on the Bank of the United States which more than anything gave his party a creed, for it pitted the gnarled 'Farmer of Tennessee' against the primary symbol of commercial progress. The bank had been chartered in 1816 for a period of twenty years, and with the approach of 1836 the case for its recharter had to be considered. Immediately after Jackson's electoral victory of 1828 the Democratic party's principal newspaper, the *United States Telegraph*, fired a warning shot at the bank, accusing it of 'having failed of the great object for which it was chartered', with the result that it had been 'converted into a great broker's shop, enriching a few individuals by the use of the Government deposites, and speculating in its own stock'. The question of rechartering it, concluded the editor, involved principles as vital as those of the recent election, 'those principles of civil liberty and equal rights, upon which the permanency of our republican institutions depend'.[8] Jackson's political opinions had never been very consistent, but this invocation of the Old Republican (and almost Bolingbrokean) critique of monied institutions was likely to touch a responsive chord in him, for he had learned the hard way of the untrustworthiness of the world of money and credit. As a young man he had been thrown massively into debt when a business associate defaulted on some notes that Jackson had endorsed, and his abiding suspicion of the financial nexus had again surfaced in 1817 when he resisted an attempt by the national bank to open a branch in his home town of Nashville. As president, Jackson's first pronouncements on the bank were somewhat circumspect, but he did reveal his sympathy with the 'large portion of our fellow-citizens' who questioned its constitutionality and expediency.[9]

To Andrew Jackson and others, the issue of a government-sponsored bank necessarily involved their conceptions of the good republic society, for such a corporation enjoyed privileges denied to others and controlled enormous financial resources which might be manipulated to enrich the favoured few, resources which furthermore might endow both itself and the federal government with illicit political power. The American Constitution had effectively guarded against a hereditary aristocracy, but it had done nothing to prevent the growth of a financial aristocracy, which, as the Jeffersonian Republicans had early pointed out, represented the chief threat to the dream of a republic of proud, equal, and independent men. Finally Jackson did decide that there was no room for a national bank in the republican system, and when a recharter bill passed Congress in 1832 he struck it down with a resounding veto. The people's president thus resorted to the new politics of democracy to protect a traditional image of the republic, for while the veto message was formally addressed to Congress it was really directed at the American people, reaching out for them in language suited to the hustings. In phrases evocative of the Republican diatribes against Hamilton's experiments, Jackson charged that the bank was the instrument of a 'self-elected directory' of rich men, a powerful and privileged oligarchy which was answerable neither to the government nor to the people. Further, implied Jackson, the interests of these rich Americans were intertwined with those of foreign (that is, British) capitalists, who had bought up some of the stock, that very connection that the Jeffersonians had espied behind the horrors of Federalism. And this unrepublican and un-American bank was quite simply also unnecessary, explained the president, for the government had need of no such agent. The true strength of the government, Jackson insisted in an illuminating exposition of Democratic principles, 'consists in leaving individuals and States as much as possible to themselves – in making itself felt, not in its power, but in its beneficence; not in its control, but in its protection; not in binding the States more closely to the center, but leaving each to move unobstructed in its proper orbit'.[10] Andrew Jackson, it seemed, was articulating a philosophy of benign neglect.

It was thus the administration's strategy to make local attachments a source of strength rather than of weakness to the federal government, whose job it saw as protection and not control. The government was to draw its energy from the people and not from powerful institutions like the national bank. When Jackson was triumphantly re-elected in 1832 he persuaded himself that the American people were with him (though he had probably lost more votes than he won by the veto), and he confidently escalated his war against the bank and its haughty president, Nicholas Biddle. In 1833 he began to remove government deposits from the bank and to place them in certain state banks, but to the dismay of the administration the rapid accumulation of public deposits led to an expansion in bank credit, which in turn helped to fuel a dangerous speculation in the land market. Ironically, this spiralling inflation had been assisted by the administration's very success in fulfilling one long-cherished Republican goal – the repayment of the national debt. As the Treasury's deficit turned into a surplus in 1835 yet more public money came to be lying in the state banks. In July 1836 Jackson struck again in an effort to end speculation and drive paper money out of circulation, the Specie Circular requiring that people pay the government quite literally with hard cash when they purchased public lands. The only money authorized by the Constitution or issued by the government itself was gold or silver coin, infinitely safer in Jackson's view than the paper notes issued by the banks and manipulated by them in their own interests. 'Recent events have proved that the paper money system of this country may be used as an engine to undermine your free institutions', Jackson warned his fellow citizens as he stepped down from office in 1837.[11]

Jackson's attacks on the Bank of the United States and the paper money system gave his party the cause that it needed. It was one thing to build an efficient political party; it was quite another to provide a *raison d'etre* for that party, a cause which would justify its existence and carry it through several elections. In a sense, there could only be one cause for any American politician of this generation – the protection of the great experiment in republican government so recently bequeathed by the Founding Fathers. But this generation was also composed of skilled political professionals, and as Jackson perhaps realized better than Van Buren, where it was necessary to mobilize a mass electorate and where electoral conditions (such as the winner-take-all principle) tended to promote a two-party system, what a party most needed was an enemy. 'Anti-voting' has long been a characteristic of American politics. The Jacksonians had stormed into power with the aid of the 'corrupt bargain' charge, but they could no longer use that to pillory their rivals. Similarly, the very success of Jackson's handling of the Nullification crisis deprived him of a permanent enemy in that quarter. Finally he found his party the perfect villain in 'the Money Power'. This was no ephemeral phenomenon, for its agents would 'continue to besiege the halls of legislation' and seek 'to mislead and deceive the public servants' for their subversive ends, and only eternal vigilance would ensure the safety of republican institutions.[12] By providing an aristocratic and privileged enemy, Jackson was able to make his party the principal beneficiary of the egalitarian and populistic currents of the day. He was also able to harness it to the potent fears of conspiracy and subversion which had long been nourished by Anglo-American constitutional thought.

Having found their cause, the Democrats could not lightly abandon it, even when their hunt for the rich rascals who were living off the people led them into politically vulnerable positions. They were becoming persuaded by their own rhetoric, and were obliged to demonstrate the sincerity of their convictions by taking other measures against the money and banking interests. The more radical Jacksonians disliked the policy of placing the deposits in selected state banks, for it exposed the party to charges of creating its own corrupt financial network and seemed to encourage the sort of speculation the Jacksonians had so virtuously denounced. 'I did not join in putting down the Bank of the United States to put up a wilderness of local banks', snorted Thomas Hart Benton, a powerful advocate of hard money.[13] When several state banks were forced to suspend specie payments during the Panic of 1837 the 'pet bank' system was discredited, and the most ardent anti-bank Democrats now pressed for a complete separation of government and banking. They proposed the creation of separate government vaults into which to put the deposits, so that the public's money need never be enmeshed in the banking system, a solution which was embodied in the Independent Treasury bill which finally passed a somewhat sceptical Congress in 1840.

The crusade against the Money Power also energized Democrats at state level. In the mid-1830s several states passed laws outlawing bank notes of small denominations. When the banks suspended payments during the Panic of 1837 and again in 1839 the public prejudice against them grew, the burning of many speculative fingers converting even some of those who had participated in the commercial bonanza to the hard money and anti-bank cause. Some Democrats wanted to abolish state banks, some wanted to sever all connections between them and the state governments, and some wanted the greater regulation of banking in the public interest. Only two states, Louisiana and Arkansas, actually went so far as to adopt constitutional prohibitions against banks within their borders, and in most states some sort of compromise was reached. But there could be no doubt that Democrats throughout the land were adopting a stance which implied a moral censure of banking and money operations.

This Democratic disapprobation of the privileged world of money and finance was felt by other institutions than banks. The Bank War fanned popular resentment against chartered monopolies of all kinds, whether state banks, turnpike companies, or railroad corporations. In many states, businessmen who wanted to form companies had to secure individual acts of incorporation from the legislature, and it was widely believed that such privileges were accorded only to the wealthy and influential few. In Jacksonian rhetoric these chartered monopolies became readily identified with that financial aristocracy ruled over by Nicholas Biddle. The Jacksonians were not hostile to business as such, but they were opposed to privileges likely to enrich the few at the expense of the many, and many supported general incorporation laws, enabling any group of men to form a corporation provided that the general conditions laid down by the state were met. 'The humblest citizens might associate together . . . ', pointed out one advocate of such a law, pooling their limited resources in such a way as to compete with 'the purse-proud men who now almost monopolize certain branches of business'.[14] In a republic, the Democrats concluded, economic affairs should not be dominated by a privileged elite any more than political affairs.

The Democrats were thus assigning to banks and other business corporations much the same position within the republican polity as they assigned to church bodies or humanitarian enterprises. They had early affirmed their strong support for the principle of the separation of church and state, even to the point of insisting that the mail be carried on the Sabbath, and in general at state level they proved less inclined than the Whigs to provide governmental support for humanitarian and moral reform measures. In the Jacksonian republic, business corporations, religious denominations, and charitable institutions were all forms of voluntary association, relying on their own resources and free of government-granted privileges. Although many Jacksonians regarded 'non-productive' businessmen like bankers and speculators as dangerous parasites and sought to curb their unrepublican activities, their attempts to divorce government from business in many ways gave encouragement to the latter. Economic (or religious or cultural) enterprises could flourish under the protecting care of a republican government, for if they did not receive its special favours nor were they subject to its control. The simple and frugal governmental system that the Jacksonians sought was almost demanded by the pluralistic nature of American society and the expansive nature of the American economy. If denominational diversity had made religious freedom all but unavoidable, the multitude of economic enterprises provided a strong case for *laissez-faire*. The Jacksonian strategy for maintaining the republic required that the federal government do little more than maintain the integrity of the Union.

The Democrats' belief that no government could be safely entrusted with the power of 'managing and directing the various general interests of . . . society', together with their tireless denunciations of the Money Power, served to identify them with the honoured libertarian movements of an earlier day.[15] Their rhetoric conjured images of a simple Jeffersonian arcadia, a republic of yeoman farmers and other virtuous small producers, which they were protecting from the subversive designs of a financial aristocracy, the forces of speculative and commercial capitalism, and the cancer of concentrated and irresponsible power. They were seeking to harness to their cause the potent emotions of early Republicanism, and indeed, their rhetoric was often closer to the 'agrarian' and 'Country' tradition of the Old Republicans than to that of the Republican moderates. The Democrats recognized that they could not hope to arrest economic change, and many prominent Democrats were themselves in hot pursuit of commercial riches, but they could hope to make the business world conform to republican principles, and in this way they could keep faith with the revolutionary past.

But if the Democrats' ideal economic order owed much to tradition and nostalgia, there was a radical and egalitarian edge to their political thought which was new. They had shed the patrician condescension of the early Republican leaders and no longer assumed a hierarchical social order. They were – or became – a voter rather than a leader-oriented party and they recognized the people as their masters. The party contest, said a correspondent of *The Globe*, was 'a mortal struggle for political supremacy between the Democracy of Numbers and the Aristocracy of Wealth'.[16] The Democrats seemed to envisage an atomistic world in which all men were of equal political weight. Yet there was no real incompatability between their economic and their political ideals, for there probably had been more economic equality in Jefferson's day, before rapid commercial growth widened the gap between rich and poor. The radical thrust of Democratic thought was consistent with the Jeffersonian promise of a land of small producers. In the Democratic world view, political innovation and economic conservatism fitted naturally together. 'Our republican spirit is restless and onward . . . ', said one Democratic campaign paper, 'Step by Step has it left behind the old Whig landmarks of limited franchise, of legislating for sections and classes, for banks, tariffs, and corporations, of governing to excess, and centralizing authority.'[17] In the perfect Jacksonian world of equal and self-reliant individuals there would be little need of government and each man would be master of his own destiny. To the self-reliant Jacksonian every regulatory law, whether economic, humanitarian or moral in its objective, impinged on his independence.

Such governmental authority as the Democrats did tend to enhance was of a supervisory rather than of a directing kind. The attempts by both federal and state administrations to regulate banking and to introduce general incorporation laws can be seen as the first uncertain steps in the direction of modern bureaucracy. As Matthew Crenson has recently shown[18], that redoubtable Jacksonian Amos Kendall spent an imaginative term as Postmaster-General turning his extensive department into an efficient administrative machine, complete with specialized bureaus and agencies and conducted according to impersonal rules and regulations. The General Land Office was also reorganized in much the same way. Hence the Jacksonians came to rely not on good character to ensure the honesty of public servants, as their patrician predecessors had done, but on complex systems of bureaucratic checks and balances. This administrative structure was highly decentralized and was closely linked to the Democratic party organization, for it was local party loyalists who were placed in the multitude of post and land offices across the country. Again, the Jacksonians were drawing strength from local communities, linking their political leaders to the federal government and yielding to their *mores* where possible, as when southern postmasters were permitted not to deliver abolitionist literature and when local customs were respected over land claims. This flexible bureaucratic system, like the party system, provided a means of maintaining order of a sort in a highly complex society without use of authoritarian forms.

The resort to bureaucratic constraints on those with power parallelled the Democrats' tendency also to impose constitutional constraints on public servants. Democratic administrations nationally sought to interpret the Constitution in such a way as to limit their own power, while in the states Democratic politicians often supported constitutional amendments to constrain state governments, such as those prohibiting banking. The Democrats were carrying the anti-power convictions inherited from the revolutionary era to their logical if not always practicable conclusions, protecting popular rights by confining governments to ever more restricting limits. The one form of government power that the Democrats did try to enhance, the executive veto, was itself seen as a popular negative on unwise legislation. Andrew Jackson cast himself as the people's tribune, whose duty it was to root out abuses in government and to forbid congressional measures which would appear to impair states rights and equal rights. The Democrats thus tended to make the presidency the focus of a system of politics in which a popularly-elected chief executive was forever defending popular rights and majority rule from the encroachments of special interests. 'Guided by the fundamental principle, that the will of the majority should, in all cases, control', wrote one admirer of Jackson, 'he has never attempted to defeat that will.'[19] In the states, too, Democrats tended to favour strengthening the veto power of the governor while circumscribing the independence of legislators through the right of instruction, which held that a particular electorate could instruct its representative how to vote on a given issue. The Democrats' concern for popular rights and their abiding distrust of government led them almost to a repudiation of government in the normal sense of the term.

These configurations of thought and feeling appear to have borne some sort of relationship, albeit an imperfect one, to the kinds of people that the Democrats spoke for. The 'agrarian', localistic, egalitarian, permissive, and anti-commercial strains in the Democratic persuasion seem roughly consonant with the possible desires and beliefs of the groups and areas that tended to vote Democratic. Few recent scholars have been able to identify a clear relationship between *class* and party in the Jacksonian era – e.g. they have not been able to establish convincingly that 'the poor' as a class voted for the Democrats – though economic considerations were not necessarily unimportant. People then, as now, tended to vote in the same way as others in the social group with which they most strongly identified, and beyond the immediate primary group of the family was the larger community, with its own particular economic, geographical, religious, and ethnic characteristics. An isolated community in need of a canal, for example, might give its allegiance to the party most likely to provide one, with both its rich and its poor citizens voting in the same way, so that their voting behaviour could be explained in economic but not class terms. At any rate, in recent years students of the Jacksonian era have been more successful in relating the party affiliations of voters to the economic, religious, and ethnic characteristics of the communities or social groups to which they belonged than to their levels of income. In the boom-and-bust period of the 1830s socioeconomic considerations may have heavily influenced voting behaviour; later, as Catholic immigrants poured into the land and nativist and religious tensions grew, ethnocultural considerations may have loomed larger.

The Democratic party was, of course, a mass party and a coalition party, and small farmers, southern planters, urban labourers, Catholics, and immigrants could all be found in its ranks. But the party's constituency can be sketched with slightly greater precision than this, although voting patterns could change over time. Both Democrats and Whigs sometimes labelled the party 'agrarian', and while it should be remembered that only a very small proportion of the American population lived in cities and that many Whig votes were necessarily cast by farmers, the association of the Democrats with certain kinds of agrarian constituencies was not without justification. In New England the Democratic banner state was New Hampshire, itself largely a land of small farmers, and the Democrats fared especially well in the smaller upland villages and the poorer agricultural regions. In neighbouring Massachusetts, too, though a Whig state, the Democrats tended to win votes among the small farmers of the western and southern counties and in the little fishing villages. In the South the most consistent Democratic states were Virginia, fallen on hard times since its tobacco-rich days and still without a commercial city, and booming Alabama. In the Old Dominion the Democrats were strong in the languishing agricultural area of the Tidewater (though the Whigs also picked up votes from disgruntled planters), the wealthy tobacco lands in the south, and in the area of small farms and mountains in the west, particularly in the poorer and more isolated counties. In Alabama, too, the more isolated and self-sufficient communities tended to be more Democratic than the economically-advanced areas. In the West the Democratic banner states were Illinois and Missouri, both frontier areas with very rapidly growing populations. In Missouri, at least, the less well-established counties were apparently more consistently Democratic than the older communities. In other states, too, notably Ohio, Tennessee, Florida, and Mississippi, there are indications of Democratic support in backward subsistence farming areas, frontier regions, and isolated communities lacking good communications. The evidence does not all point in the same direction (in both Ohio and New York, for example, there were rich farming communities that were Democratic), but the Democrats often seem to have fared well in areas that had been missed by, had been hurt by, or had not yet been overtaken by the forces of commerce and enterprise.

Certain ethnic, religious, and other groups were also more likely to vote Democrat than Whig. In the large and heterogeneous states of Pennsylvania and New York, for example, the ethnocultural make-up of a community may often have been more important than its economic character or geographical location in determining its primary political affiliation. The Scotch-Irish settlers of Pennsylvania and Ohio were early partisans of that Scotch-Irish hero, Andrew Jackson, and 'Pennsylvania Dutch' counties in both those states also regularly returned Democratic majorities. Irish Catholics almost everywhere appear to have been strongly Democratic, a fact which helped the party to maintain an ascendancy in such cities as New York and Buffalo, and most German communities, whether Catholic of Protestant, appear to have been Democratic too. Catholics of any national origin were generally Democrats, and it has been argued that the party also attracted more than its fair share of free-thinkers. It has also been suggested, particularly in relation to New York and Michigan, that communities with hedonistic (or at least 'anti-puritan') life styles, such as the hard-drinking, hard-fighting lumber towns, felt more at home in the permissive Democratic party. Finally, although it is difficult to establish that urban labourers were markedly more Democratic than Whig (unless they were Irish Catholics, which increasingly they were), the Workingmen's and other radical 'equal rights' groups that emerged in the larger cities seem at least ot have been closer to the Democracy than to its opponents and to have been more often absorbed by it. It was this connection, indeed, which gave the Democrats the popular nickname of 'locofocos', a term originally applied to an insurgent equal rights and anti-monopoly faction in New York City.

The Jacksonians had taken command of the federal government in the name of republican liberty but with only a primitive party organization and without any very coherent governmental philosophy. As the administration took up arms in the defence of the republic in the 1830s the Democratic party had taken shape around it, complete with a complex organization and a *raison d'être* of its own. As a national body, the Democratic party proved one of the most successful mechanisms for containing the host of popular and particularistic forces which had always pervaded the American system, in large part because it sought to draw strength from them. As party organization reached out across the Union, making its way into almost every town and hamlet, the party leaders became responsive to the demands of these local cadres. The Democrats' limited government and *laissez-faire* stance enabled a nation of diverse democrats to live together, each moving within his proper sphere and eschewing the aid of government.

   This image of an egalitarian society was one which had once borne some resemblance to reality, but the relatively undifferentiated social order of the colonial period had long since been destroyed by the stratification consequent upon economic growth. The Democrats were making equality a fundamental part of the American creed at a time when economic inequalities were becoming highly conspicuous. In a sense, perhaps, they made it possible for the republic to accept the growing concentration of wealth by substituting political equality for the old rough equality of economic condition. Political influence could be divorced from social status as the new mass party provided an alternative to government by notables. By grounding the government in the will of the majority, the Democratic party was simultaneously protecting the republic from the designs of ambitious men and rendering safe their pursuit of wealth.

   The Jacksonian Democrats also revived that Country and Old Republican political tradition which espied in the commercial nexus a potential threat to liberty, in turn transmitting to the later Populist generation an abiding suspicion of a corrupting association between the worlds of government and finance. They sought to quiet their unease about the growth of commercial enterprise by requiring it to conform to republican principles: businesses, like individuals, should possess no special powers or privileges in the republican polity. Governments could formulate the broad rules and regulations within which corporations – like public agencies themselves – might operate, but they should 'have as little as possible to do with the general business and interests of the people'.[20] If the federal government were to fulfil its duty of maintaining the Union within which individuals, states, and voluntary associations were free to go about their own business, it had to protect its own virtue by divorcing itself from all partial and special interests. The Democrats, in short, were pressing the old libertarian suspicions of power almost to the point of turning government into little more than a democratic bureaucracy for protecting popular rights and expressing the majority will. A degree of unity and energy was only brought to this system of politics by making the president the embodiment of the people.

Chapter 14

The Whig response

If the Democratic party was the most successful political creation of
the Jacksonian era, several important strands of American political
culture were nonetheless woven together in the Whig party. The
nature of the American electoral system, such as the rule by which
elections are won by a simple majority, has encouraged political
conflict in the United States to take the form of a two-party system,
and those interests and traditions which have not found satisfactory
expression in the dominant coalition have usually found an effective
alternative in an opposition capable of becoming the majority party.
This was the role of the Whig party in the second American party
system, a party which was in general slightly less popular than the
Democratic, was a receptacle for the many discontents that were
directed against Jacksonianism, and was on occasion able to win
national elections. In many ways the Whigs were the spokesmen for
the political culture that the Democrats seemed bent on destroying,
seeking to retain a directing role for government in the affairs of
society and regretting the passing of patrician leadership. But the
Whigs were also touched by the egalitarian currents of the day, and
they embraced the economic revolution more fervently than the
Democrats, seeing in it the forces of social progress. Like their rivals,
the Whigs were simultaneously seeking to remain true to the
revolutionary past while looking forward to the completion of the
republican mission.

One characteristic that the Whig party shared with the Democrats
was the rather slow defining of its identity. Like the Jacksonians, it
began life as an opposition party committed to little beyond saving the
republic by ousting the administration. Originating as a heterogeneous
coalition of dissident groups, too precarious to attempt to formulate a
very explicit set of policies, in course of doing battle with the
Democrats and eventually winning office themselves the Whigs came
to stand for a reasonably coherent cluster of values and doctrines. As
with their opponents too, the Whig coalition became less heterogeneous as repeated party conflict prompted some realignment of the
political ranks. Both Whigs and Democrats underwent subtle and
not-so-subtle changes in character in the first ten years of their
respective lives.

There were many who viewed the progress of the Jackson

administration with dismay and even with despair. If Jackson's most devoted admirers had seen him as a saviour of the republic, to others his actions seemed calculated to subvert the great American experiment in liberty. 'The republic is in a fearful condition, and nothing can save it from ruin, but the powerful cooperation of our ablest and best men', wrote an elitist friend of Henry Clay in the fall of 1831. 'The political condition of the country is as bad, as it can well be . . .', complained John C. Calhoun in March 1832, convinced that Jackson's use of federal patronage was rapidly reducing a nation of free men to servility. 'Nothing but a thorough reform can save us – and that cannot be long delayed, without utter ruin.' Jackson's triumphant re-election in 1832 deepened the sense of despair among his enemies, not just because they disliked Jackson, but also because they feared that the country might not survive his arrogant ways. 'What are we now to expect?' asked one. 'Will the people in their madness suffer the republic to go by the board?'[1] Many of Jackson's critics, of course, represented areas and interests which had been hurt by his policies, but there was more than self-interest in their opposition. There was too much that was novel about Jackson's style of government for it not to provoke deep anxiety. The idea of a party system had still not been generally accepted, and the Democrats' determined utilization of party devices seemed calculated to produce discord and eventually a new form of despotism. Most and perhaps all of Jackson's predecessors in office had been guided by some sort of corporate view of the republic, as were many of his critics, and even men like Calhoun who now eschewed any form of central direction conducted themselves according to some sort of systematic theory of government. By contrast, Jackson's apparently inconsistent but generally 'hands-off' policies seemed like the very abnegation of responsible government, while his placating of local interests and his appeals to the masses seemed like dangerous demagoguery. What helped to make possible the coalescing of the disparate opposition groups was the patriotic conviction that the country had to be saved from Democratic madness. As they came to see in Andrew Jackson the embodiment of all that was wrong with the republic, they moved together to arrest his reign of tyranny.

By about 1833 a richly variegated collection of enemies was arrayed against the Democratic administration. There were the National Republicans, the remnants of the old Adams-Clay coalition, demoralized after their defeat in the 1832 presidential election, and, lacking organizational strength and party discipline, beginning to wonder whether they had a future. Then there were the Antimasons, the party which had erupted in several northern states as a result of an evangelical campaign to extirpate the sinister monster of masonry. They had kept aloof from both the Democrats and the National Republicans during the 1832 presidential campaign (except in New York), when they ran their own candidate and carried the state of

Vermont. The Antimasons had little liking for Henry Clay, the titular National Republican leader and himself a mason, but the control of the federal government and of several northern state governments by the Democrats rendered many Antimasonic leaders receptive to overtures from other opposition groups. (It should be noted that the leaders did not always carry their followers with them; in Vermont and Massachusetts, for example, many Antimasonic voters seem eventually to have been absorbed by the Democrats.) In South Carolina and a few other southern states a small band of Nullifiers stood in bitter hatred of the president, flanked by a number of States Rights groups upset by Jackson's nationalistic Proclamation to South Carolina and by the force bill. In Congress and throughout the country too groups of Democrats left their party following Jackson's internal improvement and bank vetoes and his increasingly radical financial policies. Finally, many politicians still insisted that they were independent of any political grouping, though their antiparty values disposed men such as this to see little virtue in Jacksonianism. During his second term, then, Andrew Jackson was under assault from the old National Republicans, Antimasons, Nullifiers, States Rights men, ex-Democrats and self-proclaimed Independents, a shifting kaleidoscope of factional groups who seemed to share little but a common hostility to Andrew Jackson and all his works.

The electoral system itself, and in particular the winner-take-all feature of presidential elections, provided powerful incentives to these disparate groups to coalesce, for only a new majority party could oust the Democrats, but it was the Bank War which provided the occasion for the union of these groups and helped to give the new party an identity. Just as the crusade against the Money Power stamped the Democratic party with a particular character, so the Whigs too emerged from this traumatic experience with an identifiable cluster of beliefs, even though they felt it expedient not to be too explicit about them at election times. Jackson's high-handed actions in removing two Secretaries of the Treasury and in removing the deposits, the economic distress of 1834, the hard money policies of the Democratic administrations, and the severe depression following the Panic of 1837, all helped to give the Whig party a degree of rhetorical and philosophical coherence. Whig leaders seized on Jackson's actions during the Bank War as evidence of executive usurpation, a charge on which all opposition groups could agree, and they blamed the government's financial policies for the recurrent economic distress, hoping that the popular discontent would be translated into Whig votes at the polls. In its origins, then, the Whig party was an anti-Jackson coalition, which, like the anti-Adams coalition in 1827-28, hoped to ride to power by exposing the sins of the administration rather than by offering a positive programme of its own. This is not to say that the Whig strategy was wholly opportunistic; as with many Jacksonians earlier, some Whigs at least were convinced that the safety of the republican experiment imperatively demanded a change in government.

It was the recession of 1834 and the charge of executive usurpation in particular that the party managers seized on to weld the disparate opposition groups together. After Jackson had withdrawn the deposits the Bank of the United States had embarked on a policy of contraction, ostensibly to reduce its commitments now that its supply of funds had dwindled, but also to bring pressure to bear on Congress for recharter. As Biddle's deflationary policy took effect in 1834 unemployment rose. Henry Clay wrote gleefully to a friend in February that 'our city is full of distress committees. The more the better.'[2] Many did blame the recession on Jackson, and the New York historian-politician Jabez Hammond noted that it 'infused fresh spirit and vigor among the ranks of the opposition in the state and nation'.[3] The first test of the emergent party was the New York City elections of April 1834, when a group of Antimasons, National Republicans, and ex-Democrats assumed the name of Whig and ran a former Jacksonian for mayor. At national level too Henry Clay, Daniel Webster, and John C. Calhoun, despite their mutual distrust, cooperated in condemning the administration, pushing through the Senate two unprecedented censure resolutions attacking Jackson for improperly sacking a Secretary of the Treasury and removing the deposits. By the summer of 1834 the opposition coalition, both in Congress and in several states, was being labelled the Whig party.

The heterogeneous nature of this coalition, together with the unhappy history of American System measures at the polls, induced Whig leaders to avoid positive proposals and to concentrate on attacking the government. The success of the Democrats in using the bank issue to identify themselves as the people's party and their opponents as monied aristocrats persuaded men like Clay to play down measures they had once favoured. 'The Bank ought to be kept in the rear; the usurpation in the front', Clay told Biddle in 1834. 'If we take up the Bank, we play into the adversary's hands.'[4] Similarly, the political capital that Jackson had apparently made out of the Maysville Road Veto seemed to suggest that an internal improvements system would prove no more popular, while the Nullification crisis had obliged leading members of the opposition to abandon the protective tariff. By 1834 the opposition were left with no policy issues that they could safely embrace. John Quincy Adams complained that his own ambitious scheme for developing the nation's resources had been 'undisguisedly abandoned by H. Clay, ingloriously deserted by J.C. Calhoun, and silently given up by D. Webster'.[5]

The abandonment of the American System in favour of the pillorying of King Andrew may have been a necessary step in the emergence of the Whig party, but the building of a major party on a national scale took time. Even in 1836 the party had not crystallized sufficiently to allow the Whigs to hold a national convention. In

Pennsylvania the Antimasonic party still maintained a nominal independence, and in the South the large numbers of former Democrats who had broken with their party had not yet been fully absorbed into the Whig party. In Georgia, for example, the anti-Democratic States Rights party did not adopt the name Whig until 1843. In the absence of a national convention, different presidential candidates were run in different parts of the country, and state parties rallied behind the candidate they thought would serve their local interests best. 'Mr. Van Buren's election being a foregone conclusion', Thurlow Weed later recalled, 'the Whigs conducted the presidential canvass with a view to stregthening their State and congressional organizations.'[6]

Then the Panic of 1837 came to their aid. The Van Buren administration, reluctant to depart from its limited government principles, offered no solution to the depression beyond the questionable device of the Independent Treasury, and the renewed recession of 1839 further demonstrated Democratic helplessness in the face of widespread economic distress. Further, of course, the Whigs were gleefully able to attribute the depression to the Democrats' bizarre financial experiments. The party quarrels in the national and state legislatures over economic issues promoted a sense of unity among the Whigs, as did some redrawing of the party lines. Calhoun and a number of States Rights men returned to the Democratic ranks in 1837, while a number of conservative Democrats sympathetic to business swung over to the Whigs. By the late 1830s, too, the Whigs had established party organizations in most states, even in the South, where commercial interests disliked Democratic policies as much as northern businessmen. They had become a national party and were successfully submerging sectional differences under the ritual of party combat. The first national convention met in December 1839 and gave the presidential nomination to William Henry Harrison, an elderly general who had claimed victories over the Indians and the British before and during the War of 1812, one of which had earned him the popular title of 'Old Tippecanoe'. When the convention nominated John Tyler of Virginia as his running-mate, the Whigs were able to swoop into the presidential campaign of 1840 with the war cry 'Tippecanoe and Tyler Too'.

Victory in 1840 was perhaps vital to the Whigs if they were to survive. Beneath the razzamattaz of the Whig campaign was an air of desperation, a sense that 1840 was a make-or-break year. Through the 1830s the Whigs had mercilessly lacerated the Democrats for using party organization and the spoils system to maintain themselves in government, and some at least had persuaded themselves that free elections were becoming a fiction and that the republic was falling victim to a corrupt, monolithic, and all-powerful party machine. Daniel Webster wrote to a friend that if the Democratic administration was not defeated this year, 'it will be useless to renew the attempt hereafter'. A Michigan Whig described 1840 as 'the last peaceable contest we shall have' if the Democrats were re-elected, for then the Whigs must 'either submit to the tyrant contemptible and vile as he is, or resort to a mode of redress in which implements of a very different character from the ballot box will be wanted . . .'.[7] It is scarcely likely that the Whigs really would have taken up arms had they lost again, but the party may well have dissolved, desolated by this last compelling proof that the American experiment in liberty had finally been suffocated by the Democratic incubus.

Whigs throughout the country turned to Harrison as to a saviour. An *'injured* and *oppressed* PEOPLE have called this modern CINCIN-NATUS from his plough', it was said, 'to redeem their country from the *deep degradation* brought upon it by their *corrupt* and *profligate* rulers.'[8] The messiah-like nature of Harrison's candidacy was emphasized by an extraordinary campaign which owed something to the religious revivals which had swept through the northern states in the 1830s. In the Middle Atlantic states and in the Midwest in particular there seemed to be certain affinities between Whiggery and evangelical Protestantism, and it was in these areas that the great mass meetings first appeared, very like the camp revivals in character, being held in the open air, often lasting some days, with a series of orators generating an intense excitement as they foretold the advent of the Whig millenium. The Whigs, who had been identified by the Democrats as monied aristocrats, now dressed themselves in the' homespun of the common man and offered the 'Farmer of North Bend' as the people's candidate. It was Van Buren who was the real aristocrat, they insisted, as they spun false tales about the president's fondness for champagne, French perfume, and gold spoons, doing to him what the Jacksonians had done to Adams in 1828. The Democrats were unimpressed by the 'Old Granny', as they contemptuously dismissed Harrison, one editor suggesting that he would be better pensioned off to his log cabin with a barrel of hard cider to comfort him. The gibe, however, misfired, for Whig editors were quick to perceive the demotic imagery of the log cabin and hard cider, claiming that the simple old soldier did indeed live in a log cabin like any other unassuming frontiersman. In fact Harrison sprang from a distinguished Virginia family and his grandfather had been a signatory to the Declaration of Independence, but the day of the patrician candidate was now past. The Whigs now embraced the common man with uninhibited fervour. Tippecanoe clubs and log cabins appeared across the country, and barrels of cider were rolled out to delight Whig meetings. 'The Federal gentry', snorted a Democratic editor, ' . . . are making *Whiggery* synonymous with *Swiggery*.'[9]

Aided immeasurably by the economic depression, which it was all too easy to relate to twelve years of Democratic misrule, and sustained by their newly-created style of folk evangelism, the Whigs swept their saviour into the White House. The election of 1840 represented the full maturation of the second American party system, for it showed that the Whigs could now compete with the Democrats in almost every state in the Union. But although now a national party, the Whigs were still not formally committed to a programme, for the national convention had only adopted a candidate and not a platform. Like the Jacksonians in 1828, they were the beneficiaries of a popular crusade to wrest office from the evildoers in government, but once that goal was accomplished they had to face up to the responsibilities of government themselves.

The Whig saviour took his duties seriously, opening his administration by delivering the longest inaugural address ever in American history. His second historic entry in the record books followed a swift month later, when he died after having served the shortest presidential term ever. The death of Harrison elevated John Tyler to the White House, a former Democrat who had broken with Jackson because of his high-handed ways and who had never really fully embraced Whig ideology, except those aspects of it which were hostile to party forms and a strong executive. But perhaps Tyler's views did not matter, for the Whigs had long been arguing that the affairs of the country should be directed by Congress rather than by the president, and Harrison in his meandering Inaugural had promised not to interfere in the affairs of Congress. Certainly Henry Clay believed that Congress should lead and that he should lead Congress. Clay was clearly the party's most outstanding member, and given the doctrine of legislative supremacy it was logical from his point of view to regard himself as a sort of prime minister. He would mastermind the legislative programme in Congress and the president would dutifully sign the bills so passed like a constitutional monarch. Clay certainly tried to act like a prime minister. He made himself chairman of the Senate's committee on finance, and his friends moved into other important committee posts as well as the speakership of the House. Almost as soon as Congress met Clay unveiled his programme to it and it was a highly partisan one. The Democrats' Independent Treasury was to be dismantled and a new national bank established; the tariff was to be increased; the revenue from the sale of public lands was to be distributed to the states. Just as Jackson had once given his party an identity by his assaults on the Bank, so Clay was finally committing his party to a coherent set of policies. Finally, Clay hoped, his long-propounded American System would be enacted into law.

Clay energetically set about pushing his programme through Congress, so energetically indeed that he was now accused of being a dictator, but he had reckoned without the president. Tyler had always had states rights scruples about the constitutionality of a national bank and had supported Jackson's veto in 1832, and Clay's imperious manner did nothing to make the new bank bill more palatable. Tyler vetoed two bank bills that Clay had prepared, thus causing an irrevocable break with the Whig party. After his second veto his entire cabinet resigned, with the exception of Secretary of State Daniel Webster. Clay now read the president out of the Whig party, but he could not read him out of the White House and the Whigs in Congress once more found themselves in an all-too-familiar position – glowering in frustrated opposition. But there was now a difference. They were now tied to a programme, and in 1844, when Henry Clay was nominated for president, the national convention was at last bold enough to adopt a platform. The platform was admittedly short and somewhat ambiguous, but it called for 'a well-regulated currency', a tariff, distribution of the proceeds of public land sales, and one term for the president.[10] After ten years of existence the Whigs were prepared to say what they stood for. Both parties were now facing up to the implications of democracy, recognizing that the people had a right to choose the policies the federal government was to pursue, as far as was practicable. In theory, at any rate, election campaigns should be about measures and not men – the people, not the leaders, should rule.

But, of course, the Whigs had long been associated with a particular cluster of ideas and values. Like that of their opponents, the Whig persuasion subtly intertwined both conservative and progressivist impulses. Their world view combined an essentially conservative conception of the political order with a dynamic conception of the economic order, together with a conception of the moral order which was informed by evangelical Protestantism. Yet however fervently they embraced the economic revolution that was transforming America, the Whigs probably remained closer to the eighteenth century than did the Democrats in their conception of the good society. Many Whigs still nourished an organic conception of the political world and never quite shook off the idea of the hierarchical distribution of political authority. Henry Clay, who was often described as 'the embodiment of Whig principles', insisted that we 'are all – people, States, Union, banks – bound up and interwoven together, united in fortune and destiny, and all, all entitled to the protecting care of a paternal government'.[11] Political harmony, this seemed to imply, could be achieved if the affairs of government were left to an enlightened elite. 'We are in danger of forgetting that *society is a system*,' wrote one literary Whig, 'a system where all the parts have their proper function and office – and not a mere mass of elements placed in juxtaposition or jostled into a general average.'[12] The Whigs rejected the atomistic view of society towards which Democratic theorists leaned.

To maintain that society was a system was to imply the need for direction, and direction from above. According to one Democratic critic, the Whigs doubted the ability of the common people to manage the government and 'cast around for *great men* to sustain its function and regulate its principles', men of talent who were unhampered by 'the instructions of their constituents'.[13] That the Whigs did yearn for a tranquil political order in which responsible statesmen gravely pursued the public interest was revealed in their suspicion of party forms. Of course, they were obliged to resort to party organization themselves in order to protect the republic from the self-interested depredations of the unprincipled Democrats, but their construction of party machinery was slow and erratic in part because many of them found such devices distasteful. Their nostalgia for a political culture in which enlightened statesmen handed down political decisions from on high was also revealed in their attempts to resurrect the English Whig-Jeffersonian Republican conception of parliamentary government. One conse-quence of party discipline and the partisan use of spoils, they pointed out, was an improper growth in executive power, and they evolved a sophisticated critique of executive usurpation. A Whig convention in Kentucky in 1842 'Resolved, That the Executive power has increased, is increasing, and that it ought to be circumscribed . . . '.[14] As this phraseology suggests, with its echo of Dunning's famous resolution against George III in 1780, the Whig charge of executive usurpation was laden with meanings from the past. In the eighteenth century the English radicals had charged that the balanced constitution of 1688 was being subverted by an overweening executive, and the American revolutionaries in turn had solemnly listed the usurpations of George III in the Declaration of Independence. A fundamental lesson of Anglo-American history seemed to be that a primary threat to liberty lay in an overactive executive, and the Whigs feared that Jackson and his Democratic successors were similarly acquiring despotic powers. Like the English radicals and the Jeffersonian Republicans, the Whigs came to emphasize the primacy of the legislative branch in any system of government which was designed to preserve liberty, and, like earlier patricians too, they may have detected in a parliamentary system safeguards against popular tyranny. As presidential elections became plebiscitary in form and as the president was pressed into the role of popular tribune, the Whigs perceived in Congress an arena in which representative government could still function, in which the agents of the people could still deliberate and hand down decisions on the people's behalf.

But if the Whigs' concept of the polity owed something to the eighteenth century, in their social and economic views they looked forward to the new America of the city and the factory. Further, they believed that government had a vital role to play in bringing about this desirable state. A positive economic programme would promote a prosperity which would be 'general and diffusive', explained Daniel Webster, 'reacting to all classes, embracing all interests, and benefit-ing, not a part of a society, but the 'whole'. But the Whig vision went beyond even this, for economic wealth would make possible a higher civilization. 'Growth and prosperity would breed enlightenment:' argued Horace Greeley as paraphrased by his biographer, 'enlighten-ment would bring conscience, and conscience a new sense of mutuality.'[15] If the Democratic solution to the conflicting demands of the American electorate was to do as little as possible, the Whig reaction was to remove them by bringing about an economic order which rested on mutual dependence. But the Whigs were not exactly latter-day Hamiltonians, for there was a strong egalitarian streak in their rhetoric. Economic progress served not only to increase property but also to equalize it, or so they claimed, scattering it among the many. Further, an economy of equal opportunities implied a highly mobile society. 'No man in America is contented to be poor, or expects to continue so', observed the *American Review*, perceptively but uncharacteristically adding that rising status had its anxieties.[16] In contrast to the fettered serfs of Europe, the free American labourer was welcome to climb as high as his industry and talents permitted him.

The Whigs' corporatist view of society also encouraged them to look favourably on government action in social and moral matters. A responsible government could be expected to promote the well-being of society in all its aspects. Many northern Whigs, particularly those of Yankee stock, had been touched by the evangelical revivals of the era, and even those who embraced less demonstrative forms of Protestant pietism often felt it their duty to serve as their brothers' keepers. In part, this can be seen as a conservative impulse, for in enjoining such virtues as piety, sobriety, and industry on their fellow-men they were looking to the orderly functioning of society. The *American Review* held that 'forms of government are instituted for the protection and fostering of virtue . . . '.[17] Whig politicians were somewhat more likely than Democrat to support proposals for education or prison reform, and certainly Whig legislatures in several northern states showed some sympathy to temperance proposals to limit or prohibit sales of liquor. But if the evangelical spirit moved some men to call for laws to regulate behaviour, it carried others to genuinely perfectionist and egalitarian conclusion. To the Whig educationist Horace Mann, universal education enabled the poorer classes to liberate themselves from the control of the rich, and was, indeed, 'beyond all other devices of human origin, . . . the great equalizer of the conditions of men'.[18] Whigs were also more sensitive than Democrats to demands to take action against slavery and to protect Indians. 'The Whigs, as their name imports, are, or ought to be, the party of freedom', insisted Charles Sumner, as he called on his fellows in Massachusetts to avow their hostility to the monstrous evil of slavery.[19] But the perfectionist streak in Whiggery was also a source of political weakness, for those touched by it were liable to defect to more radical parties when their demands were stifled by the accommodationist strategies of pragmatic party managers. The Liberty party, a small party dedicated to the abolition of slavery, picked up some critical Whig votes in the close-run presidential election of 1844. The 'Conscience' Whigs of the North were less than enthusiastic about their alliance with the 'Cotton' Whigs of the South.

The Whigs, then, tended to see government as a sort of benevolent steward rather than a disinterested umpire. Their anachronistic quest for statesmen who were above party, their optimistic vision of a prosperous, commercial America presided over by an energetic government, and their willingness to act as their brothers' moral keepers, all implied a system of politics in which order was imposed from above. To them social order did not come naturally, as some Democrats were bold enough to argue. 'Public order is the first instinct of the Whig party', said William H. Seward. 'They have never sacrificed order or written law, whether organic or temporary, to expediency.'[20] From this perspective, the 'hands-off' governmental attitude of the Democrats could at best be interpreted as criminal irresponsibility.

The Whigs have traditionally been depicted as the party of the businessman, although it has almost equally often been remarked that there were not enough businessmen to give the Whigs all the votes they won. Like the Democratic party, the Whig party was necessarily heterogeneous and coalitional, yet the traditional stereotype was not without some justification. In New England the great Whig stronghold was Massachusetts, one of the most commercialized, industrialized and urbanized of states, well-served by a sound banking system concentrated on Boston. In particular, the Whigs could usually count on the support of all classes in Boston (though not all ethnic groups, the Irish preferring the Democrats), and were strong in the commercialized eastern counties. In Democratic New Hampshire, too, Whig support tended to come from the larger manufacturing towns and the more prosperous farming regions. At the other end of the country, Kentucky was the most consistent Whig state, in part because of the commanding influence of Henry Clay, though Tennessee also became Whig when Jackson left the presidency. Both states had developed commercial agricultural economies, and in Tennessee at least the Whigs appear to have found most favour in the commercial cities and along transportation routes. Further south, in Mississippi, the wealthier counties were more likely to be Whig than Democratic, particularly the Delta region of rich soils and large plantations, as were the state's two largest cities, and in Alabama also it was the well-developed economic communities that tended to be Whig. In the Northwest Ohio was the most Whiggish state in the region, as it was also the most sophisticated economically, the Whigs tending to do particularly well in the wealthiest constituencies, in the Yankee-settled Western Reserve, in the thriving corn and cattle-raising counties, and in mining areas. And elsewhere too, including Pennsylvania, Virginia, Georgia, Missouri, and Florida, there is scattered evidence to suggest that cities, better-established communities, commercial regions, and economically diverse areas were often – though not always – more receptive to Whiggery than to Democracy. When Whig orators spoke confidently of a prosperous economic future, they were articulating the aspirations of many of their constituents.

But Whig support was by no means confined to commercially minded farmers, planters and city-dwellers. In several northern states in particular, religious, ethnic, and cultural compulsions could lead men into Whiggery. Much of western New York, north-eastern Ohio and Michigan had been settled by Yankees, who were quick to establish churches, schools, and order, and who tended to vote Whig. The fashionable Unitarians in the vicinity of Boston and the prosperous Congregational communities of New Hampshire gave much heartier support to the Whigs than to the Democrats. The more evangelical varieties of Protestanism often leaned towards the Whigs, particularly those of Yankee heritage. In Michigan, for example, Yankee Presbyterians were strongly Whig and helped to impart an evangelical character to their party. Free blacks, where they were allowed to vote at all, voted overwhelmingly for the Whigs, and in New York and probably elsewhere the more 'Anglo-Saxon' of recent immigrants, notably the English, Scots, and Welsh, were also normally counted in the Whig camp. Protestant Irish immigrants, as might be predicted, embraced the Whig party almost as heartily as the Catholic Irish embraced the Democrats. The Whig party, then, was not a party of the native-born, though since the Democrats' immigrant groups were much the larger, and since American-born Protestants were somewhat more likely to be Whig than Democratic, the Whigs were the more likely to have connections with nativist groups. (Nativists were those who were hostile to foreign immigrants, especially Catholic immigrants.) Finally, there was one *class* which may have voted Whig. The very rich men of Boston, New York, and Detroit, at any rate, showed a marked preference for the Whig party (though perhaps for ethnocultural as well as socioeconomic reasons), even if their social inferiors felt no strong inclination to cast their votes along class lines.

The Whigs had taken shape as a party slowly and uncertainly. Even more than the Democrats, the Whigs had begun life as a coalition of leading men, at both state and national levels, originally committed to little beyond ousting the administration. In large part what had thrown these men together was outrage at Andrew Jackson's style of politics. By using the apparatus of party to mobilize popular support, and by appointing himself as the tribune of the people, Jackson was ushering in a voter-oriented system of politics, one which seemed rapidly to be becoming a kind of plebiscitary democracy. By this time most American conservatives had accepted the inevitability of universal suffrage (for white men) and other democratic principles, but they were loathe to surrender a system of politics in which talented men resolved the issues of the day. From their perspective, Jackson's innovations seriously endangered the republican polity, and they united in heartfelt opposition to executive usurpation. In so doing they were able to draw on eighteenth-century critiques of ministerial tyranny and corruption, showing how liberty could be extirpated by a power-hungry and patronage-laden executive. But as they exploited fears inherited from the past, the Whigs also sought to harness Americans' hopes for a more prosperous and happier future, aligning themselves with the forces of commercial change. In the expansive economy of the mid-nineteenth century, they could hope to recruit the support of ambitious and public-spirited citizens throughout the Union.

But if the Whigs adapted successfully to the emerging socioeconomic order, their adaption to the highly egalitarian and individualistic political environment of Jacksonian America was less than wholly successful. They remained the proponents of order in a society which was casting off restraints (other than those protecting equal rights), whether that order was imposed by a social if self-made elite, a paternal government, an integrated economy, or a public code of morality. This stance exposed the Whigs to the charge of being aristocrats, of wishing to establish a political system in which a governing elite handed down laws for the good of the people rather than at the behest of the people. It was also an uncomfortable stance, for in order to win power the Whigs were obliged to adopt the same organizational and campaign techniques as the Democrats, which exposed them to the charge of hypocrisy. Nonetheless the Whigs too in time emerged as a mass political party, an administrative device for channelling the disparate demands of a host of interest groups upwards to the seat of government. As they did so they came to reinforce the new political order.

Chapter 15

The disruption of
the second party system

The second American party system reached its apogee in the early 1840s. In the presidential election of 1840 the Whigs and Democrats slogged it out with one another in almost every state of the Union, achieving a parity throughout the country unsurpassed in American history. It was by now quite clear too that the two parties gave expression to contrasting political persuasions. The Whigs of 1840 may not have been formally committed to any platform, and the hullabaloo with which they dowsed their candidates deflected attention away from issues, but their past battles with the Democrats and speakers like Clay and Webster made it clear enough what they stood for. Then over the next two or three years the parties confronted one another in Congress, not to mention the state legislatures, over such issues as money and banking, the tariff, the distribution of land revenue, and internal improvements. The fact that for most of this time the White House was occupied by a man who had broken with his party, and whose protracted duel with Clay was so dramatic, has tended to disguise the more important fact that this was the high tide of the second party system, when the major parties each had national constituencies, were clearly divided on ideology and issues, and when partisan cohesion was very high.

But the triumph of this particular party system was short-lived. Within a few years both the major parties were being riven by deadly strains. If sectional and popular pressures had been used to help build up the second party system, they also contributed to its destruction. For a while it looked as if it might be the Democratic party which crumbled, but in the event it was the Whig party which was to be torn apart by the forces of sectionalism and nativism in the 1850s. As ever, there was an ideological dimension to the events which helped to bring about this disturbed situation. Some Americans had come to believe that the next logical step in the nation's historic mission was to extend the blessings of their unique democracy across the globe. In a sense, expansionism represented the high tide of democratic reform, though it also proved highly disruptive to the polity. Other Americans were fearful that their great experiment in republican government would be undone by the admission of aliens incapable of respecting the principles of freedom. Nativism, like expansionism, was in its way a form of patriotism and it too proved disruptive. The major parties had each originated as coalitions of factional chieftains, but as they were transformed into mass parties with organizations reaching into every locality, they perhaps became more vulnerable to grassroots pressures. The professional politicians who had politicized and mobilized the mass electorate found that their control was precarious in the extreme.

In some measure, as we have seen, the creation of the second American party system can be viewed as a response to the local and sectional pressures which perenially threatened the American Union. When Van Buren, John C. Calhoun, and others had moved to fashion a national party coalition in the 1820s, sectionalism had seemed the most serious menace. By 1840 sectional issues seemed to have been quieted. 'Sectional jealousies, and geographical distinctions are forgotten', proclaimed the *Log Cabin Patriot* in August of that year, while stressing nonetheless the vulnerability of American institutions. 'A deep sense of impending danger rests upon all', insisted the editor, locating the issue in 'Rational Liberty protected by Law', or 'Licentiousness with all its attendant vices . . . '.[1] The voters were being invited to choose between Whig order and Democratic permissiveness. It was almost as if the party system had saved the Union by creating new issues for politicians to do combat over. Party leaders seemed to sense that slavery in particular was too hazardous a topic for political debate; instead, they provided themselves and their followers with emotive issues like executive usurpation and the Money Power, issues which enabled men to fight fiercely for their vision of the American republic without sundering the Union. This is not to suggest that these party battles were empty or cynical affairs. Unquestionably both leaders and followers were energized by their particular party creeds. Yet somehow, perhaps both consciously and unconsciously, they had created a political culture in which they could battle passionately yet safely for the destiny of the republic.

The success of the party system depended on the extent to which it contained divisive issues, which in a sense were always local issues. The South Carolinians who fought bitterly in Congress against the protective tariff early in the Jacksonian era, and the Bostonians and Philadelphians who later deserted the major parties to rally behind nativist organizations, were all responding to particularistic pressures. The preservation of the party system depended on containing these potentially anarchic forces, on conciliation, on compromise, on avoiding disruptive issues – and on finding other causes to war over. And in the early 1840s the national parties succeeded briefly in doing all these things.

In a sense what finally brought down the second American party system was a series of folk movements. The imposing edifice of party was to be undermined by the trickles of sand beneath its foundations. One important movement was of American citizens themselves, as they pressed into the Southwest and Far West in search of land, riches, and opportunity, subtly changing the balance between the sections and precipitating a series of events which unleashed the ferocious passions of sectionalism. Another important set of folk migrations was of European immigrants into the northern states. As Irish and German Catholics in particular crowded into the cities, many native Protestants felt threatened by these alien hordes and new tensions began to eat into the party coalitions that the politicians had so painfully constructed. If the migrations both across the continent and to it from Europe were of ordinary people, so too were the sectional and nativist emotions that were aroused. That American democracy had left the deferential world of Anglo-American politics far behind became clear when the second American party system was pulled apart by the resentments, fears, ideals, and ambitions of the people.

Martin Van Buren had long recognized that the strength of the Democratic party, and indeed of the party system as a whole, depended on its ability to contain sectional issues. He also seemed to perceive that the nation's expansion westwards contained grave dangers for the American polity, for expansionism could all too readily ignite sectional jealousies. It had after all been the Missouri Crisis which in a sense had ushered in the style of politics associated with the Jacksonian era, with its emphasis on sectional compromise, and although a formula had been found for the admission of new states carved out of the Louisiana Purchase, any attempt to add further territory to the American Union would imperil the balance between free and slave states and risk a new and ruinous confrontation. But in the 1840s Van Buren and his cautious contemporaries were losing control of the Democratic party. A younger generation of politicos, impatient with the increasingly anachronistic crusade against the Money Power, were looking for a new cause with which to identify the Democracy and they found it in expansionism. There was some logic in the Democrats' decision to make Manifest Destiny their mission, but ultimately it served to disrupt their party by reviving the deep-seated fears of the evil of slavery.

The actions of the politicians followed the movements of the people. Americans had been moving into the wilderness for years, of course, but increasing numbers of them were not confining themselves to undisputed American territory. In the Southwest Americans had long been invading the spacious and empty plains of Texas and some were making their intrepid way to distant California, though both these areas were under Mexican jurisdiction. In the Northwest restless and ambitious Americans had been beckoned by the furs and fertile lands of Oregon, to which both Britain and the United States laid claim. The hard times following 1837 persuaded many struggling Mississippi Valley farmers that there were greener pastures over the western horizon.

By 1836 there were over 30,000 Americans in Texas, and in that year they threw off Mexican restrictions and declared their independence. The Texan war of independence was brief and bloody and took the lives of such celebrated frontiersmen as Davy Crockett and Jim Bowie, but the Texans succeeded in wrenching themselves away from the faltering Mexican government. The United States would have bought Texas if Mexico had been willing to sell, but the Mexicans refused even recognition of Texan independence. Presidents Jackson and Van Buren moved cautiously, realizing that an annexation of Texas might mean war with Mexico and would be resisted by northern antislavery men, for the American settlers had planted cotton and raised slaves in their new land. For several years Texas thus remained independent as the Lone Star republic. But the expansionist forces could not be held back indefinitely. By the mid-1840s Americans were casting speculative glances at both Texas and Oregon and were arguing that they should be brought fully into the American republic. In part this expansionism was a product of a popular conviction in the superiority of America's democratic institutions that successive election campaigns had fostered. Democracy, said the Jacksonians' *Globe*, had brought 'this country to a place in the family of nations, which is the envy and admiration of the world'.[2] It was but a short step to the logical conclusion that the sum of human felicity would be enlarged with each advance of the American frontier. This, at any rate, was the message of Manifest Destiny, which held quite simply that God had specially reserved the whole of the North American continent – and perhaps beyond – for the great political experiment that the United States was conducting. 'We are the nation of human progress', trumpeted John L. O'Sullivan, 'and who will, what can, set limits to our onward march?'[3]

Reinforcing the messianic emotions of Manifest Destiny were considerations of a more tough-minded nature. Territorial aggrandizement promised economic gains: cotton was the nation's largest export and yet more of it could be grown in Texas; the fur trade of Oregon was lucrative and the valleys fertile; more territory would mean a larger domestic market for American manufacturers; the superb natural harbours at San Francisco, San Diego, and in the Puget Sound offered the hope of trade expansion with China and India. And there were certainly sectional motives behind expansionism. Many southerners were becoming pathologically sensitive about the South's role in the country, for the population of the free states was growing fast and attacks on slavery were mounting. Calhoun for one wanted Texas in order to increase the weight of the slave South in the American Union. Southerners also feared that an independent Texas might abolish slavery under British pressure, so that free land would menace the South to the west as well as to the north. Conversely, southerners were not enthusiastic about acquiring Oregon, for that would only augment the free states. For their part, the inhabitants of the Northwest, what is today the Midwest, saw some advantages for their section in American advancement to the Pacific. With the peopling and development of the Far West, cities like Chicago would become important communications and commercial centres.

Considerations of American security also weighed with those who were seeking to formulate policy. They perceived signs that the European powers, particularly Britain, were seeking to establish their influence in neighbouring territories. British and French activities in Texas and Mexico and the British presence in Oregon seemed to presage a further expansion of European influence in the New World. Britain indeed seemed to be pressing in on the United States on all sides, with her presence in Canada and her navy on the Atlantic. The American republic, it was suggested, was being menaced by the jealous monarchies of Europe, who had become alarmed at her rapid and auspicious growth. In this context, the annexation of Texas and Oregon could be defended as a pre-emptive move in the interests of American security.

Yet the economic, sectional, and security considerations which bore on American politicians do not wholly explain Manifest Destiny. As in so much of early American political history, ideology and rhetoric played a persuasive part. Economic interests varied, and in any case the development of the territories in question under any jurisdiction would have brought economic opportunities for Americans. The Whig party itself, the most reliable political vehicle of the commercial interests, was cool towards expansion. Sectional influences were important, but many slaveholders in fact opposed the annexation of Texas, fearing the confrontation it might bring with the North. And the fears over security were largely imaginary, much of the Anglophobic bombast serving as a smokescreen for America's own ambitions. What immeasurably strengthened and certainly legitimized expansionism was a set of emotions and beliefs concerning the nation's historic purpose in the world. A sense of mission had been inherited from the Puritans, and in the revolutionary era Americans had secularized it and offered the United States to the world as a model of how men could live together in liberty. It was America's unique destiny, Andrew Jackson advised his countrymen as he left the White House in 1837, to act as the guardian of freedom and 'to preserve it for the benefit of the human race'.[4]

There was, of course, nothing very novel about the Americans' pride in their free institutions. As the English traveller E.S. Adby observed in 1834, it was no wonder that Americans believed they were 'the greatest people under the canopy of heaven', for they were so often told it in 'fourth of July orations, in sermons, and speeches, and reviews, and magazines, and newspapers, and prefaces to literary works . . . '.[5] But by the 1840s an evangelical spirit was energizing the American sense of mission. No longer was it thought enough to set a benign example to the world; now the world had to be converted by positive action. A number of influences had contributed to this more aggressive stance. One perhaps was the so-called Second Awakening itself, the series of religious revivals which had scorched the land in the 1820s and 1830s and had helped to create a sense that the millenium was at hand. Another was the exuberant celebration of democracy which the incessant election campaigns had generated, a secular version of the evangelical revival which contained an imperative to carry to others the inestimable blessings of freedom. Manifest Destiny also offered to Democrats in particular a new cause to justify their existence. The Monster Bank had long been slain and Democrats needed a new crusade to which to summon the people. Since their conception of American progress held little room for economic development, the alternative was to carry the American mission across space. They could fulfil their duty to carry forward the great experiment in republican government by extending it across the continent. At any rate, the American mission to promote liberty had taken on a proselytizing edge by the 1840s, and Democrats proved far more vulnerable to this impulse than Whigs.

What pointed up the identification of expansion with the American commitment to free government was the alleged involvement of European powers in Texas and Mexico. The designing presence of Britain and France raised once more the spectre of monarchism in the New World. The American continent, perhaps, was about to witness its last great confrontation between monarchy and republicanism, between despotism and freedom, between the American creed and the detested doctrines of Europe. Even earlier the war between Mexico and Texas in 1836 had been depicted as 'a war of barbarism against civilization, of despotism against liberty, of Mexicans against Americans'.[6] Now Americans were more convinced than ever that only the United States possessed the key to freedom. If other peoples had not followed the American example after all these years, it began to be reasoned, it must be because they lacked the capacity to do so. It became even more incumbent on the United States to replace tyranny and misery with freedom and happiness in neighbouring territories and to banish forever the evil influence of Europe from the American continent. 'One thing is very certain', argued one Democratic orator, 'that as you extend the empire of the Anglo-Saxon race, particularly that portion of it which has been bred under the benign auspices of American freedom, you extend the principles of civil liberty, you free the oppressed from bondage and secure to them the blessings of "life, liberty and the pursuit of happiness".'[7] Manifest Destiny was the extension of the American Revolution across space.

But many Americans opposed an impetuous annexation of Texas or a confrontation with Britain over Oregon. Whigs throughout the Union were generally unenthusiastic about the implications of Manifest Destiny and northerners of all persuasions were worried that the acquisition of Texas would enlarge the slave South and revive sectional issues. Not least among the opponents of annexation was Martin Van Buren, the leader of the Democratic party and its probable

candidate in the 1844 election. At least he seemed the probable
candidate early in 1844, but elements in his party were now beginning
to chafe under the prolonged Jackson-Van Buren hegemony. Van
Buren had led the party to its first ever national defeat in 1840, and his
limited government-hard money brand of politics no longer seemed
very relevant to many southern and western politicos who were
becoming infected with the expansionist ambitions of their constituents. But Van Buren was determined to maintain the political
strategy of the 1820s, which called for the containment and avoidance
of sectional issues, and in April 1844 he published a letter arguing that
annexation was unwise at that time because it would bring about war
with Mexico. On the same day the Whig leader Henry Clay published a
similar statement, and it may be that those two old advocates of
sectional compromise and conciliation had conspired together to
remove the dangerous issue of Texas from the campaign. If so their
tactic failed, for Van Buren's letter precipitated a rebellion against him
within the party ranks. In May the Virginia Democrats deserted Van
Buren, thus severing the New York-Virginia alliance around which the
Democratic party had been organized since the 1820s, and other
southern and western Democrats speedily followed. The Democratic
national convention found itself impossibly deadlocked between Van
Buren and Lewis Cass, a portly western expansionist, and the
nomination eventually went to an obscure but able party regular from
Tennessee, James K. Polk. As an expansionist Polk was acceptable to
western and southern Democrats, as a hard money man he was
acceptable to the Van Burenites, and as a protégé of Old Hickory
himself he was an authentic Jacksonian.

Meanwhile the role of the slave South in expansionism was being
ruthlessly spelled out by John C. Calhoun. An embattled President
Tyler had determined to attempt to restore his foundering political
fortunes by embracing the mounting annexationist cause, and he
appointed Calhoun as Secretary of State to try to speed the entry of
Texas to the Union. In May 1844 Calhoun wrote to the British minister
in Washington, and hence to the world, that the American government
had decided to annex Texas in order to prevent the British from
securing the abolition of slavery there, for that would 'place in the
power of Great Britain the most efficient means of effecting in the
neighboring States of this Union what she avows to be her desire to do
in all countries where slavery exists'.[8] He then proceeded to extol the
virtues of slavery. This extraordinary and very explicit linking of the
annexationist cause with slavery by one of the highest officers in the
government served to confirm the uneasy suspicions of many
northerners. In part because of Calhoun's letter and the public
reaction to it the Senate frustrated the Tyler-Calhoun bid to annex
Texas in 1844, but the fateful day was not long delayed. The
Democrats, swinging into line behind Polk on the platform 'the
reoccupation of Oregon and the re-annexation of Texas', narrowly

won the presidential election. In December 1845 Texas became the twenty-eighth state in the Union.

But, as the elder statesmen had warned, annexation did mean war with Mexico. Polk asked Congress for $2 million to buy Mexican territory, which American troops rapidly conquered. It early became clear that the United States would emerge from the war with considerably more than Texas, and indeed the eventual peace treaty awarded her a vast new empire in the Southwest. Northern politicians grew increasingly unhappy at these signs of an expanded South and in August 1846 the Pennsylvania Democrat, David Wilmot, raised the pertinent question in Congress – would slavery be allowed in these new lands? He thought it should not be and introduced his famous Proviso to debar it. He reaffirmed his commitment to support slavery in the South, but reminded Congress that 'the issue now presented is not whether slavery shall exist unmolested where it now is, but whether it shall be carried to new and distant regions, now free, where the footprint of a slave cannot be found.'[9] Calhoun, now in the Senate, ferociously counter-attacked for the South, submitting a series of resolutions which argued that Congress had no power to bar slavery from any territory. Both Wilmot's and Calhoun's proposals were unacceptable to Congress, but they became the rallying points for radicals in both sections. The dread issue of slavery had finally burst to the forefront of American politics. 'It is apparent, that the conflict between North and South is every day becoming more pointed and determined', wrote a satisfied Calhoun to a friend in 1847, 'If nothing else should be in the way it, of itself, will do much to break up the old party organizations.'[10]

The Democratic party was becoming acutely aware of its own fragility. To many northern and western Democrats it seemed as if Polk's administration was primarily serving southern interests. Expansionist Democrats in the Northwest had felt betrayed when the president had not pursued the Oregon claim as avidly as he had pursued Mexican lands, the dispute with Britain being resolved by a compromise which gave the United States less than half of the area in question. Some westerners were also outraged when Polk vetoed a rivers and harbours improvements bill in 1846, for the river network was now proving insufficient for the booming commerce of the West. But to accuse Polk of leading a southern administration was somewhat unfair. Polk's political philosophy seemed to be close to the Old Republicanism of Andrew Jackson, betraying the same dislike of economic and political privilege, the same hostility to the idea of a positive central government, and the same strict constructionism. In securing a reduction of the tariff, the re-establishment of the Independent Treasury, and in resolutely vetoing internal improvements bills, Polk was remaining true to the old Jacksonian faith. But his war on Mexico looked to many northern Democrats to be designed to secure the extension of slavery, and his failure to appoint hard money men to his cabinet raised doubts about his soundness on that tenet of Jacksonianism.

But despite the grievances of expansionist and commercially-oriented westerners, antislavery northerners, and hard money radicals, the Democratic party continued to hang precariously together until the national convention of 1848. On that occasion the presidential nomination went to Lewis Cass of Michigan. This was too much for the old Van Burenites and the antislavery Democrats. Cass was an expansionist who was prepared to conciliate both the slavery and the commercial interest. The Van Buren group in particular loathed him because they considered him at the centre of the intrigue which had unseated their chief in 1844. Finally they bolted. At a hastily called convention at Buffalo a curious amalgam of New York radicals, antislavery Democrats, old Liberty party men, and Conscience Whigs raised the banner of Free Soil and nominated Martin Van Buren to the presidency. That elderly architect of the Democratic party, champion of party regularity, and long-time practitioner of sectional conciliation, now found himself leading a breakaway party committed to keeping slavery out of the newly-acquired territories. The recent Democratic and Whig conventions, declared the Free Soilers, had 'dissolved the national party organizations heretofore existing' by nominating for president 'under Slaveholding dictation', candidates tolerant of the extension of slavery.[11]

The major parties hardly considered themselves dissolved, although these defections aroused deep forebodings. President Polk regarded the secession of the Free Soil Democrats as 'more threatening to the Union than anything which has occurred since the meeting of the Hartford convention in 1814'.[12] But while the Free Soilers won an ominous 10 per cent of the vote, mainly in New York, Pennsylvania, and New England, they carried no states and the major parties survived. Democratic defections helped the Whigs to their second national victory, and again they put an old soldier in the White House, General Zachary Taylor, a hero of the Mexican War. But nothing had been solved by the election and the sectional rumblings continued, becoming increasingly ill-tempered as the politicians analysed the implications of yet another popular folk migration, this time to California where gold had been found. Americans swarmed to this western honey-pot in their thousands, and suddenly California had a large enough population to qualify for admission to the Union as a fully fledged state. Finally Congress would have to answer the pertinent question that David Wilmot had so impertinently raised in 1846 – was slavery to be permitted in the free territories acquired from Mexico?

As talk of secession rustled through the South, the old political leaders once more summonsed the creaky machinery of party to the cause of the Union. As in 1820 and in 1833, pragmatic politicians of all sections and persuasions engaged one another in a complex colloquy as they searched for a formula which would remove the unwanted issue of slavery from national politics. The outcome of their deliberations was the Compromise of 1850. Concession was traded for concession in this remarkable political package, the principal provisions of which were the admission of California as a free state and a more effective fugitive slave law to enforce the return of runaway slaves to the South. The party ranks by no means held firm in the face of these contentious measures, but prominent men from both parties laboured for the Compromise, the old Whig leaders Clay and Webster performing this last service for their Union before the rising young Democrat, Stephen A. Douglas of Illinois, took command of the bills in question and steered them through Congress with the variable support of most Democrats, northern and southern, and of southern Whigs. Several congressmen maintained a precarious loyalty to their party by absenting themselves from votes on measures that their constituents found particularly offensive. The Compromise then became the vital test of a politician's willingness to put party and Union before section, and in the 1852 presidential election both party conventions remained determinedly unmoved by the local tears of outrage and pledged their support to Congress's final solution. The major parties were reading the slavery issue out of national politics, the Democrats promising to resist its revived agitation, 'under whatever shape or color the attempt may be made'.[13] The Whigs made similar pledges but less convincingly, for nothing could conceal the antislavery sympathies of many Whig politicians in New England and the middle states, and old Whig voters in the South began to stay away from the polls.

But it was not only in the South that Whig voters were losing faith in their party. Northern Whig voters too were beginning to feel that their political leaders were stretching their loyalties too far. In part theirs was the reverse of the southern experience. Many northern Whigs, particularly those of Yankee stock and of evangelical or liberal Protestant faith, were highly susceptible to the antislavery appeals of the abolitionists and the Free Soilers. They needed no convincing that slavery was a sin, that the Slave Power had the national government in its wicked grasp, and that resistance to slavery extension was both a moral and a political necessity. Thus the Whig parties in several northern states tended to suffer defections when antislavery candidates were in the field. But the Whigs' hold on their voters was also weakening for other reasons. Again population movements were largely responsible for injecting new and divisive issues into American politics. The mid-nineteenth century witnessed a massive influx of Catholic immigrants, mainly Irish and German, who not only threatened the jobs of native workmen but also brought with them cultural *mores* which comported ill with those of God-fearing, Sunday-observing, temperate-drinking, middle-class Protestants. 'The flood-gates of intemperance, pauperism, and crime are thrown open by them', said *The American Protestant Magazine* of these newcomers in 1849.[14] The liberty-loving republic, it seemed to some, might not survive the assault of these degenerate hordes.

The reaction to the large-scale Catholic immigration fed on a number of fears and resentments, but whatever its social and psychological roots, nativism was a force to be reckoned with in many northern cities by the 1840s and 1850s. In 1844, for example, a nativist political group calling itself the American Republican party success-fully contested the mayoral election in New York City, their candidate apparently drawing most of his votes from men who had previously voted Whig. Most of the new immigrants, and certainly the Catholics, were absorbed by the Democratic party, a circumstance which may have prompted some of the party's more zealous Protestant voters to swing to the Whigs. Certainly some northern Whig organizations – though not all – flirted with nativism, hoping to capitalize on the resentments of native-born urban Americans. But there was a limit to which the Whig party could embrace the nativist cause, its more liberal members finding xenophobia distasteful and un-American and its more hard-headed politicos not wanting to lose such foreign-born voters as were in their camp.

What most troubled many ordinary Americans living in the northern cities around 1850, then, was not slavery, the tariff, the banking system or any of the other issues that appeared regularly in the major party platforms. It was the complex of issues associated with the Catholic immigrant. Both major parties suffered from grassroots defections by voters sensitive to anti-Catholic, anti-foreign and pro-temperance appeals, but since the Whigs relied most heavily on such votes they were the more vulnerable. At first much nativism was covert, as unhappy Americans nourished their grievances and pre-judices in non-partisan secret societies, but in the early 1850s the Order of the Star Spangled Banner emerged to unite these local chapters and to groom political candidates of its own. Dubbed the 'Know-Nothings' because of its propensity for organizational secrecy, this new political movement was soon attracting the support of those who wanted to end the corrupt practices of the party machines and to keep Catholics and immigrants out of politics. Thus might the republic's free institutions be secured. The Democratic party was able to survive the Know-Nothing raids on its votes, but the Whig party, already suffering from antislavery schisms, was now irreparably crippled.

The anti-Catholic frenzy reached its peak at about the same time as antislavery emotions were riding high once more. In 1854 Stephen A. Douglas squeezed through Congress his infamous Kansas-Nebraska bill, which among other things repealed the Missouri Compromise, declaring that the people living in the western territories could decide for themselves whether or not to have slavery. Since this opened up to potential southern colonization a large area which had previously been designated as permanently free, it provoked an explosive reaction

202 The triumph of party

from antislavery northerners who felt betrayed and cheated by their representatives in Congress. The Kansas-Nebraska bill unleashed a virulent anti-Southernism which finally killed off the Whig party and provided a new platform for northern politicians. In the South former Whigs sought refuge in the Democratic party, its soundness on the slavery question now being more important to them than its questionable attitude towards business enterprise. In the North the ex-Whigs, antislavery Democrats, Know-Nothings, and evangelicals of all kinds found a common cause in resisting Douglas's odious bill. In the mid- and late 1850s the various anti-Democratic groups fused together as the Republican party, in which a mixture of base and noble emotions fuelled a popular crusade against southern arrogance and alien subversion. The old national coalitions of the second American party system were being replaced by sectional parties and the nation was heading irresistibly for civil war.

In the end, then, the old political managers had lost control, at least temporarily. In a sense democracy had worked too well in the United States, for the professional politicians had not been able to contain the passions of the people. The fierce parochial forces of nativism and sectionalism had pulled people away from their old political moorings and put an end to the ritualized party conflict of the Jacksonian era. In the gentlemanly days of Washington and Jefferson, one suspects, when politicians could still hope to lead as well as to follow their constituents, the patrician elite might have resolved these destructive issues by earnest deliberations at the seat of government. By the mid-nineteenth century a remarkably democratic political system had been created by and for white Americans; but they were still learning how to master it.

Yet learn they did. If the second American party system itself proved short-lived, other party systems followed which were remarkably similar to it. A new two-party system was fashioned in the late 1850s, and only the highly sectional character of the major parties distinguished them clearly from their predecessors. The old Democratic party, indeed, although divided never entirely disappeared, maintaining an institutional continuity from the Jacksonian era to the present day. And after the turmoil and nightmare of the Civil War and Reconstruction years had ended it was possible to build national party coalitions once more. Ever since the Jacksonian period, despite periodic upheavals, American politics have generally been ordered by a two-party system, and in structure and function these parties have closely resembled those which did battle with one another in the 1840s. In this sense, the American polity fashioned by Martin Van Buren and Henry Clay and their contemporaries has never disappeared.

Part 6

American politics as mass politics

The concept of mass society, it is sometimes said, had its origins in Alexis de Tocqueville's remarkable book, *Democracy in America*, which appeared in two parts in 1835 and 1840. In Jacksonian America Tocqueville believed that he had discovered a people who had achieved a conspicuous 'equality of condition', who were marked by a 'restless temper', and whose greatest potential enemy lay in their very egalitarianism, which made possible a 'tyranny of the majority'. He was evidently witnessing a political society which was profoundly different to that of mid-eighteenth-century England, which some colonial Americans had once wanted to emulate. In the traditional society, it has been argued, men were bound by strong ties to their local communities, which were often hierarchical in structure and within which social, economic, and political influence went together. The mass society, on the other hand, is an aggregation of rootless individuals, an atomized society in which community ties are weak and central governing authorities distant. Jacksonian America was hardly the mass society postulated by modern sociological theory, but, as Tocqueville perceived, it could no longer be adequately explained in Old-World terms. Tocqueville had to employ a new term, individualism, to describe the central social and political ethic of the New American World.

The image of the United States as a nation of questing individuals is not altogether accurate, but it may help to explain some of the characteristics of American politics. One attribute of the mass society possessed by Jacksonian America was fluidity. Rapid economic change and a highly mobile population made for a society in flux, at least outside the slave South, where the survival of something like the patrician republic of the eighteenth century underlined the receptivity to change of the rest of the country. Change and diversity stimulated anxieties as well as optimism, and Americans of this generation were at least as prone as their predecessors to espy subversive designs on the republic. One way in which this mass of restless individuals might find a measure of security was through the creation of a common political culture, an important function of the new mass political parties, which between them absorbed the great majority of white men into a national system of politics. The national focus of popular politics tended to be the presidency, the one office for which Americans throughout the land could vote, and by the 1840s men were participating in presidential elections in unprecedented numbers. The people's tribune was linked to his scattered electoral masters by the medium of party, which came to have a very conservative function in the protean republican polity, serving as a great voluntary association for the political socialization and integration of the masses. American politics had in some measure become a folk activity, as ordinary citizens throughout the land were caught up in the campaign drama. The mass political party provided the uprooted individual with a new sense of community, enrolling him in a brotherhood which transcended time and space. Its rituals provided him with a contact with the revolutionary past and gave him a sense of participating in the great republican mission. The incessant election campaigns were giving rise to a popular political culture which went some way towards making Americans one people.

Chapter 16

The protean republic

'All strangers who come among us remark the excessive anxiety written in the American countenance', remarked a writer in *The American Whig Review* in 1845, locating the source of the trouble in 'the excitement, the commercial activity, the restlessness' that America's free and equal society had generated in such abundance.[1] Hope and fear, optimism and unease, have gone together in American history. One source of this divided temperament has been the utopian yearning which has afflicted Americans since the Puritans began to build their city upon a hill and which was perhaps even stronger than ever in the heady days of Andrew Jackson. 'If it be the duty of the individual to strive after a perfection like the perfection of God', declared the high priest of Jacksonian democracy, George Bancroft, 'how much more ought a nation to be the image of Deity'.[2] But the greater the aspiration the greater the insecurity. Even as Americans boasted of their unexcelled freedom and prophesied of yet greater things to come, they could not quite suppress the uneasy thought that the republic might somehow be going astray. And this lurking anxiety was made the greater by the highly fluid nature of American society and the very pace of social and economic change. As Americans were shaken out of the settled ways of their fathers, they looked to the future with a mixture of hope and apprehension. If some found the spirit of progress exhilarating, others feared lest it vanquish the republic of their dreams.

The Austrian traveller Francis Grund, surveying the incessant bustle of the United States, was moved to observe that 'Life consists in motion'.[3] For many Americans of the mid-nineteenth century life undoubtedly did consist in motion. Never had Americans witnessed a period of such extraordinary growth or rapid change. The swift rate of change was made possible by – and in turn helped to promote – a high degree of mobility, as men moved from place to place, from occupation to occupation, from class to class. Such features were not universal, however, for a more traditional social order survived in the slave South, sustaining in turn something of an older style of politics. Change and mobility were related to a third important feature of American life, its diversity or heterogeneity. There had always been profound differences between Americans, for reasons related to the geography of the continent and the circumstances of its settlement, but economic growth and newer population movements were adding considerably to the varieties of American experience. Rapid change, mobility, and diversity, then, were major characteristics of American society in the ante-bellum period. Many Americans benefited by these conditions and gladly seized the opportunities afforded them, but others reacted by stabbing out blindly at the forces they thought were making their lives and futures less secure and certain. The emergence of the mass society was inevitably accompanied by political tensions.

In some ways American society was changing more rapidly than ever before or ever since. Demographic figures strikingly illustrate certain kinds of change. The number of people in the United States more than doubled between 1825 and 1850, when the total reached 23·26 million, the fastest expansion being in the 1840s. The West, of course, was the most rapidly-growing section, holding less than a quarter of all Americans in 1830, nearly a third by 1850, and about thirty-eight per cent in 1860, by which time it had outpaced both the Northeast and the South. And if some Americans were moving west, others were leaving the farms for the cities. In the ante-bellum years urban population was growing at its fastest rate ever in American history, the most stupendous increase being in the 1840s when it grew by over ninety-two per cent. By 1850 six cities had exceeded a population of 100,000, and had lost their small town status and were fast becoming great metropolises, with an urban environment and culture unfamiliar to most Americans. These demographic changes can largely be accounted for by natural increase and internal migration. Americans were having large families, the death rate was relatively low, and the transportation revolution facilitated the movements to the West and to the cities. But immigration was becoming an increasingly important source of population. In the first fifty years of Independence foreign immigration had been relatively low, first reaching as many as 10,000 in a single year only in 1825. Thereafter the figures mounted rapidly, reaching nearly 600,000 in the decade of the 1830s and 1·7 million in the 1840s. The most massive influx came in the very middle of the century, 1845-54, when three million people poured into American ports, most of them Irishmen and Germans fleeing the hunger in their own lands. In proportion to resident population, this mid-century invasion was never to be surpassed.

The sheer pace of various forms of economic change was also unprecedented. The hard times following the Panic of 1837 did little to arrest the commercial revolution, which, it could be argued, was in turn ushering in an industrial revolution. At any rate, commercial and manufacturing enterprises were soon multiplying at a breathtaking rate, aided by the continued improvements in transportation. The locomotive made its appearance for the first time in many communities, careering along 2,818 miles of track in 1840, over 9,000 miles in 1850 and 30,626 miles in 1860. A crude idea of how fast the economy was changing is conveyed by the increase in the number of workers gainfully employed in manufacturing, hand trades, and construction. Together these industrial sectors of the economy employed an estimated 350,000 people in 1820, 790,000 in 1840, nearly 1·3 million in 1850 and over 1·9 million in 1860. The expansion of those so employed in the 1840s was the fastest ever in American history, unequalled even in the great industrializing decade of the 1880s, if the figures are to be believed. The rate of increase in the number of men engaged in mining in the two decades before the Civil War was also never again to be surpassed. Of course, most Americans remained engaged in various forms of agriculture and the real industrial revolution was not accomplished until the late nineteenth century, but the pace of change was startling, particularly perhaps in the 1840s. In 1839 manufacturing contributed seventeen per cent of the nation's output of commodities, compared with seventy-two per cent for agriculture. By 1849 the respective shares were thirty and sixty per cent, while by 1859 manufacturing accounted for thirty-two per cent of the total and agriculture fifty-six per cent. Economic historians have never agreed on the interpretation of the fragmentary data that they have culled from the ante-bellum records, but there seems little doubt that the economic world in which most Americans lived in the mid-nineteenth century was changing fast.[4]

American society was thus being transformed at an exhilarating and even unnerving rate. The rapid swelling of the West, the mushrooming cities, the tidal wave of foreign immigrants, the transportation and commercial revolutions, the acceleration in manufacturing activities, not to mention the faster communications made possible by these technological improvements and the invention of the telegraph, meant that Americans found much that was unfamiliar to them in their own land. These novelties and changes were related to another important characteristic of the American people – a high degree of mobility, particularly geographical mobility. Michel Chevalier thought that 'a locomotive engine or a steamboat' was 'the most suitable emblem' for the American people for they were constantly in motion.[5] 'Such a thing as rest or quiescence does not even enter the mind of an American', observed another European traveller, 'and its presence would to him be actually insupportable.'[6] The popularity of the rocking-chair among Americans, it has been said, was due to a desire to keep moving even when sitting still. Detailed statistical evidence on mobility remains to be compiled, but the surge of population (and to) the West and the cities provides some indication of the extent that Americans were prepared to move.

Recent studies suggest that even the working class, or perhaps especially the working class, were ever on the move, if not always on the make. It was possible for a city to experience an almost complete turnover in residents in the course of a decade or so. Indeed in ante-bellum Boston, Peter R. Knights's researches into population movements suggest that total turnover during a decade 'could reach several times the city's total population'.[7] Many workers did not find good jobs or homes and they apparently drifted from town to town, earning a precarious living in a succession of different employments. This large shiftless, restless population occupied a perhaps important but as yet ill-defined role in the Jacksonian social and political order. On the one hand, these footloose workers testify to the fluidity of American society. Yet their very rootlessness perhaps prevented them from being a threat to the established political structure. Trade unions or radical labour organizations, for example, could not easily flourish when their potential supporters were constantly disappearing over the horizon. And a certain degree of upward social mobility also served to mute class strife. Historians have disagreed about the extent of upward mobility in this period, and it certainly varied from community to community, but it is at least possible that the relatively broad if unequal distribution of property, the general availability of education, the ever receding frontier and the expansive economy provided more opportunities for social advancement (and decline) than was the case in most other countries or in most earlier periods. The growing stratification was not necessarily accompanied by a diminution of economic opportunity. At any rate, as Stephan Thernstrom and others have shown, there was apparently sufficient upward mobility, limited though it may have been, for men to *believe* that America was the land of opportunity and to behave accordingly.[8] 'There is no such thing in America as being contented with one's position or condition . . .', observed Thomas Low Nichols. 'Every one is tugging, trying, scheming to advance – to get ahead.'[9]

The rapidity of social and economic change and the high mobility of the American people, together with the vast and still growing extent of the American Union, accentuated a third characteristic of American society, its extraordinary diversity. Foreign travellers in the United States bemusedly recorded their encounters with wealthy Boston merchants, western fur-trappers, Virginia planters, black slaves, Indians, New England factory girls, Irish navvies, backwoods farmers, and Yankee evangelists. Indeed, travelling Americans themselves often attempted their own intrigued comparisons of regional characteristics, such publications as Charles Fenno Hoffman's *A Winter in the West* and A. De Puy Van Buren's *Jottings of a Year's Sojourn in the South* testifying to the fascination that Americans had with one another. But the differences were more than regional and sectional. The distinction between town and country was becoming ever more apparent, and, perhaps more important, the differences between the small town and the big city. In the larger commercial and industrial communities the distance between rich and poor had become very marked, both economically and geographically, and the emergence both of trade unions and of employers' associations was evidence of a degree of class conflict. Immigration added to the diversity of the population. The principal immigrant groups in this period were Irish and German, though there were also significant numbers of newcomers from England, Scotland, Scandinavia, Switzerland, and France. This influx of Europeans also added to the religious diversity of the United States. There had been few Roman Catholics in the American colonies, but between 1790 and 1850 about a million of them came into the country, making their church larger than any single Protestant sect, though the Protestants together continued to predominate.

American society, then, was becoming ever more heterogeneous, a perplexing conglomeration of sectional, economic, ethnic, and religious groups. There was often friction between these different elements, but perhaps the most ominous cleavage was that which increasingly seemed to be separating the South from the rest of the country. However diverse and divided the American people may have been, northerners and westerners probably felt more in common with one another, socially, politically, and economically, than either felt with the South. ' . . . American society has a peculiar development in Virginia', observed Alexander Mackay, adding that the peculiarities also extended 'to some of the adjacent States, particularly to Maryland and South Carolina'.[10] There were certain ways, at any rate, in which large parts of the South seemed to be diverging from the political and social trends of the rest of the country. For one thing, the South was less imbued with the spirit of frantic change. Cities and industry were slow to develop in the South, and relatively few foreign immigrants found their way there. Those twin symbols of progress, the railroad and the public school, made only a laggardly appearance in several southern states. 'If you call Long Island behind the times, I don't know what you would call North Carolina', wrote the northern wife of one southern planter. 'It has been rightly termed Rip Van Winkle.'[11]

This is not to suggest that the South was static. Some planters and farmers, particularly in the Upper South, experimented with new techniques and new crops. Cotton production was increasing and both the number and the size of plantations were expanding. Most scholars today accept that slavery was profitable, although they may disagree on the degree of profitability, and there seems little doubt that much of southern agriculture was prospering. Economic growth in the South in the middle decades of the nineteenth century, measured in terms of *per capita* income, appears to have been at least as fast as for the rest of the country. But to a large extent, southern prosperity was based on more of the same – more cotton and more slaves. Plantation agriculture had proved very successful and southerners with money to invest frequently spent it on yet more plantation agriculture. For the most part, the South expanded by expanding its traditional institutions rather than by introducing new ones. In this sense social change in the South was of quite a different kind from change in the North. The southerner, concluded one thoughtful New Yorker, 'has much less curiosity than the Northerner; less originating genius, less inventive talent, less patient and persevering energy'.[12]

Contemporary writers often argued that, unlike the free states, much of the South was still subject to the will of an aristocracy. Several modern scholars have patiently pointed to the extensive suffrage and vigorous two-party systems in many southern states as evidence that democracy did after all exist in the South, but it is difficult to escape the conclusion that the great planters did exert a disproportionate political influence. Eugene Genovese, in seeking to avoid the ambiguous word 'feudalism', has labelled the social system of the slave South 'seigneurial', and the term appears well chosen.[13] On the large plantation the owner was the head of an extensive community, comprising his family, sometimes a tutor for his children, perhaps a white overseer or other white employees, and a variety of household and field slaves, some of them skilled workers themselves. Each person had his or her place in this ordered – if sometimes inefficient – community. The master recognized an obligation to protect his slaves, who had no alternative but to serve him. The plantation was not an industrial enterprise from which the workers returned to their own homes at night: it was a community, a social and cultural as well as an economic institution, whose members lived and worked together. 'The estate of a Virginian landlord is, in some of its features, very closely assimilated to an English manor . . . ', noted one Scottish traveller. 'In the most convenient part of the estate is generally to be found the manor-house, and, with the exception of his family and his guests, all who live upon it are the vassals or slaves of the proprietor.'[14]

The nature of plantation life, then, fostered a paternalistic ethos. All authority rested with the lordly planter, who lived up to his role by adopting the life-style of an aristocrat. This is not to suggest that planters were indifferent to making profits. Many of them administered their plantations efficiently and marketed their crops with an eye to reaping the highest return. But the plantation was no more simply a business enterprise to them than it was to those who laboured on it. They saw themselves as heads of an extensive family more readily than they saw themselves as directors of an economic unit, and they behaved accordingly. Indeed, finding themselves thrown into the role of lord of the manor, they recognized that the well-being of their community rested on more than profitability, and they tended even to disdain enterprises of purely an economic character. 'The leading planters of South Carolina are generally men who, having inherited large estates with numerous slaves born upon them, and received liberal educations, consider themselves . . . *the gentlemen of America*', wrote one visiting Englishman, 'looking down upon the trading communities in the Northern States. . . . '[15] They did not plough all their profits back into their business, as did the more capitalistic-minded businessmen and farmers of the North and the West, but like the old European aristocracies spent money on conspicuous consumption, a typical aristocratic device for asserting rank and intimidating the lesser orders. Hence southern planters hired tutors for their children or sent them to private schools and colleges. They built fine mansions, stocked them with French wine and French furniture, rode in expensive carriages, and went out hunting with their peers. And the great planters in some measure succeeded in having themselves accepted as an aristocracy. Their lesser neighbours deferred to them socially and politically. The large planter might not only be the lord of his own plantation, but also of the surrounding region. Local small farmers, for example, often sold their products to the planter, as they used his ginning and marketing services. Some of them might be related to him. The paternalistic ethos generated on the plantation thus often spread outwards, exerting an influence well beyond the estate itself. In parts of the South, at any rate, the social order continued to be ruled by a patrician elite, whose commanding position was sustained by wealth, patronage, and deference.

These great planters also continued to wield disproportionate political power. Political influence still tended to follow wealth and status in the South, even as the old relationship between social and political position was being destroyed in the North. Most southern states, it is true, had adopted much the same liberal suffrage provisions as the free states, and the great majority of white men enjoyed the right to vote. But the older South was slow to develop the new organizational techniques, and the planting gentry and their allies continued to be elected to office. In Virginia, for example, (where the franchise was limited until 1851), the principal organ of local government was the powerful county court, consisting of magistrates appointed by the legislature. These non-elective county courts were dominated by the local gentry, and in general political careers had to be routed through these bodies. This oligarchical system, the small number of elective offices at any level, and the cohesiveness of Virginia's planting class, all helped to perpetuate a patrician style of politics. Virginia's elite did divide themselves into Whigs and Democrats, but the party organizations remained relatively crude and party discipline weak. South Carolina was even less receptive to democratic pressures. White manhood suffrage had been adopted in the state as early as 1810, but almost the only officers that voters could vote for were congressmen and state legislators. Most other officials, including the governor and presidential electors, were appointed by the legislature, and high property qualifications for office-holding helped to keep government in the hands of the rich. The legislature itself was dominated by a conservative planting class which despised and feared the apparatus of party, and South Carolina alone did not develop a two-party system in the Jacksonian era. In South Carolina, as one patrician politician expressed it, the people expected their leaders to 'think for them'.[16]

The most sophisticated champion of a patrician political order in the South was John C. Calhoun, whose increasingly anachronistic views clearly owed much to South Carolina's peculiar polity. In the later part of his life Calhoun resurrected and rewrote the republicanism of the

Founding Fathers after his own image. He became one of the fiercest critics of the style of government personified by Martin Van Buren, arguing that republican liberty was fast disappearing as unscrupulous party bosses acquired despotic power by the cunning deployment of spoils and demagoguery. One of his fundamental objections to the measures associated with the American System was that they put patronage into the hands of the government. As a recent scholar had written, 'By exorcising the new political brokers Calhoun could hope to bring the republic back to the enlightened rule of disinterested patricians, fulfill his presidential ambitions, and develop national political movements based on principles rather than spoils.'[17] But Calhoun's revision of eighteenth-century republicanism was southern conservatism at its most attenuated. In most of the South the old elites had been obliged to adapt to newer political styles. Nonetheless, in the slave South generally the wealthy planters appear to have retained an influential voice in political affairs, party discipline was weaker and the two-party structure was somewhat slower to develop than in the North. The two-party system may also have been more precarious than elsewhere, for the semblance of balance achieved by the early 1840s was being destroyed again by the end of the decade by the revived issue of slavery.

Ante-bellum America was a highly variegated and fragmented society. Even where the social order was not characterized by rapid change, as in the South, this in itself pointed up the differences in the American experience. The mobility and diversity of the American people, together with the onward rush of progress, provided patriotic orators with grounds for celebration, but they also occasioned much mistrust and unease. People could not help but wonder what fate awaited them and the republic as they were whirled into the future. Tensions of many kinds were probably increasing in the unsettled middle decades of the nineteenth-century. The rapid advance of commerce and industry saddened those who still nourished the Jeffersonian dream of a land of sturdy small farmers, as the limited government and anti-banking attitudes of many Democratic administrations, state and federal, distressed many of those who wanted some protection for their business pursuits. In the major cities class tensions grew as the gulf between rich and poor yawned ever wider, erupting occasionally in working class riots. The unprecedented flood of immigrants created ugly prejudices between native and foreigner, and the massive invasion of Roman Catholics, coinciding with an evangelical Protestant revival, exacerbated religious friction. The immigrants sometimes brought their own animosities with them, as those between English and Irish or Irish Protestant and Irish Catholic. These class, ethnic, and religious tensions were at their most acute in the northern states in general and in the larger cities in particular, though from the mid-1840s sectional antagonisms were reawakening too. The war with

Mexico brought in its turbulent wake a complex of issues related to the place of slavery in the American republic, envenoming sectional hatreds as never before.

The United States of the mid-nineteenth century, then, was a far from happy republic. One measure of this was the frequency of mob action. In the first three decades of the century there was relatively little mob violence, but from the 1830s rioting became quite a popular pastime, and by the Civil War over a thousand people had been killed as a result. 'Accounts of outrages committed by mobs form the every-day news of the times', mourned the young Abraham Lincoln. 'They have pervaded the country, from New England to Louisiana; they are neither peculiar to the eternal snows of the former, nor the burning suns of the latter. . . . '[18] Some riots were the products of economic distress, such as the 'flour riots' in New York City in 1837, and many bloody disturbances were generated by the hysteria of election day, but probably most riots were directed against an unpopular minority group. Thus there were large numbers of anti-Catholic outbreaks, the Irish suffered from and participated in the so-called 'Irish riots', German immigrants were the victims of the celebrated 'beer riots' of the 1840s and 1850s, when righteous nativists took exception to the relaxed European Sunday, and Mormons suffered repeated violent harassments, even to the extent of the murder of their leader, Joseph Smith. The best-remembered were the anti-abolition riots, for even in northern cities those who demanded the abolition of slavery incurred considerable odium for their disruptive doctrines. By the 1850s, however, many Yankees had been won over by the evangelical crusade, and antislavery men then precipitated more sympathetic disturbances when they tried to free runaway slaves. But almost anything, it seemed, could spark a riot. In 1849 the nation was shocked by the Astor Place riots in New York City, when the rivalry between two famous actors and their partisans erupted in a spate of bloody scenes in which over twenty people lost their lives. Lawless behaviour of this sort exposed the tensions within American society and increased the anxieties of orderly Americans. Mob action may perhaps have been encouraged by the democratic ethos of Jacksonian America, by the sense that the people were the masters, but to many it seemed to presage total social disintegration.

It was as easy as ever, then, to believe that the American republic was experiencing – or was about to experience – a serious degeneration. Since these ill-assorted Americans nursed different conceptions of the good republic, a variety of sinister designs on it were perceived. Americans had been uneasily watching for evidence of subversion since the earliest days of nationhood, and convictions that there were conspiracies afoot had seemingly touched almost every part of American public life. The rapid change, social disintegration, and insecurity of the mid-nineteenth century probably served to strengthen this paranoid temper, and accusing fingers were pointed in all directions. The Money Power, the spoils system, the demon drink, degenerate immigrants, the Slave Power, the abolitionists, Mormonism, the mob, Popery and a host of other 'powers' too, were each variously identified as the real enemies of the republic. Only when these evils were rooted out, it was suggested, would the great experiment be safe.

Concern about the fate of the American people was not necessarily irrational. Politicians of all parties, after all, were in some measure moved by a determination to transmit republican institutions unimpaired to later generations. A similar rationale lay behind many of the religious and reforming enterprises of the period. In the northern states in particular the rapid and endless change was one reason for the growth of evangelical and reform movements of all types, as missionaries were dispatched to save souls in the burgeoning slums and on the distant frontier, as temperance crusaders called on their reckless fellows to give up drink, as educationists laboured to ensure that the rising generation received the right civic and moral training in the schools. These movements were propelled both by a fear of a pervasive moral erosion and by a millennial conviction that American society was perfectible. The old social restraints of the church, the family, the local magistrate, and the force of community opinion could not operate very effectively on a people in motion, and new means of regulating behaviour had to be found. A fluid society could only be made safe if its individual members remained virtuous, and a principal object of the host of religious, benevolent, and educational bodies was to give citizens an internalized code of behaviour. Internal constraints were to replace the disappearing external agencies. The religious and social reformers' ultimate goal was in a sense political, for they were acting on the old belief that the key to the survival of a republic was the virtue of its citizens. 'The safety and glory of the Republic', a reforming Buffalo editor pointed out, 'depends on the education and training of the children.'[19]

But all too often this natural anxiety to protect the republic from destructive influences was replaced by an irrational conviction that alien and sinister forces were consciously conspiring to deprive the American people of their liberties. An early victim of this state of mind was the institution of freemasonry, whose secrecy and arcane rituals had long aroused the suspicions of outsiders. After the disappearance of a renegade freemason and the apparent hushing-up of the affair by the authorities, a remarkable display of antimasonic sentiment burst across the northern states in the late 1820s and early 1830s. Freemasons, it was said, had burrowed their way into the very heart of government, where they advanced the interests of their fellows and subordinated the public good to that end. In this respect, Antimasonry was an egalitarian crusade, based on the conviction that masons-in-government were denying to all citizens their equal rights. But this egalitarian impulse sometimes tipped over into paranoia, into the belief that masons were actively at work to take over the republic. 'When the citizen of these United States kneels at the alter of masonry, when he swears allegiance to her laws', cried one antimason, 'he snaps asunder the ties that bind him to his country.'[20] The republic, it seemed, was being eaten away by this cancer within.

Similar charges were levelled at Mormons and Catholics, who, it was said, gave their first loyalty to their church and not to their country. The luckless Mormons were harried right across the country – for a variety of reasons – until they were all but pushed out of it when they took refuge in the wilds of Utah in the 1840s. The Catholic hordes were held to be even more dangerous, in part because righteous Protestants believed that their faith encouraged a depraved morality which was inimical to republicanism, and in part because the Catholic church was identified with the authoritarian regimes of Europe. The fact that at this time Catholicism was so closely associated with foreign immigrants made it seem doubly alien or un-American. Samuel F.B. Morse, just before turning his prodigious imagination to the invention of the telegraph, warned his fellows of a giant conspiracy master-minded by Prince Metternich, the Pope, and the Austrian Emperor to use the 'unlettered Catholic emigrant' to seize control of American institutions and crush the cause of liberty.[21] Sensing in the growing pluralism of nineteenth-century society a shattering of the organic republic of old, insecure Protestant patriots responded with accusations that their world was being subverted by alien conspiracies.

Some Americans, of course, espied conspiracies nearer home. As was the case with some other popular movements, among the forces behind the antislavery crusade was a dynamic evangelical Protestantism and a more secular desire to fulfil the libertarian promise of the Revolution, and it now seemed to antislavery men that the slave South was diverting the republic from its proper course. To them, at least, slavery was demonstrably incompatible with the republican faith. And as they found their cause repeatedly rebuffed by Congress, the president and the Supreme Court, they came to believe that slave interests were conspiring to infiltrate the organs of government and bend it to their will. The destruction of the national bank, the annexation of Texas, the Mexican War, the Kansas-Nebraska Act, and other infamous measures too, were recited as cumulative proof that the Slave Power had seized control of the government and was subverting the republic to its despotic ends. For 'the Slave Power dares anything;' argued Charles Sumner, 'and it can be conquered only by the united masses of the People.'[22] But apprehensive southerners too were espying conspiracies. As the surging population of the free states underlined their minority status, southerners increasingly felt themselves in a state of siege as the antislavery campaign mounted. Noting the connections between British and American antislavery men, some southerners even charged that abolitionism was the product of a British plot to divide and destroy the American republic, 'a great concentrated effort . . . against the good name and well being of the United States . . . '.[23] In their eyes, it was the anarchistic and demagoguic ways of the antislavery crusaders that were alien to the American republican tradition.

To maintain a system of politics responsive to the needs of American society was evidently no easy task. Politicians operating in the national arena in the mid-nineteenth century were confronted with a political nation which was almost as diverse as it was extensive, encompassing among many other features the seigneurial sociopolitical order of the slave South, where the patrician republicanism of the eighteenth century died hard, the fragmented polities of the major cities, where resistance to the idea of a pluralistic society was often bitter, the rich, commercial farming communities throughout the Union, many of which wanted a political system which would foster a dynamic economy, and the rapidly-expanding frontier societies in the West, where subsistence farmers, miners, and adventurers of all kinds nurtured the self-help ethic. The rapid pace of economic change and high geographical mobility added immeasurably to the uncertainties of American life, as did the rapid expansion of 'alien' ethnic groups and religions. The individualistic thrust of the entrepreneurial economy and of evangelical religion, as well as of other aspects of American life, also served to create the impression of a social order close to disintegration, and Americans feared for their own fates and that of the republic even as the onward rush of progress promised them a yet greater future. In this uncertain milieu some insecure Americans perceived conscious conspiracies to undo the republic, while others searched for security in familiar forms.

The major political parties had an important role to play in this nation of rootless individuals and mutually suspicious groups. As the community-oriented traditional society disappeared, the major parties could offer men new loyalties and seek to create a national political culture of a kind. Attention was becoming more directed towards the centre in American politics, as the popularization of presidential elections in particular enabled the two mass parties to try to inculcate common values among their diverse supporters throughout the Union. The citizens of this protean republic could hope in some measure to submerge their anxieties and their differences in the popular community of party.

Chapter 17

The presidency, parties, and the people

'Politics are much discussed', noted Charles Dickens after travelling on an American railroad, 'so are banks, so is cotton'.[1] The incessant election campaigns which characterized the American polity, he continued, provided 'comfort to all strong politicians and true lovers of their country: that is to say, to ninety-nine men and boys out of every ninety-nine and a quarter'. In the United States politics was a pursuit of the many as well as of the few. The ancient belief that democracy could function successfully only in a state limited in area and population had been magnificently disproved, at least to the satisfaction of most white American males, and in the ante-bellum decades curious Europeans crossed the Atlantic in their hundreds to examine for themselves this novel governmental experiment and to report back on it to their Old-World audiences. Where colonial Americans had once looked to England for a model of political society, Englishmen and others were now beginning to wonder what political lessons they could learn from the presumptuous American republic. Many in fact doubted that the American example could safely be followed. Something of the difference between the American and British political worlds was rather grotesquely captured in a dispute at Cambridge University in 1866, when conservatives damned a proposal to allow Harvard to send a scholar to lecture on American history and institutions as an attempt to instil 'in the youth of the governing classes a love for democratic principles and democratic institutions'. The British system, it seemed, was allergic to American influences: 'Government, authority, faith, submission, reverence – these are indissolubly bound together, and any shock to one part of the system must be felt throughout the whole.'[2]

Such hierarchical, deferential, and organic images were now rarely reflected in American conceptions of the good political society, except in the slave South. By the mid-nineteenth century the United States had developed a mature and distinctive political system of her own, one which was roughly in accord with the social and economic realities of the New-World environment. A number of conditions and influences had nurtured the individualistic ethic in America, among them the absence of an entrenched hereditary aristocracy, the relatively broad distribution of property, the expansive entrepreneurial economy, a dynamic evangelical Protestantism, and the natural rights creed of the Revolution. The new American man was the free individual, answerable to no higher authority, secular or ecclesiastical, and possessed of the capacity to govern himself. The revolutionary proposition that all men were created equal thus led ultimately to universal suffrage, the abolition of property qualifications for office-holding, the separation of church and state (and to a large degree of business and state), and to constitutions which put almost crippling constraints on government in order to protect individual liberties. It also led to denials that blacks were really men, at least on a par with white men, as it eventually contributed as well to their liberation – and to that of women. The proposition that all men were equal also pointed logically to majority rule, an ideal which was translated into crude reality by the device of party. By the 1840s the majority were deciding not merely who would serve them in government but also what they would do, for the party platforms gave the people the choice, albeit a limited one. The two-party system itself enabled a wide array of interests and ideals to find political expression, and sustained a public discourse over the appropriate functions of republican government and the success of the American experiment.

In one perspective, then, the political nation of ante-bellum America can be viewed as a mass of equal individuals. The national political system which held them together was, of course, considerably more complex than this, with its ingenious constitutional structure, its dispersal of powers among the different branches of government and among a host of state and local polities, its tolerance of slavery, and its unofficial use of the Christian faith. But Americans were now actively functioning as members of a national political community as well as of their town and local communities, one encompassing the people as a whole. At the apex of this national system was the president, whose role had tended to become more important with the growth of democracy. The presidency, with the vice-presidency, was the one office for which Americans throughout the land could vote as one people. 'All things are gravitating to one grand centre', observed the Philadelphia *Public Ledger* in 1836. 'The Presidency is becoming a potent maelstrom, ingulfing and breaking down to pieces all other powers.'[3] The presidency was not nearly as powerful as this comment suggested, but it was certainly not the constitutional monarchy that it had once seemed to be turning into, and the advent of the popular election of the president pointed the American system of politics even more firmly in a direction of its own. Perhaps most important, the popular presidential election did much to facilitate the creation of the national political parties, which provided the mass polity with a measure of integration, absorbing the politically-active citizenry into great voluntary associations of equals. The parties harnessed the energies of the people to the cause of republican government, and the people demonstrated their conviction in their sovereignty by their massive turnouts at the polls and by their enthusiastic participation in political activity of all kinds. Great mass meetings became common, the carnival atmosphere of campaigns attracted the attention of countless numbers, and, indeed, the excitement was such that popular action sometimes degenerated into mob action. American politics at this level had become a folk activity. The party rallies provided the American individual with a new sense of community, and the rites and rituals of the endless election campaigns seemed to make politics a kind of substitute religion, enabling ordinary men throughout the Union to participate in the historic mission that Providence had assigned to the American people.

The restoration of the political energy of the presidency helped to reshape the American political order. The framers of the Constitution had intended to make a clear separation between the executive and the legislative branches of the federal government, making the Chief Magistrate the head only of the administration and denying him and his executive officers places in Congress. In the early years of the republic the principle of the separation of powers had in some measure been undermined by the close relationship which developed between president and Congress. Jefferson had sought to bind Congress to him, infiltrating its committees with his men and shaping its legislation, while his successors had found themselves very much beholden to Congress, which had played a major part in placing them in the White House. But the popular election of the president from the 1820s served to weaken any influence Congress might have over the executive. The president now had a power base in the electorate and was more genuinely independent of Congress than ever before. Andrew Jackson finally restored the old separation of powers by striking down a number of congressional measures and securing vindication for his belligerent vetoes in his re-election of 1832. Congress itself had long shown itself to be too disorganized and fragmented to provide the nation with very decisive leadership. The establishment of a direct link between the people and the presidency provided a new pattern of government. The Democrats indeed seemed almost to be turning the traditional polity upside down, for they tended to present the executive as the true popular branch of the government, whose duty it was to protect the people's rights from the designs of a corruptible legislature filled with partial interests.

The advent of the popular election of president thus ensured that the American system of politics would not revert to anything resembling the British model. In addition to frustrating the tendency towards a form of parliamentary government by re-establishing the independence of the executive, it also opened the highest office in the land to men outside the governing elite in the nation's capital. In Britain, Parliament remained the principal route to political preferment. Prime ministers customarily reached that eminence after several years in the public service, usually after holding other great offices of state. A similar route was still possible for the ambitious American politician, but the favoured candidate of federal officeholders and Washington legislators might still be defeated by an outsider or a newcomer with greater popular appeal. Such a man might also appoint other political parvenus to senior posts in his administration. In the American polity it would always remain possible for new men to grasp for the federal government in the name of the people.

The presidency itself became more powerful once it was freed from its dependence on Congress. Under Madison and Monroe presidential authority had reached perhaps its weakest condition ever, but Andrew Jackson reversed this trend. With his power base in the electorate rather than in Congress, and with the temperament of a clan chieftain, Jackson made the president the undoubted head of the government. Far from deferring to his cabinet, as Monroe and John Quincy Adams had done, Jackson insisted that his cabinet members take their instructions from him, and he did not hesitate to dismiss them when they failed to do so. Further, he made extensive use of an unofficial group of advisers, the so-called 'kitchen cabinet', a practice which again downgraded the official cabinet and which marked a primitive stage in the evolution of a White House staff. Jackson further increased presidential power by the vigorous employment of the veto, striking down more bills than all his predecessors combined, not to mention making use of the pocket veto. Traditionally, presidents had been moved to the extremity of vetoing a bill only if they thought it unconstitutional, or so they said, but Jackson was also prepared to weigh the desirability of a measure, insisting on 'the undoubted right of the Executive to withhold his assent from bills on other grounds than their constitutionality'.[4] In short, Jackson taught his successors how they could use the veto power to promote their own policies, or at least to frustrate those of their enemies. The presidential veto was 'a sort of appeal to the people', said Tocqueville[5], and the supporters of a later embattled president, John Tyler, tried vainly to invest him with a certain folk appeal by dubbing him 'Old Veto'. Not all of Jackson's successors used the powers of the presidential office as successfully as he, but at least they found them greatly enhanced.

The Jacksonians tended to justify this exercise of executive authority by casting the president as the dutiful agent of the democratic people. 'The people . . . and not the States', said Jackson in refuting the nullificationist doctrines of South Carolina, 'are represented in the executive branch'.[6] The Democrats' assault on the monster bank, in reviving the old Country nightmare of a corrupt alliance between the worlds of money and politics, managed to suggest that Congress was a less reliable guardian of the people's liberty than the president himself. It was a fallacy, argued James Buchanan in 1842, to assume that Congress 'in every situation and under every circumstance, truly represent the deliberate will of the people'.[7] By depicting the president as the people's tribune the Jacksonians were able to strengthen executive authority, which skilful presidents extended yet further by exploiting their powers as party chieftains. Where earlier presidents had been reluctant to use the federal patronage at their disposal for political and partisan purposes, Jackson and his successors soon lost any such inhibitions, employing the spoils system to assert their leadership and to cement their party support.

If the advent of the popular presidential election (together with the device of party) made possible an enhancement of presidential authority, it also profoundly influenced the development of the party system itself. In Britain the principal object of the emerging political parties was to obtain as many seats as possible in the House of Commons. In the United States parties were certainly interested in maximizing their representation in Congress, but of increasing concern to them was control of the White House, with its strategic importance on the political battlefield. 'The presidential question absorbs everything else', complained John J. Crittenden in the spring of 1840, 'and but little is doing, or will be done, in Congress at the present session, though the session will, in all probability, be a long one.'[8] The widespread obsession with president-making was perhaps related to the pluralistic and democratic nature of American political society. It was hardly an accident that the renewal of the contest for the presidency occurred in the 1820s, when the Missouri Crisis in particular was modifying perceptions of the nature of the American polity. 'At the approach of every election for president, every section of the union, appears anxious to furnish the man', wrote a correspondent of the *Washington Gazette* in 1822, arguing that the North, the West, the South, and the East should be allowed to take it in turns to furnish a president, a bizarre proposal which illustrated the growing tendency to see the Union as composed of separate, powerful, and permanent sections.[9] In succeeding years such forces as geographical expansion, rapid economic growth, and large-scale immigration further eroded the old ideal of a harmonious and cohesive political order. But as it seemed that America was becoming a pluralistic society of competing individuals, groups, and sections, it was also evident that the political system was becoming more democratic, exposing minority interests to the risk of oppression by a majority coalition. Or so some observers believed, including John C. Calhoun and Alexis de Tocqueville, who in very different ways warned Americans of a potential 'tyranny of the majority'. In a pluralistic and democratic political culture access to the White House was of critical importance. The president helped to shape public policy, but, perhaps more important, he could veto any measure he thought improper, and any sensitive sectional or other interest could feel more secure with a friend in the White House.

Party managers also discovered that the dramatic battles for the White House were capable of arousing an unusual interest among the voters at large, and this too may partly explain why the presidency tended to command the centre of the American political stage. 'The election of the President, being one affecting the whole country', noted one English visitor, 'the respective candidates for that office were the butts at which all political shafts were aimed, and to which every other election was rendered subservient . . . ', whether for governor, congressman or even 'constable of the obscure ward of an obscure town'.[10] On such occasions, Alexis de Tocqueville added, 'the whole nation glows with feverish excitement'.[11] In the early republic voters had tended to turn out for state and local elections in greater numbers than they did for presidential elections, but from the 1840s this pattern was being reversed, with turnout in elections for congressional and state offices falling away and that for presidential elections reaching an astonishing height, nearly eighty per cent of adult white males in 1840. It may be that the very mobility and fluidity of American society in the Jacksonian era served to increase popular interest in presidents and presidential elections. Restless Americans, detached from their old communities, perhaps came to invest national campaigns with greater significance.

The advent of the popular election of the president thus served to make the White House the focus of the American system of politics. It made possible the conception of the president as the true spokesman of the people, it arrested the earlier trend towards congressional or parliamentary government, and it opened high federal office to men outside the Washington community. The White House occupied a strategic position in a highly democratic political society frayed by intense sectional jealousies, and the major party coalitions were built largely with the object of winning it, harnessing the energies of citizens throughout the Union to this dramatic cause. These ritualistic party battles gave rise to a kind of popular political culture, and, once the electorate had been politicized, the national parties came to perform important supportive functions for the American polity.

Alexis de Tocqueville himself related the American compulsion to form associations in part to the absence of a hierarchical social order and the weakness of traditional habits of deference. 'The English often perform great things singly', he observed, 'whereas the Americans form associations for the smallest undertakings.' In aristocratic communities men of wealth and standing could provide a lead in public enterprises and could often expect their sentiments to be 'easily introduced into the minds or hearts of all around'. In democratic nations, in contrast, 'associations ought . . . to stand in lieu of those powerful private individuals whom the equality of conditions has swept away'.[12] Americans were not as equal in their economic and social conditions as Tocqueville seemed to think, and it may be that the egalitarian ethos was as important as material circumstances in prompting Americans to band together. But associate they did. Temperance and charitable societies, business corporations, insurance associations, cultural and scientific institutions, church organizations and all manner of reform societies were proliferating rapidly. In 1830 the Rev. William Ellery Channing, who had himself organized the American Unitarian Association, remarked on 'the disposition, which now prevails, to form Associations, and to accomplish all objects by organized masses'.[13] Americans were also electing presidents and other public officers by organized masses, that is by political parties. These were the institutions which provided the link between the isolated individual and the distant governing bodies. The political party, with its network of local organizations and its reassuring rhetoric, helped to integrate the individual American into the larger political system. The political party gave him a new sense of fellowship and helped to generate loyalty to the American polity. Politics revolved less around local communities in which notables dominated; rather, a man's political ties were increasingly with some supra-local organization. By the 1840s party organization existed at every level, congressional, state, and local, and politicians had largely succeeded in mobilizing the electorate.

Perhaps the most striking evidence of popular participation in politics was the extraordinarily high voter turnout in elections. The sheer numbers of people involved were quite unlike anything known in the Old World. Even after the Reform Bill of 1832 Britain had an electorate of only about 800,000 in a population of over sixteen million. In the presidential election of 1832 probably over two million men were qualified to vote in a population of under fourteen million, and about one and a quarter million actually did so. By the early 1840s the population of the United States was almost equal to that of Britain. In the presidential election of 1840 over 2·4 million people cast votes; in the British general election of the following year probably less than a million men were even qualified to vote, and many of them simply could not do so because nearly half the parliamentary seats were not contested. In Britain politics was still largely a game for the aristocratic and commercial elites; in America politics was a game for the masses. And not only were millions of Americans going to the polls in the 1840s; the turnout in presidential elections was higher than ever before and higher than anything achieved in the twentieth century so far. In 1840 and 1844 the turnout in the presidential elections reached seventy-eight and seventy-five per cent respectively and despite some falling off it remained high thereafter. By contrast only fifty-five per cent of the electorate were attracted to the polls in 1972 and only fifty-three per cent in 1976, and turnout in congressional elections has been even lower.

Americans flocked to the polls in such numbers in part because they were responding to the call of party. Unlike his modern successor, the nineteenth-century American voted solidly down the party line. When a man went to the polls he normally voted for all his party's nominees for the various offices being contested, split-ticket voting being rare, demonstrating a degree of partisan commitment which was also revealed by the low swings between the parties at elections. There were few landslides in presidential elections, Andrew Jackson's fifty-six per cent of the popular vote in 1828 being the greatest proportion received by any presidential candidate in the nineteenth century, whereas twentieth-century candidates have not infrequently exceeded sixty per cent. Where a party did fare abnormally well in a nineteenth-century election, as the Democratic party did in several southern states in 1852, it was probably because its opponents' erstwhile supporters stayed away from the polls in disproportionate numbers. The unprecedented popular participation in electoral politics in the mid-nineteenth century was thus also a highly partisan participation, though it was not only the closeness of the competition at the polls which pulled people to them. The whole apparatus of party, the furious battles in the partisan press, the cataclysmic rhetorical harangues, and the hullabaloo and excitement surrounding campaigns at every level all contributed to the politicization of the electorate. The English publisher William Chambers found that 'party spirit is . . . the soul of American society – regulating and controlling everything'.[14]

Once the mass electorate had been successfully mobilized and the party organizations had been completed, the major parties came to perform some rather conservative functions for the political system. The parties of the Jacksonian era held a virtual monopoly of political education. There were almost no impartial newspapers and no ostensibly objective radio and television news reports. Virtually all political information was conveyed by the party politicians and the partisan press, and this near monopoly of the media may have been partly responsible for the high degree of political excitement and the striking party solidarity. As the primary agents of political socialization, the parties helped to integrate the nation's scattered and mobile citizens into the political system. Their incessant campaign propaganda, with its ritual celebration of liberty, democracy, and Union, served to instil common political values among partisans throughout the land.

It was the task of party managers to attempt to absorb new groups as they appeared and to suppress seriously divisive issues. The emergence of Workingmen's parties in several cities around 1830 was in part the product of a nascent class consciousness, a consciousness potentially hostile to American middle class norms, but as the major parties developed in the 1830s they succeeded in sucking in these dissident groups. There were similar attempts to recruit newly arrived immigrants into the party ranks, as when the Whigs in the 1840 presidential election formed German Tippecanoe clubs in many cities and published campaign literature in German. Conversely, the major parties worked hard to avoid, suppress, or compromise issues which might tear them and the Union apart, most notably the issue of slavery. In 1836 the northern and southern Democrats and the southern Whigs in Congress agreed to the so-called 'gag rule', which attempted to bar the congressional discussion of slavery, and it was that patrician foe of party, John Quincy Adams, who led the campaign against this infamous resolution. And when slavery did break into national politics, in 1843 when it became linked to the issue of the annexation of Texas, it was another pair of antiparty men, John Tyler and John C. Calhoun, who were largely responsible. The attempt by the major parties to suppress disruptive issues was also reflected in their intense hostility to third party movements, one Whig editor in 1852 characteristically labelling the members of a Free Soil convention as 'three hundred open and avowed traitors'.[15]

If the patrician leaders of the early republic had once wanted to preserve the *status quo* of the Era of Good Feelings, the established political parties wanted to preserve the *status quo* of the 1840s. The parties themselves did not change much in structure after this period, although the Whig party was replaced by the Republican party. It has been said that the American party system has long been in a state of arrested development, in striking contrast to the dynamism of the socioeconomic system.[16] The only significant innovation in party form since the 1840s has been the direct primary. The parties early became bureaucratic structures with an in-built resistance to change.

The party system has also served to preserve the American constitutional structure much as the Founding Fathers designed it. In a system in which the state was the primary political unit, national parties were naturally coalitions of state parties, and hence had a certain interest in preserving the autonomy of the state. State bosses have looked to the federal government for patronage, but they have not welcomed central control. Hence, while other countries such as Britain were becoming increasingly centralized, the United States remained largely decentralized. But the United States has preserved even more from the eighteenth century than its confederal political structure. The Constitution of 1787 enshrined many of the preoccupations of the political theorists of the seventeenth and eighteenth centuries, such as the doctrine of the separation of powers, the system of checks and balances, and the suspicion of a strong, central executive. A number of conditions have conspired to preserve the eighteenth-century polity, but among them have been the American party systems. Once the American political parties had accommodated themselves to the constitutional structure they shared an interest in preserving it largely intact. While the British political system was moving away from the idealized constitution of 1688 with the abandonment of the old equipoise in favour of a concentration of political authority in the House of Commons, the American political system perpetuated its ancient forms. Even today much American political debate revolves around the same constitutional issues that preoccupied the generations of Thomas Jefferson and Andrew Jackson, such as the balance of power between president and Congress, the strength and size of the federal bureaucracy, and the rights of the separate states. The shape of the party system was in large part dictated by the constitutional structure, but the parties in turn have helped to conserve that structure. Power has remained dispersed in the American polity.

With the emergence of mass politics, then, the national political parties came to perform integrative and conservative functions for American political society. But there was also another dimension to the phenomenon of mass politics. By the 1840s political movements were in some measure folk movements. Not only were people turning out to vote in such unprecedented numbers, but they were also participating in the campaigns themselves. Election campaigns did not simply consist of the candidates, their surrogates, or the party editors formally addressing themselves to the people, as had once been the case. The people themselves were now participating in the ritual of democracy, in rallies, parades, mass meetings, riots, popular activity of all kinds. Just as revivalistic religion and such causes as the temperance crusade were being transformed into folk movements, with the displacement of their old conservative and patrician leaderships, so too election campaigns were acquiring some of the characteristics of popular mass movements. There is no question that astute party managers planned these extraordinary campaign gatherings, but people attended them of their own volition. This too was an important aspect of the American way of politics.

The mass meeting perhaps provided the best example of politics as a folk activity. It was the Whigs in 1840 who first pioneered the mass meeting as an electoral device. Large campaign rallies had been known for years, but they did not compare with the 'immense assemblages' of 1840, at which, grumbled John Quincy Adams, 'twenty, thirty, fifty thousand souls' congregated to hear 'the first orators of the nation address the multitude, not one in ten of whom can hear them'.[17] The first of these massive rallies was held at Columbus, Ohio, on Washington's birthday, attracting an estimated 20,000 people from all over the state and even beyond. Thereafter mass meetings became a regular feature of election campaigns for both parties. In 1844 editor Hezekiah Niles reported that the numbers attending the political rallies that year were 'certainly beyond all precedent', citing as an example 'a rank of mounted men, carriages and wagons, *six miles long*' making its way to a mere district meeting in western New York, and observing that assemblies of ten, twelve, or fifteen thousand people were but 'an every day occurrence'.[18] A reported 50,000 Democrats crammed into the city of Nashville, Tennessee, in August, jamming every road into the city and testing the skills of the organizers, who rose to the occasion by providing a dinner table two miles long.

It was more than entertainment and excitement that drew people to such spectacular gatherings, or, for that matter, to the polls. In the mass society of Jacksonian America the political party offered a new

form of community. As the heightened change and mobility of the
nineteenth century severed or weakened the individual's ties with his
local community, he tended to look elsewhere for security and
reassurance. Among other institutions, the political party came to
function as a brotherhood, a church, a community of believers. A man
might grow old in the party fold, and he might move from Maine to
Missouri, but whatever his age and wherever his place, he could
participate in the same comforting rites and rituals, in the same
exhilarating declarations against executive tyranny or the monster
bank, in the same reassuring celebrations of republican virtue. Men
often travelled long distances to the mass meetings of the mid-
nineteenth century, perhaps hundreds of miles, on horseback, in
bumpy waggons, on hazardous rivers, over muddy roads. These
meetings frequently lasted for some days, obliging people to sleep on
the ground, under tents, on hard floors, on overcrowded mattresses.
Their reward for exposing themselves to such dangers and discomforts
was to be received within the great community of party, a community
which stretched across space and over time.

The newspaper accounts of campaign rallies repeatedly stressed the
way in which such activities transcended the barriers of age, sex,
distance, and occupation. A meeting at Springfield, Illinois, in 1840
was officially designated 'The young men's convention and old
soldier's [sic] meeting', an invitation to young and old to march side by
side in the cause.[19] Even women and children were given a role at such
gatherings, despite the fact that they could not vote, the massive
Democratic rally in Nashville in 1844 being well patronized by women,
their 'white handkerchiefs waving from almost every house, and their
bright smiles beaming from every window, in approval of the
magnificent display'.[20] And just as these meetings brought together the
different ages and sexes, so they also united people of different regions
and occupations. At a state rally, each county would send a delegation,
equipped with a proud banner proclaiming whence it came. Similarly,
these parades frequently included groups of farmers, blacksmiths,
joiners, brickmakers, shoemakers, and other tradesmen, each carrying
a banner and the insignia of its trade. The great fellowship of party
embraced Americans of all ages and occupations, welding them
together in the common cause.

And it was not only a community of the present. A part of the power
of community is its sense of continuity with the past. Much of the ritual
and rhetoric of an election campaign was designed to invoke the
blessing of an earlier generation, and in particular of the heroes of the
Revolution. If Americans feared that their republic was going awry,
the incessant campaign rallies reassured them, for their message was
that they were fighting the good old fight of '76. Revolutionary
symbolism was everywhere. Old flags, weapons, drums, and other
relics of the revolutionary war were conspicuously displayed at
election rallies, which not infrequently were held on revolutionary

sites such as Bunker's Hill, all designed to provide the party faithful with vicarious contact with the revolutionary past. Among the relics of the Revolution were old men who had actually – or allegedly – fought in it, and election parades were frequently headed by a small band of veterans of the war. A mass meeting at Rochester in 1844 was brought to a patriotic close by 'an old Revolutionary soldier, who played Yankee-doodle on the same old fife on which he had played the same old tune at the battle of Bunker's Hill'.[21] When the campaign organizers could no longer find any revolutionary survivors they pressed veterans of the War of 1812 into service. Through the medium of these old men the party rallies offered the new generation a contact with the past. In place of the organic community of old, the displaced individual of Jacksonian America was offered the community of party, which enrolled him in a fellowship both with his contemporaries and with his ancestors. The party gave him a place in society and a place in history.

If party rituals and election campaigns gave comfort to the individual, they also gave sustenance to the American political system by generating support for the republican faith. Yet as ritual re-enactments of the Revolution, such contests obliged each party to identify itself with the true republican cause and to cast its opponents as the un-American enemy. A typical editorial of 1836 insisted that 'the triumph of the opposition would be a death blow to Republican Institutions', while another partisan claimed that the election of 1840 would determine the survival of 'the free institutions of Republican America'.[22] Each election was depicted as a new battle for the republic. Presidential elections in particular gave the voters an opportunity to identify with the republican mission. Every four years Americans were called on to rally to the flag of liberty and to purify the nation of its unrepublican excrescences. Underlying the exuberance of the ante-bellum campaigns was an anxiety for the American mission, an unease lest the new generation betray the sacred trust handed down to them from the past. As the patriotic citizen cast his vote for his favoured candidate he was striking a blow for liberty, he was riding with Paul Revere, and suffering at Valley Forge. Uneasy that the American mission was being diverted and republican virtue eroded, he was telling his ancestors – and himself – that he was still with them.

Of course it was a ritual combat. Ballots had been substituted for bullets, enabling Americans to reaffirm the revolutionary faith without tearing down the structure they had created. The act of participating in the election also implied a willingness to accept the result. But this too served as a further confirmation of dedication to American ideals. A willingness to submit to democratic processes and the will of the majority was at the heart of American republicanism, and a rejection of those institutions which enshrined the concept of popular sovereignty would of itself have been to betray the Fathers. Such was the observation of Hezekiah Niles of the presidential election of 1844:

Every voter in the broad expanse of the Union knows and feels that the PEOPLE are this day SOVEREIGNS; one of whom he is. . . . All acquiescing in the decision bow to the majority of the people, and with one accord each one returns to his occupation recognizing the choice of the majority as being the CHIEF OF THE NATION for the ensuing four years, feeling as though his duty to his country had for this occasion been performed. This is the test *and the* proof *too, of republican virtue.* [23]

American nationality was defined not so much by geographical boundaries or an ancient cultural inheritance as by a cluster of beliefs, in particular by the libertarian principles enshrined in the Declaration of Independence and the democratic convictions which could be derived from them. The ritualistic ceremonies of American politics were a form of worship, and in the polling booths Americans reaffirmed their commitment to the republican religion. The popularization of American political culture did something, if not quite enough, to strengthen those 'mystic chords of memory, stretching from every battle-field and patriot grave to every living heart and hearthstone all over this broad land', which President Lincoln was to summon to the defence of the people's republic.[24]

References

Preface

1. **Michel Chevalier,** *Society, Manners, and Politics in the United States: Letters on North America,* ed. **John William Ward,** Doubleday, 1961, p.308, p.410.
2. **Saul K. Padover,** ed., *The World of the Founding Fathers: Their Basic Ideas on Freedom and Self-Government,* Thomas Yoseloff, 1960, p. 573.

Chapter 1: The politics of Old England

1. Quoted by John Brooke in **Sir Lewis Namier** and **John Brooke,** *The History of Parliament,* H.M.S.O., 1964, i, 146.
2. **W.E. Gladstone,** ed., *The Works of Joseph Butler,* Clarendon P., 1896, ii, 305.
3. Quoted by **Brooke,** op. cit., p. 26.
4. Quotes in: **Gordon S. Wood,** *The Creation of the American Republic, 1776-1787,* Norton, 1972, p. 11; **Asa Briggs,** *The Age of Improvement, 1783-1867,* Longmans, 3rd impr., 1962, p. 88; *New York Gazette,* 11-18 March 1733/34, in **Lawrence H. Leder,** ed., *Dimensions of Change: Problems and Issues of American Colonial History,* Burgess, 1972, p. 174.
5. **John Wise,** *A Vindication of the Government of New-England Churches,* 1717, in ibid., p. 169.
6. Charles I's Answer to the 19 Propositions of Parliament, 18 June 1642, in ibid., p. 166.
7. **E.N. Williams,** ed., *The Eighteenth Century Constitution: Documents and Commentary,* Cambridge U.P., 1960, p. 75.
8. **John B. Owen,** *The Eighteenth Century, 1714-1815,* Nelson, 1974, p. 103.
9. For a good brief discussion of Englishmen's perceptions of party see **Caroline Robbins,** ' "Discordant Parties": A Study of the Acceptance of Party by Englishmen', *Pol. Sc. Qu.,* lxxiii, 1958, 505-29. More detailed is **Michael Wallace,** 'The Ideology of Party in the Age of Jackson', Ph.D. thesis, Columbia University, 1973, pp. 9-48. **John Brewer,** *Party Ideology and Popular Politics at the Accession of George III,* Cambridge U.P., 1976, was published after this chapter was written but is recommended to students.
10. Quoted by **Bernard Bailyn,** *The Origins of American Politics,* Vintage Books, 1970, p. 42.
11. See ibid; **Bailyn,** *The Ideological Origins of the American Revolution,* Belknap Press of Harvard U.P., 1967; **Wood,** op.cit.; **Lance Gilbert Banning,** 'The Quarrel with Federalism: A Study in the Origins and Character of Republican Thought', University Microfilms, Ph.D. thesis, Washington University, 1972.
12. Quoted by **Bailyn,** *Origins,* p. 46.
13. See **Isaac Kramnick,** *Bolingbroke and His Circle: The Politics of Nostalgia in the Age of Walpole,* Harvard U.P., 1968; **Banning,** op. cit., pp. 86-91.
14. **Michael Wallace,** 'The Ideology of Party', pp. 1-184.
15. **Ian Christie,** *Wilkes, Wyvill and Reform,* Macmillian, 1962, pp. 15-16, quoted in **Bailyn,** *Ideological Origins,* p. 283 n.
16. **John Brooke,** op. cit., p. 99.

17. Quoted by **G.D.H. Cole** and **Raymond Postgate,** *The Common People, 1746-1946,* Methuen, 1961, p. 96.

Chapter 2: Politics in colonial America

1. **Bernard Bailyn,** *Ideological Origins,* p. 303.
2. **Perry Miller** and **Thomas H. Johnson,** eds., *The Puritans: A Sourcebook of Their Writings,* Harper Torchbooks, 1963, i, 195.
3. Quoted by **Jack P. Greene,** 'The Preconditions for American Republicanism: A Comment', *The Development of a Revolutionary Mentality,* Library of Congress, 1972, p. 122.
4. Quoted by **Wesley Frank Craven,** *The Colonies in Transition, 1660-1713,* Harper & Row, 1968, p. 186.
5. See **Page Smith,** 'Anxiety and Despair in American History, *William and Mary Qu.,* xxiv (July 1969), 416-24; quote on p. 48.
6. **Patrick M'Robert,** *A Tour through part of the North Provinces of America,* quoted by **Jackson Turner Main,** *The Social Structure of Revolutionary America,* Princeton U.P., 1965, p. 222.
7. Quoted by **Richard L. Bushman,** *From Puritan to Yankee: Character and the Social Order in Connecticut, 1690-1765,* Norton, 1970, p. 267.
8. **William Smith,** 1734, in **Leder,** *Dimensions of Change,* p. 176.
9. **J.R. Pole,** ed., *The Revolution in America 1754-1788: Documents and Commentaries,* Macmillan, 1970, p. 11.
10. For example see **Jack P. Greene,** 'Search for Identity: An Interpretation of the Meaning of Selected Patterns of Social Response in Eighteenth-Century America', *J. Soc. Hist.,* iii (Spring 1970), 189-220; **John M. Murrin,** 'The Legal Transformation: The Bench and Bar of Eighteenth-Century Massachusetts', in **Stanley N. Katz,** ed., *Colonial America: Essays in Politics and Social Development,* Little, Brown, 1971, 415-49.
11. William Franklin to Elizabeth Graeme, 9 Dec. 1757, **Leonard W. Labaree,** ed., *The Papers of Benjamin Franklin,* Yale U.P., 1963, vii, 290.
12. Quoted by **Leonard Woods Labaree,** *Royal Government in America,* Ungar, 1930, p. 206.
13. **Merrill Jensen,** ed., *English Historical Documents,* Eyre & Spottiswoode, 1955, ix, 196.
14. **Robert E.** and **B. Katherine Brown,** *Virginia 1705-1786: Democracy or Aristocracy?,* Michigan State U.P., 1964, pp. 225-6.
15. Quoted in ibid., p. 158.
16. **Jack P. Greene,** 'Changing Interpretations of Early American Politics', in **Ray Allen Billington,** ed., *The Reinterpretation of Early American History,* Huntington Library, 1966, p. 176.
17. See **Patricia U. Bonomi,** *A Factious People, Politics and Society in Colonial New York,* Columbia U.P., 1971, and 'The Politics of Disorder', *Revs. in Am. Hist.,* i, (June 1973), 208-13.
18. On the theme of deference, see **J.R. Pole,** 'Historians and the Problem of Early American Democracy', *Am. Hist. Rev.,* lxvii (April 1962), 626-46; **Richard Buel,** jr., 'Democracy and the American Revolution: A Frame of Reference', *William and Mary Qu.,* xxi (April 1964), 165-90; **J.G.A. Pocock,** 'The Classical Theory of Deference', *Am. Hist. Rev.,* lxxxi (June 1976), 516-23.
19. *Pennsylvania Journal,* 28 Sept. 1758. in **Clinton Rossiter,** *Seedtime of the Republic,* Harcourt, Brace, 1953, p. 143.

Chapter 3: The spirit of 'seventy-six

1. Quoted by **Russel Blaine Nye,** *The Cultural Life of the New Nation, 1776-1830,* Harper & Row, 1963, p. 51.

2. **Moncure Daniel Conway,** ed., *The Writings of Thomas Paine,* Burt Franklin, 1902-08, ii, 137.
3. Ibid., i, 154, 97.
4. Adams to Horatio Gates, 23 March 1776, **E.C. Burnett,** ed., *Letters of the Members of the Continental Congress,* Carnegie Inst. Washington, 1921-36, i. 406.
5. Stamp Act Resolutions, in **Richard B. Morris,** *The American Revolution: A Short History,* Van Nostrand, 1955, p. 92.
6. **Pole,** ed., *Rev. in America,* p. 22.
7. **Wood,** *Creation of the Am. Rep.,* p. 10.
8. **Pole,** ed., *Rev. in America,* p. 20.
9. Ibid., p. 453.
10. Adams to James Warren, 22 April 1776, **Samuel E. Morison,** ed., *Sources and Documents illustrating the American Revolution, 1764-1788,* 2nd edn., Oxford U.P., 1929, p. 147.
11. **Jackson Turner Main,** 'Government By the People: The American Revolution and the Democratization of the Legislatures', *William and Mary Qu.,* 3rd ser., xxiii (July 1966), 391-407, quotation on p. 407. See also **Main,** *Political Parties Before the Constitution,* Norton, 1974.
12. Quoted by **Merrill Jensen,** *The New Nation,* Knopf, 1953, p. 43.
13. Quoted by **Chilton Williamson,** *American Suffrage from Property to Democracy, 1760-1860,* Princeton U.P., 1960, p. 107.
14. **J.R. Pole,** *Political Representation in England and the Origins of the American Republic,* Macmillan, 1966, p. 170, pp. 172-89, pp. 372-3, and *Foundations of American Independence, 1763-1815,* Fontana, 1973, pp. 89-90.
15. Quoted by **Duncan J. MacLeod,** *Slavery, Race and the American Revolution,* Cambridge U.P., 1974, p. 17.
16. **William G. McLoughlin,** ed., *Isaac Backus on Church, State, and Calvinism: Pamphlets, 1754-1789,* Harvard U.P., 1968, p. 333, p. 338, p. 436.
17. Quoted by **Merrill Jensen,** *The Making of the American Constitution,* Van Nostrand, 1964, p. 30.

Chapter 4: A quest for republican security

1. **Max Farrand,** ed., *The Records of the Federal Convention of 1787,* Yale U.P., 1937, i, 27.
2. **Charles Francis Adams,** ed., *The Works of John Adams,* Boston; Little, Brown, 1850-56, vi, 219.
3. **Saul K. Padover,** ed., *The World of the Founding Fathers,* p. 415.
4. Jefferson to Madison, 1 July 1784, **Julian P. Boyd,** ed., *The Papers of Thomas Jefferson,* Princeton U.P., 1953, vii, 356.
5. **Pole,** ed., *Rev. in America,* p. 388.
6. Quoted by **Jensen,** *New Nation,* p. 45.
7. Quoted in ibid., p. 62.
8. Henry Lee to George Washington, 17 Oct. 1786, **Burnett,** ed., *Letters Members Cont. Congr.,* viii, 486.
9. **Jensen,** *Making of Constitution,* p.34.
10. Quoted by **Jackson Turner Main,** *The Antifederalists: Critics of the Constitution, 1781-1788,* U. North Carolina P., 1961, p.64.

Chapter 5: An American Constitution

1. **J. Franklin Jameson,** ed., *Essays in the Constitutional History of the United States in the Formative Period, 1775-1789,* Houghton, Mifflin, 1889, p. 46.
2. **Farrand,** ed., *Records Federal Convention,* i, 552; i, 26; ii, 273.
3. Ibid., ii, 89.
4. Ibid., ii, 221.
5. Amendment X (1791).

6. **Padover,** ed., *World of the Founding Fathers:,* pp. 500-1.
7. Quoted by **Charles C. Thach,** *The Creation of the Presidency, 1775-1789: A Study in Constitutional History,* Johns Hopkins P., 1922, p. 98.
8. Quoted in ibid., p. 96.
9. **Padover,** ed., op. cit., p. 448.
10. **Alexander Hamilton, James Madison** and **John Jay,** *The Federalist or, The New Constitution,* J.M. Dent, 1971, No.lxii, p.318.
11. Quoted by **Wood,** *Creation of the Am. Rep.,* p. 595.
12. For the theme of representation see ibid., pp. 162-255, pp. 593-600, Madison quotation on p. 596.
13. *Federalist,* No. x, p. 47.
14. Ibid., p. 47.
15. Ibid., p. 45.
16. Ibid., No. lxviii, p. 349.
17. **Padover,** ed., op. cit., p. 327.
18. Quoted by **Clinton Rossiter,** *1787: The Grand Convention,* Macmillan, 1966, p.170.
19. Quoted in ibid., p. 283.
20. **Padover,** ed., op. cit., p. 250; *Independent Gazetteer,* 29 Oct. 1787, in **John B. McMaster** and **Frederick D. Stone,** eds., *Pennsylvania and the Federal Constitution, 1787-1788,* Lancaster, Pa., 1888, i, 174.
21. Quoted by **Jensen,** *Making of Constitution,* p. 123.
22. *Federalist,* No. xxxix, 194, 196.
23. On association of Federalism with wealth and standing, see **Main,** *Antifederalists,* pp.221-48; Morris quotation in **Rossiter,** *1787,* p.287.
24. Smith to Abraham Yates, jr., 28 Jan. 1788, in **Main,** *Antifederalists,* p. 203.
25. *Federalist,* No. xxxv, p. 167.
26. Jay to George Washington, 27 June 1786, **Morison,** ed., *Sources and Documents,* p.215.
27. *Federalist,* No. xxxv, p. 168.

Chapter 6: The Federalist design

1. **Marcus Cunliffe,** *American Presidents and the Presidency,* Eyre & Spottiswoode, 1969, pp. 37-8, briefly discusses the monarchical aspects of the presidency and quotes Washington Irving.
2. **Richard B. Morris,** ed., *Alexander Hamilton and the Founding of the Nation,* Dial Press, 1957, p. 495; Lafayette quoted in **Marcus Cunliffe,** *George Washington: Man and Monument,* Collins, 1959, p. 122; **John C. Fitzpatrick,** ed., *The Writings of George Washington . . . ,* G. Washington Bicentennial Commission, 1939, xxx, 66-7, n. 80.
3. The title dispute is well-described in **James H. Hutson,** 'John Adams' Title Campaign', *New England Qu.,* xli, (March 1968), 30-9.
4. **Leonard D. White,** *The Federalists: A Study in Administrative History,* Macmillan, 1956, pp. 67-8.
5. **Harold C. Syrett,** ed., *The Papers of Alexander Hamilton,* Columbia U.P., 1966, xi, 429.
6. Quoted by **Gerald Stourzh,** *Alexander Hamilton and the Idea of Republican Government,* Stanford U.P., 1970, p. 175.
7. Quoted in ibid., p. 180.
8. Quoted by **Richard Buel** jr., *Securing the Revolution: Ideology in American Politics, 1789-1815,* Cornell U.P., 1972, p. 11.
9. **Henry Cabot Lodge,** ed., *The Works of Alexander Hamilton,* Putnam, 1904, x, 425.
10. **Padover,** ed., *World of the Founding Fathers:,* p. 213.
11. **Lodge,** ed., op. cit., iii, 332.
12. The continuing impact of English constitutional thought on American politics, and the role of fears of constitutional degeneration, have been splendidly analysed by

Lance Banning, and the discussion of these themes is much influenced by his writings. See **Banning,** 'Republican Ideology and the Triumph of the Constitution, 1789 to 1793', *William and Mary Qu.,* xxxi (April 1974), 167-88, and 'The Quarrel with Federalism'. The Virginia legislature is quoted in ibid., p. 245. See also **John Robert Zvesper,** 'Republican Ideology and the Origins of American Party Government, 1789-1801', Ph.D. thesis, Cambridge University, 1973.

13. **John C. Miller,** *The Federalist Era, 1789-1801,* Harper & Row, 1960, p. 56.
14. Quoted by **Banning,** 'The Quarrel with Federalism', p. 267.
15. Quoted in ibid., p. 275.
16. Quoted in ibid., p. 320.

Chapter 7: The spectre of party

1. **Robert McColley,** ed., *Federalists, Republicans, and Foreign Entanglements, 1789-1815,* Prentice-Hall, 1969, p. 82.
2. **Andrew A. Lipscomb,** ed., *The Writings of Thomas Jefferson,* Thomas Jefferson Memorial Association, 1903, ix, 359.
3. Quoted by **Banning,** 'The Quarrel with Federalism', p. 396.
4. Quoted in ibid., pp. 396-7.
5. Quoted by **Miller,** *Federalist Era,* p. 249.
6. Ibid., p. 262.
7. Quoted in ibid., p. 265.
8. **Lipscomb,** ed., op. cit., p. 136.
9. **Fitzpatrick,** ed., *Writings of George Washington,* xxxv, 228.
10. **Noble E. Cunningham,** jr., ed., *The Making of the American Party System, 1789-1809,* Prentice-Hall, 1956, p. 21.
11. Ibid., p.17.
12. **Syrett,** ed., *Papers of Hamilton,* xi, 433, 429.

Chapter 8: Towards republican harmony

1. Quoted by **Richard E. Ellis,** *The Jeffersonian Crisis: Courts and Politics in the Young Republic,* Oxford U.P., 1971, p. 27. This book is more wide-ranging than the title suggests and has influenced the approach in this chapter.
2. **Lipscomb,** ed., *Writings of Thomas Jefferson,* x, 175.
3. Ibid., ii, 162.
4. Ibid., iii, 320.
5. Quoted by **Herbert Agar,** *The United States: The Presidents, the Parties and the Constitution,* Eyre & Spottiswoode, 1950, p. 72.
6. **Lipscomb,** ed., op. cit., iii, 317-24.
7. Ibid., x, 79.
8. Quoted by **Richard Hofstadter,** *The American Political Tradition,* Jonathan Cape, 1962, p. 34.
9. Jefferson to William Duane, 24 July 1803, in **Raymond Walters,** jr., *The Virginia Dynasty,* Van Nostrand, 1965, p. 107.
10. Theodore Dwight, 7 July 1801, in ibid., p. 104.
11. **Lipscomb,** ed., op. cit., xii, 324.
12. Ibid., xii, 324.
13. Quoted by **Ellis,** op. cit., p. 281.
14. **Lipscomb,** ed., op. cit., xiv, 391.
15. Quoted by **Ellis,** op. cit., p. 57.
16. **Lipscomb,** ed., op. cit., xv, 213.
17. Quoted by **Ellis,** op. cit., p. 102.
18. Theodore Dwight, 1801, in **Walters,** op. cit., p. 104; **Samuel E. Morison,** *The Life and Letters of Harrison Gray Otis: Federalist, 1765-1848,* Houghton Mifflin, 1913, i, 279.

19. Quoted by **Norman K. Risjord,** *The Old Republicans: Southern Conservatism in the Age of Jefferson,* Columbia U.P., 1965, p. 47.
20. Quoted by **Russell Kirk,** *Randolph of Roanoke: A Study in Conservative Thought,* U. of Chicago P., 1951, p. 21.
21. Quoted by **Leonard W. Levy,** *Jefferson and Civil Liberties: The Darker Side,* Harvard U.P., 1963, p. 71.
22. **Henry Adams,** *History of the United States of America,* Charles Scribner's Sons, 1890, iv, 417.
23. See **Leonard W. Levy,** op. cit., for an unfavourable analysis of Jefferson's record on civil liberties. The quotation is on p. 120.
24. Gallatin to Jefferson, 18 Dec. 1807, in **Walters,** op. cit., p. 130.
25. Quoted by **Levy,** op. cit., p. 133.
26. Daniel Blaisdell, quoted by **David Hackett Fischer,** *The Revolution of American Convervatism*, Harper Torchbooks, 1969, p.234.
27. **Charles R. King,** ed., *The Life and Correspondence of Rufus King,* Putnam, 1898, v, 187-8.
28. Quoted by **Roger H. Brown,** *The Republic in Peril: 1812,* Norton, 1971, p. 31.
29. **McColley,** ed., *Federalists, Republicans, and Foreign Entanglements,* 157-8.
30. Quoted by **Roger H. Brown,** p.84.
31. **King,** ed., *Corr. of King,* v, 345.
32. Quoted by **Fischer,** p. 180 n.

Chapter 9: The patrician order of the early republic

1. Quoted by **Raymond Walters** jr., *Albert Gallatin: Jeffersonian Financier and Diplomat,* Macmillan, 1957, p. 288.
2. Quoted by **Williamson,** *Am. Suffrage from Property to Democracy,* p. 137.
3. Quoted by **Fischer,** *The Revolution of Am. Conserv.,* p. 156.
4. Quoted by **Buel,** *Securing the Revolution,* p. 256.
5. **Lipscomb,** ed., *Writings of Thomas Jefferson,* xv, 442.
6. For the association of the less secure elites with Federalism and of the more secure elites with Republicanism, see **Buel,** *Securing the Revolution,* Ch. 4.
7. **Lester J. Cappon,** ed., *The Adams-Jefferson Letters,* U. of North Carolina P., 1959, ii, 388.
8. **Pole,** *Political Representation,* pp. 543-64; **Richard P. McCormick,** 'New Perspectives on Jacksonian Politics', *Am. Hist. Rev.,* lxv (Jan. 1960), 288-301.
9. Quoted by **Williamson,** op. cit., p. 135.
10. **Noble E. Cunningham,** *The Jeffersonian Republicans: The Formation of Party Organisation, 1789-1801,* U. of North Carolina P., 1957, p. 105.
11. **White,** *The Federalists,* p. 258.
12. **Lipscomb,** ed., op. cit., xi, 423.
13. Quoted by **Leonard D. White,** *The Jeffersonians,* Macmillan, 1956, p. 356.
14. **Lipscomb,** ed., op. cit., x, 134.
15. **Cunningham,** ed., op. cit., p. 130.
16. **Lipscomb,** ed., op. cit., ix, 351.
17. **Ralph Volney Harlow,** *The History of Legislative Methods in the Period Before 1825,* Yale U.P., 1917, p.168 n; Adams in **White,** *The Jeffersonians*, p.48 n.
18. **Lipscomb,** ed., op. cit., xi, 117.
19. Quoted by **James Sterling Young,** *The Washington Community, 1800-1828,* Columbia U.P., 1966, p. 187.
20. Quoted by **White,** *The Jeffersonians,* p. 39.
21. **Young,** op. cit.
22. *Zanesville Express,* 20 Jan. 1813, in **Donald J. Ratcliffe,** 'The Experience of Revolution and the Beginnings of Party Politics in Ohio, 1776-1816', *Ohio History,* lxxxv, (Summer 1976), p. 221.
23. Quoted in ibid., p. 222.
24. **Cappon,** ed., op. cit., ii, 427.

Chapter 10: The old structure crumbles

1. Morris Birkbeck, quoted by **Harold U. Faulkner,** *American Economic History*, 8th edn., Harper & Row, 1963, p.182.
2. **Francis J. Grund,** *Aristocracy in America,* Harper Torchbooks, 1959, p. 245.
3. *Am. Quarterly Rev.,* xix (March and June 1836), 29.
4. W.L. Marcy to Van Buren, 29 Jan. 1828, in **George Dangerfield,** *The Awakening of American Nationalism, 1815-1828,* Harper Torchbooks, 1965, p. 279 n.
5. 'A Southron', *To the People of South Carolina. An Address on the subject of the approaching Presidential Election . . .* (1824), p. 8.
6. Quoted by **Glyndon G. Van Deusen,** *The Life of Henry Clay*, Little, Brown, 1937, p.134.
7. 'FRANKLIN' in *The Nose,* (Jersey Shore, Pa.,), 7 Aug. 1828, pp. 26-7.
8. **Allan Nevins,** ed., *The Diary of John Quincy Adams, 1794-1845,* Charles Scribner's Sons, 1951, p. 386.
9. **Merrill D. Peterson,** ed., *Democracy, Liberty, and Property: The State Constitutional Conventions of the 1820's,* Bobbs-Merrill Co., 1966, p. 400.
10. *National Advocate,* 24 July 1821, in **Williamson,** op. cit., p. 207.
11. *Annals of Congress,* 2nd sess., p. 149 (13 Jan. 1819).
12. *Albany Argus,* 27 Feb. 1824.
13. *Delaware Gazette,* 25 Mar. 1823, in **Robert P. Hay,** ' "The Presidential Question": Letters to Southern Editors, 1823-24', *Tennessee Hist. Qu.,* xxxi (Summer 1972), p. 182.
14. *Richmond Enquirer,* 6 May 1823.
15. **Henry Thomas Shanks,** ed., *The Papers of Willie Person Mangum,* N. Carolina State Dept. of Archives and History, 1950, i, 137.
16. *National Journal,* 20 Nov. 1824.
17. *Western Volunteer,* (Frankfort, Ky.), 20 Oct. 1824.
18. *Argus of Western America* (Frankfort, Ky.), 29 Oct. 1828.
19. **Everett S. Brown,** ed., *The Missouri Compromises and Presidential Politics, 1820-1825,* Missouri Historical Society, 1926, p. 51.
20. Quoted by **Dangerfield,** op. cit., p. 232.

Chapter 11: The politicians respond

1. Quoted by **M. Ostrogorski,** *Democracy and the Organization of Political Parties,* Macmillan, 1902, ii, 44.
2. Van Buren to Thomas Ritchie, 13 Jan. 1827, Van Buren Papers, L.C.
3. **Peterson,** ed., *Democracy, Liberty, and Property*, p.435.
4. Ibid., p. 155.
5. Quoted by **Jane L. Mesick,** *The English Traveller in America, 1785-1835,* Columbia U.P., 1922, p. 324.
6. *Register of Debates in Congress,* 19th cong., 1st sess., p. 1370 (15 Feb. 1826).
7. *Letters and Other Writings of James Madison,* Lippincott, 1865, iii, 334.
8. *National Journal,* 20 Nov. 1824.
9. *Suggestions on Presidential Elections, with Particular Reference to a Letter of William C. Somerville, Esq.,* Boston, 1825, p. 4.
10. First Annual Message, 1825, **Glyndon G. Van Deusen,** *The Rise and Decline of Jacksonian Democracy,* Van Nostrand Reinhold, 1970, p. 123.
11. Clay in 1824, **Walters,** *Virginia Dynasty,* p. 165.
12. Quoted by **Dangerfield,** *Awakening of Am. Nationalism,* p. 18.
13. Quoted by **William Appleton Williams,** *The Contours of American History,* Jonathan Cape, 1961, p. 209.
14. Message to Legislature, 1819, **Frank Otto Gatell** and **John M. McFaul,** eds, *Jacksonian America, 1815-1840: New Society, Changing Politics,* Prentice-Hall, 1970, p. 11.

15. First Annual Message, 1825, **Van Deusen,** op. cit., p. 123.
16. Dallas to Calhoun, 24 Dec. 1815, **Walters,** op. cit., p. 128.
17. **Clement Eaton,** ed., *The Leaven of Democracy,* George Braziller, 1963, p. 49.
18. Quoted by **Denis Tilden Lynch,** *An Epoch and a Man: Martin Van Buren and His Times,* Horace Leveright, 1929, p. 243.
19. **Fletcher Webster,** ed., *The Private Correspondence of Daniel Webster,* Boston, 1857, i, 371.
20. Quoted by **Cyrus T. Brady,** *The True Andrew Jackson,* Lippincott, 1906, p.288.
21. *Richmond Enquirer,* 30 July 1822.
22. Quoted by **Charles Grier Sellers,** jr., 'Jackson Men with Feet of Clay', *Am. Hist. Rev.,* lxii (April 1957), p. 545.
23. *Corr. of Webster,* i. 346.
24. *Nashville Gazette* in *Richmond Enquirer,* 30 July 1822.
25. Quoted by **Robert V. Remini,** *The Election of Andrew Jackson,* Lippincott, 1963, p.28.
26. For the exploitation of Jackson's earthy image against Adams' professorial image, see **John William Ward,** *Andrew Jackson: Symbol for an Age,* Oxford U.P., 1962, esp. Ch. 4.
27. Quoted by **Edwin L. Green,** *George McDuffie,* State Co., 1936, pp. 49-50.
28. Van Buren to Thomas Ritchie, 13 Jan. 1827, Van Buren Papers, L.C.
29. Ibid.

Chapter 12: The new American party system

1. *Albany Argus,* 14 May 1824.
2. *Speech of Mr. Stevenson, of Virginia, on the Proposition to Amend the Constitution of the United States, respecting the Election of President and Vice President,* Washington, 1826, p. 27.
3. Francis P. Blair to Martin Van Buren, 30 Sept. 1832, Van Buren Papers, L.C.
4. See **Michael Wallace,** 'Changing Concepts of Party in the United States: New York, 1815-1828', *Am. Hist. Rev.,* lxxiv (1968), 453-91; **Wallace,** 'The Ideology of Party in the Age of Jackson', doctoral thesis, Columbia Univ., 1973; **Richard Hofstadter,** *The Idea of a Party System: The Rise of Legitimate Opposition in the United States, 1780-1840,* California U.P., 1970.
5. *Register of Debates in Congress,* 19th cong., 1st sess., p. 1678 (14 Mar. 1826).
6. Mangum to Duncan Cameron, 7 Feb. 1834, **Henry Thomas Shanks,** ed., *The Papers of Willie Person Mangum,* N. Carolina State Dept. of Archives and History, 1950, ii, 74.
7. See **Richard P. McCormick,** *The Second American Party System: Party Formation in the Jacksonian Era,* North Carolina U.P., 1966.
8. *Summary of the Proceedings of a Convention of Republican Delegates, from the several states in the Union, for the purpose of nominating a candidate for the office of Vice-President of the United States; ...,* Albany, 1832, p. 13.
9. *Baltimore Republican,* 21 May 1835.
10. *Boston Statesman,* 11 Feb. 1835.
11. **James D. Richardson,** *A Compilation of the Messages and Papers of the Presidents,* New York, 1910, ii, 449; **Henry Steele Commager,** ed., *Documents of American History* (7th edn.), Appleton-Century-Crofts, 1963, p. 255.
12. **Harriet Langdon Pruyn Rice,** *Harmanus Bleecker: An Albany Dutchman, 1779-1849,* Albany, 1924, p. 189.
13. Mangum to Duncan Cameron, 7 Feb. 1834, **Henry Thomas Shanks,** op. cit., ii, 74.
14. *National Intelligencer,* 22 March 1827; Augustus L.G. Fischer to McLean, 23 Aug. 1843, John McLean Papers, L.C.
15. *Columbian Centinel,* 24 Sept. 1836.
16. *Niles's Weekly Register,* 1 (30 Jan. 1836), 384.
17. **George E. Baker,** ed., *The Works of William H. Seward,* Boston, 1884, iii, 261.

Chapter 13: The Democratic strategy

1. *United States Telegraph*, 24 Nov. 1828.
2. Bank Veto Message, **George Rogers Taylor,** ed., *Jackson Versus Biddle: The Struggle Over the Second Bank of the United States*, D.C. Heath, 1949, p. 19.
3. **John C. Fitzpatrick,** ed., *The Autobiography of Martin Van Buren,* Da Capo Press, 1973, i, 320, 322.
4. **William W. Freehling,** ed., *The Nullification Era; A Documentary Record,* Harper & Row, 1967, p. 103.
5. Ibid., p. 162.
6. **Francis J. Grund,** *The Americans in Their Moral, Social, and Political Relations,* Boston, 1837, p. 202.
7. William Foster to Silas Wright Jr., 3 Jan. 1835, Van Buren Papers, L.C.
8. *United States Weekly Telegraph,* 6 Dec. 1828, p. 3.
9. **Richardson,** ed., *Messages and Papers,* ii, 462.
10. **Taylor,** ed., op. cit., p. 19.
11. Farewell Address, in **Joseph L. Blau,** ed., *Social Theories of Jacksonian Democracy: Representative Writings of the Period 1825-1850,* Bobbs-Merrill, 1954, p. 14.
12. Ibid., p. 18.
13. *Register of Debates,* 24th cong., 2nd sess., p. 610 (27 Jan. 1837).
14. *New York Evening Post,* 30 Dec. 1834, in **Edwin C. Rozwenc,** ed., *Ideology and Power in the Age of Jackson,* Doubleday, 1964, p. 225.
15. *The United States Magazine and Democratic Review,* i (Oct. 1837), p. 6.
16. 'GRATTAN', *The Globe* (Washington), 10 Oct. 1840.
17. *Papers for the People,* (New York), i, June 1852, p. 4.
18. See **Matthew A. Crenson,** *The Federal Machine: Beginnings of Bureaucracy in Jacksonian America,* Johns Hopkins U.P., 1975.
19. **William M. Holland,** *The Life and Political Opinions of Martin Van Buren, Vice President of the United States,* Hartford, Conn., 1835, p. 359.
20. *Democratic Rev.,* i (Oct. 1837), p. 6.

Chapter 14: The Whig response

1. Gen. Dearborn to Clay, 2 Oct. 1831, Clay Papers, L.C.; Calhoun to Christopher Van Deventer, 31 March 1832, **J. Franklin Jameson,** ed., 'Correspondence of John C. Calhoun', Am. Hist. Assoc., *Annual Report,* 1899, ii, 317; R.W. Stoddard to Henry Clay, 12 Nov. 1832, Clay Papers, L.C.
2. Clay to Francis Brooke, 10 Feb. 1834, **Calvin Colton,** ed., *The Private Correspondence of Henry Clay,* Boston, 1856, p. 378.
3. **Jabez D. Hammond,** *History of Political Parties in the State of New York,* Albany, 1842, ii, 439.
4. Clay to Biddle, 2 Feb. 1834, **Reginald C. McGrane,** ed., *The Correspondence of Nicholas Biddle,* Houghton Mifflin, 1919, p. 220.
5. **Charles Francis Adams,** ed., *Memoirs of John Quincy Adams,* Philadelphia, 1874-77, ix, 162 (30 July 1843).
6. **Thurlow Weed,** *Autobiography,* ed. Harriet A. Weed, Boston, 1883, p. 443.
7. Webster to Samuel Jaudon, 23 June 1840, **Fletcher Webster,** ed., *The Private Correspondence of Daniel Webster,* Boston, 1857, ii, 88; John Van Fossen to Thurlow Weed, 20 July 1840, Weed Papers, L.C.
8. *The Harrison Medal Minstrel,* Philadelphia, 1840, p. 3.
9. *The Rough-Hewer* (Albany), 21 May 1840.
10. **Kirk H. Porter** and **Donald Bruce Johnson,** compilers, *National Party Platforms, 1840-1964,* Illinois U.P., 1966, p. 9.
11. Quoted by **William G. Carleton,** 'Political Aspects of the Van Buren Era', in **Frank Otto Gatell,** ed., *Essays on Jacksonian America,* Holt, Rinehart and Winston, 1970, p. 200.

12. Quoted by **Rush Welter,** *The Mind of America, 1820-1860,* Columbia U.P., 1975, p.128.
13. **Holland,** *Life of Martin Van Buren,* pp. 79-80.
14. *National Intelligencer,* 4 Nov. 1842.
15. **Rozwenc,** ed., *Ideology and Power,* p. 39; **William H. Hale,** *Horace Greeley: The Voice of the People,* Harper, 1950, pp. 37-8.
16. **Rozwenc,** ed., op. cit., p. 48.
17. *The American Review: A Whig Journal . . . ,* vi, Sept. 1847, 242.
18. **George E. Probst,** ed., *The Happy Republic: A Reader in Tocqueville's America,* Harper, 1962, p. 433.
19. **Daniel Walker Howe,** ed., *The American Whigs: An Anthology,* John Wiley, 1973, p. 219.
20. **Baker,** ed., *Works of Seward,* iii, 261.

Chapter 15: The disruption of the second party system

1. *Log Cabin Patriot,* (E. Bridgewater, Mass.), 7 Aug. 1840.
2. *The Globe,* 15 Dec. 1837.
3. *Democratic Rev.,* vi (1839), p. 427.
4. Farewell address, in **Blau,** ed., *Social Theories of Jacksonian Democracy:,* p. 20.
5. **E.S. Abdy,** *Journal of a Residence and Tour in the United States of North America, from April, 1833, to October, 1834,* London, 1835, ii, 337.
6. 'Appeal by Stephen F. Austin', 15 April 1836, **John Spenser Bassett,** ed., *Correspondence of Andrew Jackson,* Carnegie Institution of Washington, 1926-35, v, 397.
7. *Address of the Democratic State Convention, to the People of New Jersey, as reported by James C. Zabriskie, Esq., Chairman of the Committee,* Trenton, N.J., 1844, p.10. For an interesting analysis of the relationship between libertarian ideas and expansionism see **Major L. Wilson,** *Space, Time and Freedom,* Greenwood P., 1974, Ch. v.
8. Calhoun to Richard Pakenham, 18 April 1844, **Glyndon G. Van Deusen,** *The Rise and Decline of Jacksonian Democracy,* Van Nostrand Reinhold, 1970, p. 233.
9. **Joel H. Silbey,** ed., *The Transformation of American Politics, 1840-1860,* Prentice-Hall, 1967, p. 70.
10. Calhoun to Thomas G. Clemson, 24 July 1847, **Jameson,** ed., 'Corr. of Calhoun', 736.
11. **Porter** and **Johnson,** *National Party Platforms,* p. 13.
12. **M.M. Quaife,** ed., *Diary of James K. Polk during His Presidency, 1845-1849,* Chicago, 1910, iii, 502.
13. **Porter** and **Johnson,** ibid., p. 17.
14. **Silbey,** ed., op. cit., p. 61.

Chapter 16: The protean republic

1. **Rozwenc,** ed., *Ideology and Power,* pp. 48-9.
2. **Blau,** ed., *Social Theories of Jacksonian Democracy* , p. 267.
3. **Grund,** *Americans – Moral, Social, and Political Relations,* p. 323.
4. Statistics cited in preceding paragraphs are drawn principally from *Historical Statistics of the United States, Colonial Times to 1957,* U.S. Bureau of the Census, 1960; see also **George Rogers Taylor,** *The Transportation Revolution, 1815-1860,* Rinehart, 1951, p. 4, p. 388, and **Stuart Bruchey,** *The Roots of American Economic Growth, 1607-1861,* Harper & Row, 1968, p. 82.
5. **Michael Chevalier,** *Society, Manners, and Politics in the United States: Letters on North America,* ed., John William Ward, Doubleday, 1961, p. 60.
6. **Grund,** op. cit. (1837), p. 323.

7. **Peter R. Knights,** *The Plain People of Boston, 1830-1860: A Study in City Growth,* Oxford U.P., 1971, p. 59.
8. See **Stephan Thernstrom,** *Poverty and Progress: Social Mobility in a Nineteenth Century City,* Harvard U.P., 1964.
9. **Probst,** ed., *The Happy Republic.,* p. 30.
10. **Alexander Mackay,** *The Western World, or Travels in the United States in 1846-47,* London, 1849, ii, 77.
11. **Eaton,** ed., *The Leaven of Democracy,* p. 181.
12. Ibid., p. 481.
13. **Eugene D. Genovese,** *The World the Slaveholders Made: Two Essays in Interpretation,* Vintage Books, 1971, p. 16.
14. **Mackay,** op. cit., ii, 79.
15. **Eaton,** ed., op. cit., p. 197.
16. Quoted by **William W. Freehling,** 'Spoilsmen and Interests in the Thought and Career of John C. Calhoun', *J.A.H.,* ii (June 1965), p. 37.
17. Ibid., p. 40.
18. **Roy P. Basler,** ed., *The Collected Works of Abraham Lincoln,* Rutgers U.P., 1953, i, 109.
19. *Buffalo Morning Express,* 30 Dec. 1856.
20. **David Brion Davis,** ed., *The Fear of Conspiracy: Images of Un-American Subversion from the Revolution to the Present,* Cornell U.P., p. 80.
21. Ibid., p. 98.
22. **Silbey,** ed., *Transformation of Am. Politics,* p. 82.
23. **Davis,** ed., op. cit., p. 137.

Chapter 17: The presidency, parties and the people

1. **Charles Dickens,** *American Notes for General Circulation and Pictures from Italy,* Chapman & Hall, 1913, p. 54.
2. Quoted by **Ged Martin,** 'The Cambridge Lectureship of 1866: A False Start in American Studies', *J. Am. St.,* vii (April 1973), p. 24.
3. *Public Ledger* (Philadelphia), 15 Sept. 1836.
4. Quoted by **Leonard D. White,** *The Jacksonians: A Study in Administrative History, 1829-1861,* Free Press, 1965, p. 29.
5. **Alexis de Tocqueville,** *Democracy in America,* Vintage Books, 1954, i, 126.
6. **Rozwenc,** ed., *Ideology and Power,* p. 201.
7. Quoted by **White,** op. cit., p. 32.
8. **Chapman Coleman** (ed.), *The Life of John J. Crittenden,* Philadelphia, 1871, ii, 118.
9. 'A FARMER', *Washington Gazette,* 9 Feb. 1822.
10. **Eaton,** ed., *The Leaven of Democracy,* p. 50.
11. **Tocqueville,** op. cit., i, 141.
12. Ibid., ii, 115, 117.
13. Probst, ed., *The Happy Republic,* p. 288.
14. Quoted by **Max Berger,** *The British Traveller in America, 1836-1860,* Columbia U.P., 1943, p. 98.
15. *Daily Pennsylvanian,* 14 Aug. 1852.
16. See **Walter Dean Burnham,** 'Party Systems and the Political Process', in **William Nisbet Chambers** and **Walter Dean Burnham,** eds., *The American Party Systems: Stages of Political Development,* Oxford U.P., 1967, esp. pp. 277-9.
17. Quoted by **Robert Gray Gunderson,** *The Log-Cabin Campaign,* U. of Kentucky P., 1957; p. 115.
18. *Niles's National Register,* lxvi (13 July 1844), p. 314.
19. Ibid., lviii, (18 July 1840), p. 309.
20. Ibid., lxvii, (7 Sept. 1844), p. 3.

21. 'W' in *National Intelligencer*, 7 Oct. 1844.
22. *The Pennsylvanian*, 27 July 1836; *Richmond Whig*, 1 May 1840.
23. *Niles's National Register*, lxvii (9 Nov. 1844), p. 149.
24. **Commager,** ed., *Documents*, p. 388.

Select bibliography

This bibliography is not meant to be exhaustive. It is designed mainly as a guide for further reading, and is confined to secondary works which students should find fairly accessible. It also enables the author to acknowledge some of the books and articles which have been of most value to him. The publishing dates given are not necessarily those of first publication. For primary sources on this period, students are referred to Oscar Handlin et al., *Harvard Guide to American History*, Harvard U.P., 1954.

A. General

Herbert Agar, *The United States: The Presidents, the Parties, and the Constitution,* Eyre & Spottiswoode, 1950.

Rowland Berthoff, 'The American Social Order: A Conservative Hypothesis', *Am. Hist. Rev.,* lxv, (April 1960), 495-514.

Rowland Berthoff, *An Unsettled People,* Harper & Row, 1971.

Richard D. Brown, 'Modernisation and the Modern Personality in Early America, 1600-1865: A Sketch of a Synthesis', *J. Interdisciplinary Hist.,* ii (Winter 1972), 201-28.

William Nisbet Chambers and **Walter Dean Burnham,** eds., *The American Party Systems,* Oxford U.P., 1967.

Edward S. Corwin, *The President: Office and Powers, 1787-1957,* 4th edn, New York U.P., 1957.

Marcus Cunliffe, *American Presidents and the Presidency,* Eyre & Spottiswoode, 1969.

Marcus Cunliffe, *The Nation Takes Shape, 1789-1837,* U. Chicago P., 1959.

Robert A. Dahl, *Who Governs? Democracy and Power in an American City,* Yale U.P., 1961.

Arthur A. Ekirch, jr., *The American Democratic Tradition,* Macmillan, 1963.

Ronald P. Formisano, 'Deferential-Participant Politics: The Early Republic's Political Culture, 1789-1840', *Am. Pol. Sc. Rev.,* lxviii (June 1974), 473-87.

Frank Otto Gatell, Paul Goodman and **Allen Weinstein,** eds., *The Growth of American Politics,* Oxford U.P., 1972, i.

Louis Hartz, *The Liberal Tradition in America,* Harcourt, Brace & World, 1955.

Richard Hofstadter, *The American Political Tradition and the Men Who Made It,* Cape, 1962.

Richard Hofstadter, *The Idea of a Party System: The Rise of Legitimate Opposition in the United States, 1780-1840,* California U.P., 1970.

Richard Hofstadter, *The Paranoid Style in American Politics,* Cape, 1966.

John R. Howe, *From the Revolution Through the Age of Jackson,* Prentice-Hall, 1973.

Sidney E. Mead, *The Lively Experiment,* Harper & Row, 1963.

Roy F. Nichols, *The Invention of the American Political Parties,* Macmillan, 1967.

M. Ostrogorski, *Democracy and the Organization of Political Parties,* Macmillan, 1902, ii.

J.R. Pole, ed., *The Advance of Democracy,* Harper & Row, 1967.

J.R. Pole, *The Foundations of American Independence, 1763-1815,* Fontana, 1973.

Eugene H. Roseboom, *A History of Presidential Elections,* Macmillan, 1958.

Page Smith, 'Anxiety and Despair in American History', *William and Mary Qu.,* xxvi, (July 1969), 416-24.

Cushing Strout, *The New Heavens and New Earth: Political Religion in America,* Harper & Row, 1974.

William Appleton Williams, *The Contours of American History,* Cape, 1961.

Chilton Williamson, *American Suffrage from Property to Democracy, 1760-1860,* Princeton U.P., 1960.

B. The English and colonial background

Charles M. Andrews, *The Colonial Background of the American Revolution,* Yale U.P. (rev. edn), 1931.

Bernard Bailyn, *The Origins of American Politics,* Vintage Books, 1970.

Ray Allen Billington, ed., *The Reinterpretation of Early American History,* Huntington Library, 1966.

Patricia U. Bonomi, *A Factious People, Politics and Society in Colonial New York,* Columbia U.P., 1971.

John Brewer, *Party Ideology and Popular Politics at the Accession of George III,* Cambridge U.P., 1976.

John Brooke, *The House of Commons, 1754-1790: Introductory Survey,* Oxford U.P., 1968.

Richard L. Bushman, *From Puritan to Yankee: Character and the Social Order in Connecticut, 1690-1765,* Norton, 1970.

Wesley Frank Craven, *The Colonies in Transition, 1660-1713,* Harper Torchbooks, 1968.

Paul Goodman, ed., *Essays in American Colonial History,* Holt, Rinehart and Winston, 1967.

Jack P. Greene, 'Political Mimesis: a Consideration of the Historical and Cultural Roots of Legislative Behavior in the British Colonies in the Eighteenth Century', *Am. Hist. Rev.,* lxxv (Dec. 1969), 337-60.

Jack P. Greene, *The Quest for Power: The Lower Houses of Assembly in the Southern Royal Colonies,* U. North Carolina P., 1963.

Jack P. Greene, 'The Role of the Lower Houses of Assembly in Eighteenth-Century Politics', *J. Southern Hist.,* xxvii (1961), 451-74.

James A. Henretta, *The Evolution of American Society, 1700-1815,* Heath, 1973.

Geoffrey Holmes, *The Electorate and the National Will in the First Age of Party,* University of Lancaster, 1976.

Stanley N. Katz, ed., *Colonial America: Essays in Politics and Social Development,* Little, Brown, 1971.

Stanley Nider Katz, *Newcastle's New York: Anglo-American Politics, 1732-1753,* Harvard U.P., 1968.

Leonard W. Labaree, *Conservatism in Early American History,* Cornell U.P., 1959.

Peter Laslett, *The World We Have Lost* (2nd edn), Methuen, 1971.

Paul Lucas, 'A Note on the Comparative Study of the Structure of Politics in Mid-Eighteenth-Century Britain and Its American Colonies', *William and Mary Qu.,* xxviii (April 1971), 301-9.

Sir Lewis Namier, *The Structure of Politics at the Accession of George III,* Macmillan, 1929.

Alison G. Olson, *Anglo-American Politics, 1660-1775,* Clarendon P., 1973.

John B. Owen, *The Eighteenth Century, 1714-1815,* Nelson, 1974.

J.R. Pole, 'Historians and the Problem of Early American Democracy', *Am. Hist. Rev.,* lxvii (April 1962), 626-46.

J.R. Pole, *Political Representation in England and the Origins of the American Republic,* Macmillan, 1966.

244   *Bibliography*

Caroline Robbins, ' "Discordant Parties": A Study of the Acceptance of Party by Englishmen', *Pol. Sc. Qu.*, lxxiii, 1958, 505-29.
Clinton Rossiter, *Seedtime of the Republic*, Harcourt, Brace, 1953.
R.C. Simmons, *The American Colonies*, Longman, 1976.
Charles Sydnor, *Gentlemen Freeholders: Political Practices in Washington's Virginia*, U. North Carolina P., 1952.
Clarence L. Ver Steeg, *The Formative Years, 1607-1763*, Macmillan, 1965.
Michael Zuckerman, *Peaceable Kingdoms: New England Towns in the Eighteenth Century*, Knopf, 1970.

C.   The Revolution, Confederation, and Constitution

Bernard Bailyn, *The Ideological Origins of the American Revolution*, Harvard U.P., 1967.
Robert E. Brown, *Middle Class Democracy and the Revolution in Massachusetts, 1691-1780*, Cornell U.P., 1955.
Richard Buel, jr., 'Democracy and the American Revolution: A Frame of Reference', *William and Mary Qu.*, xxi (April 1964), 165-90.
E. James Ferguson, *The American Revolution: A General History, 1763-1790*, Dorsey, 1974.
E. James Ferguson, *The Power of the Purse: A History of American Public Finance, 1776-1790*, U. North Carolina P., 1961.
Merrill Jensen, *The American Revolution within America*, New York U.P., 1974.
Merrill Jensen, *The Articles of Confederation, 1774-1781*, Wisconsin U.P., 1940.
Merrill Jensen, *The New Nation . . . 1781-1789*, Knopf, 1953.
Stephen G. Kurtz and James H. Hutson, eds, *Essays on the American Revolution*, U. North Carolina P., 1973.
Forrest McDonald, *E Pluribus Unum: The Formation of the American Republic, 1776-1790*, Houghton Mifflin, 1965.
Duncan J. MacLeod, *Slavery, Race and the American Revolution*, Cambridge U.P., 1974.
Pauline Maier, *From Resistance to Revolution*, Knopf, 1972.
Pauline Maier and Jack P. Greene, eds, 'Interdisciplinary Studies of the American Revolution', *J. Interdisciplinary Hist.*, vi, (Spring 1976).
Jackson Turner Main, *The Antifederalists: Critics of the Constitution, 1781-1788*, U. North Carolina P., 1961.
Jackson Turner Main, 'Government By the People: The American Revolution and the Democratization of the Legislatures', *William and Mary Qu.*, xxiii (July 1966), 391-407.
Jackson Turner Main, *Political Parties Before the Constitution*, Norton, 1974.
Jackson Turner Main, *The Social Structure of Revolutionary America*, Princeton U.P., 1965.
Jackson Turner Main, *The Sovereign States, 1775-1783*, Franklin Watts, 1973.
Edmund S. Morgan, *The Birth of the Republic, 1763-89*, U. Chicago P., 1956.
Clinton Rossiter, *1787: The Grand Convention*, Macmillan, 1966.
Robert E. Shalhope, 'Toward a Republican Synthesis: The Emergence of an Understanding of Republicanism in American Historiography', *William and Mary Qu.*, xxix (Jan. 1972), 49-80.
Gordon S. Wood, *The Creation of the American Republic, 1776-1787*, Norton, 1972.
Esmond Wright, *Fabric of Freedom, 1763-1800*, Macmillan, 1965.

D.   The era of Hamilton and Jefferson

James M. Banner, jr., *To the Hartford Convention: The Federalists and the Origins of Party Politics in Massachusetts, 1789-1815*, Knopf, 1970.
Lance Banning, 'Republican Ideology and the Triumph of the Constitution, 1789-1793', *William and Mary Qu.*, xxxi (April 1974), 167-88.

Rudolph M. Bell, *Party and Faction in American Politics: The House of Representatives, 1789-1801,* Greenwood P., 1973.
Roger H. Brown, *The Republic in Peril: 1812,* Norton, 1971.
Richard Buel jr., *Securing the Revolution: Ideology in American Politics, 1789-1815,* Cornell U.P., 1972.
William Nisbet Chambers, *Political Parties in a New Nation: The American Experience, 1776-1809,* Oxford U.P., 1963.
Joseph Charles, *The Origins of the American Party System,* Harper Torchbooks, 1961.
Marcus Cunliffe, *George Washington: Man and Monument,* Collins, 1959.
Noble E. Cunningham, *The Jeffersonian Republicans: The Formation of Party Organization, 1789-1801,* U. North Carolina P., 1957.
Noble E. Cunningham, *The Jeffersonian Republicans in Power,* U. North Carolina P., 1963.
Richard E. Ellis, *The Jeffersonian Crisis: Courts and Politics in the Young Republic,* Oxford U.P., 1971.
David Hackett Fischer, *The Revolution of American Conservatism,* Harper Torchbooks, 1969.
John R. Howe, jr., 'Republican Thought and the Political Violence of the 1790's', *Am. Qu.,* xix (Summer 1967); 147-65.
Leonard W. Levy, *Jefferson and Civil Liberties: The Darker Side,* Harvard U.P., 1963.
Forrest McDonald, *We, The People: The Economic Origins of the Constitution,* Chicago U.P., 1963.
John C. Miller, *The Federalist Era, 1789-1801,* Harper & Row, 1960.
Donald J. Ratcliffe, 'The Experience of Revolution and the Beginnings of Party Politics in Ohio, 1776-1816', *Ohio Hist.,* lxxxv (Summer 1976), 186-230.
Norman K. Risjord, *The Old Republicans: Southern Conservatism in the Age of Jefferson,* Columbia U.P., 1965.
Marshall Smelser, *The Democratic Republic, 1801-1815,* Harper Torchbooks, 1968.
Gerald Stourzh, *Alexander Hamilton and the Idea of Republican Government,* Stanford U.P., 1970.
Raymond Walters, jr., *The Virginia Dynasty,* Van Nostrand, 1965.
Leonard D. White, *The Federalists: A Study in Administrative History,* Macmillan, 1956.
Leonard D. White, *The Jeffersonians,* Macmillan, 1956.
James Sterling Young, *The Washington Community, 1800-1828,* Columbia U.P., 1966.

E.   The Jacksonian era and beyond

Lee Benson, *The Concept of Jacksonian Democracy: New York as a Test Case,* Princeton U.P., 1961.
William R. Brock, *Conflict and Transformation: The United States, 1844-1877,* Penguin, 1973.
Richard H. Brown, 'The Missouri Crisis, Slavery, and the Politics of Jacksonianism', *S. Atlantic Qu.,* lxv (Winter 1966), 55-72.
B.W. Collins, 'Community and Consensus in Ante-Bellum America', *Hist.J.* xix (Sept. 1976), 635-63.
Matthew A. Crenson, *The Federal Machine: Beginnings of Bureaucracy in Jacksonian America,* Johns Hopkins U.P., 1975.
George Dangerfield, *The Awakening of American Nationalism, 1815-1828,* Harper & Row, 1965.
David Brion Davis, 'Some Themes of Counter-Subversion: An Analysis of Anti-Masonic, Anti-Catholic, and Anti-Mormon Literature', *Miss. Valley Hist. Rev.,* xlvii (Sept. 1960), 205-24.
David Donald, *Lincoln Reconsidered,* Vintage Books, 1956.
Herbert Ershkowitz and **William G. Shade,** 'Consensus or Conflict? Political Behavior in the State Legislatures During the Jacksonian Era', *J. Am., Hist.,* lviii, 591-621.
Eric Foner, *Free Soil, Free Labor, Free Men: The Ideology of the Republican Party Before the Civil War,* Oxford U.P., 1970.

Ronald P. Formisano, *The Birth of Mass Political Parties: Michigan, 1827-1861,* Princeton U.P., 1971.

Ronald P. Formisano, 'Political Character, Antipartyism, and the Second Party System', *American Qu.,* xxi (Winter 1969), 683-709.

Ronald P. Formisano, 'Toward a Reorientation of Jacksonian Politics: A Review of the Literature, 1959-1975', *J. Am., Hist.,* lxiii (June 1976), 42-65.

William W. Freehling, *Prelude to Civil War: The Nullification Controversy in South Carolina, 1816-1836,* Harper & Row, 1966.

William W. Freehling, 'Spoilsmen and Interests in the Thought and Career of John C. Calhoun', *J. Am. Hist.,* lii (June 1965), 25-42.

Frank Otto Gatell, ed., *Essays on Jacksonian America,* Holt, Rinehart and Winston, 1970.

Eugene D. Genovese, *The World the Slaveholders Made,* Vintage Books, 1971.

Norman A. Graebner, *Empire on the Pacific,* Ronald, 1955.

David Grimsted, 'Rioting in Its Jacksonian Setting', *Am. Hist. Rev.,* lxxvii (April 1972), 361-97.

Michael F. Holt, *Forging a Majority: The Formation of the Republican Party in Pittsburgh, 1848-1860,* Yale U.P., 1969.

Peter R. Knights, *The Plain People of Boston, 1830-1860: A Study in City Growth,* Oxford U.P., 1971.

Shaw Livermore, *The Twilight of Federalism,* Princeton U.P., 1962.

Richard P. McCormick, 'New Perspectives on Jacksonian Politics', *Am. Hist. Rev.,* lxv (Jan. 1960), 288-301.

Richard P. McCormick, *The Second American Party System: Party Formation in the Jacksonian Era,* U. North Carolina P., 1966.

John M. McFaul, *The Politics of Jacksonian Finance,* Cornell U.P., 1972.

Lynn L. Marshall, 'The Strange Stillbirth of the Whig Party', *Am. Hist. Rev.,* lxxii (Jan. 1967), 445-68.

Frederick Merk, *The Monroe Doctrine and American Expansionism,* Knopf, 1966.

Marvin Meyers, *The Jacksonian Persuasion,* Stanford U.P., 1957.

Edward Pessen, *Jacksonian America: Society, Personality, Politics,* Dorsey P., 1969.

Edward Pessen, *Riches, Class, and Power Before the Civil War,* Heath & Co., 1973.

Lorman Ratner, *Antimasonry: The Crusade and the Party,* Prentice-Hall, 1969.

Robert V. Remini, *Andrew Jackson and the Bank War,* Norton, 1967.

Robert V. Remini, *The Election of Andrew Jackson,* Lippincott, 1963.

Robert V. Remini, *Martin Van Buren and the Making of the Democratic Party,* Columbia U.P., 1959.

Arthur M. Schlesinger, *The Age of Jackson,* Eyre & Spottiswoode, 1946.

Charles G. Sellers, 'Jackson Men with Feet of Clay', *Am. Hist. Rev.,* lxii (April 1957), 537-51.

Charles S. Sellers, 'Who Were the Southern Whigs?', *Am. Hist. Rev.,* lix (Jan. 1954), 335-46.

James Roger Sharp, *The Jacksonians versus the Banks,* Columbia U.P., 1970.

Joel Silbey, *The Shrine of Party: Congressional Voting Behavior, 1841-1852,* U. Pittsburgh P., 1967.

Fred Somkin, *Unquiet Eagle: Memory and Desire in the Idea of American Freedom, 1815-1860,* Cornell U.P., 1967.

Stephan Thernstrom, *Poverty and Progress: Social Mobility in a Nineteenth Century City,* Harvard U.P., 1964.

Stephan Thernstrom and **Peter R. Knights,** 'Men in Motion: Some Data and Speculations about Urban Population Mobility in Nineteenth-Century America', *J. Interdisciplinary Hist.,* i (Autumn 1970), 7-35.

Glyndon G. Van Deusen, *The Jacksonian Era, 1825-1848,* Harper & Row, 1959.

Glyndon G. Van Deusen, *The Rise and Decline of Jacksonian Democracy,* Van Nostrand Reinhold, 1970.

Glyndon G. Van Deusen, 'Some Aspects of Whig Thought and Theory in the Jacksonian Period', *Am. Hist. Rev.,* lxiii (Jan. 1958), 305-22.

Michael Wallace, 'Changing Concepts of Party in the United States: New York, 1815-1828', *Am. Hist. Rev.,* lxxiv (1968), 453-91.

John William Ward, *Andrew Jackson: Symbol for an Age,* Oxford U.P., 1962.

Rush Welter, *The Mind of America, 1820-1860,* Columbia U.P., 1975.

Leonard D. White, *The Jacksonians: A Study in Administrative History, 1829-1861,* Free Press, 1965.

Major L. Wilson, *Space, Time and Freedom: The Quest for Nationality and the Irrepressible Conflict, 1815-1861,* Greenwood P., 1974.

Index

Polk, James K.,   197, 198, 199
Political Disquisitions, see Burgh, James
Political nation,
  colonial,   1, 21, 24, 29
  English,   1, 7, 11, 14, 15
  United States,   32, 40, 44, 89, 103,
    112, 152, 216, 218
Popular pressures,   29
  in revolutionary era,   32-3, 36, 43
  in 1810s and 1820s,   116, 122-8
  and mass political parties,   226-9
Population,
  growth of, in free states,   121
  and immigration,   200-1
  increasing,   206
  mobility of,   207-8
  represented in colonial and revolutio-
    nary assemblies,   25, 39
  represented in House of Representa-
    tives,   56, 58
  spreads west,   117, 120, 128, 192,
    207
Populism,   116, 122, 170
  see also Popular pressures
Post Office,   173
Presbyterians,
  in New York colony,   26
  and Scots-Irish,   18
  and Whig party,   189
Presidency,
  in Constitution,   57-8, 60
  decline in political authority of,   104,
    108-12, 115
  effects of popular election of,   146-7,
    218
  and first Congress,   69-70
  focal point of second party system,
    146-7, 155-6
  role of in mass polity,   218-19, 221-2
  strengthened by Jacksonian Democ-
    rats,   174, 219-21
President, system of electing,
  in Constitution,   57
  dangers in,   133
  limited popular participation in,
    107-8
  and modes of choosing electors,
    107-8
  proposed amendments in relation to,
    133-5
  trend towards popular election,   124,
    127-8
Press, *see* Newspapers
Prime minister,
  attacked by Bolingbroke,   13
  in English politics,   9, 10, 15, 68, 71

Professional politician, emergence of,
  157
Property, colonial distribution of,   19,
  24
Protestantism,
  in colonies,   18
  individualistic dynamic of,   19-20
  and republicanism,   42, 215
  and Whiggery, association with,   183,
    187, 189
Providence, R.I.,   19, 52
Puritans,
  Congregational churches established
    by, in New England,   18
  mission of,   18, 31
  political views of,   16

Quakers, in colonies,   18
Quid Schism, *see* Tertium Quids
Quincy, Josiah,   106
Quitrents,   40

Radicals, (English),   11, 23
  influence in U.S.,   74, 77, 88, 92, 96,
    110
Randolph, Edmund,   55, 63, 71
Randolph, John,   95, 96, 109, 131
Ratification of U.S. Constitution,   60-3
Reform Bill of 1832 (British),   223
Reformation (British and European),   18
Religious liberty,
  and pluralism,   41, 59
  and separation of church and state,
    42
Religious tolerance, in middle colonies,
  18
Report on Manufactures (Alexander
  Hamilton),   73, 75
Representative principle,
  in colonies,   25
  in House of Representatives,   58
  in revolutionary era,   33, 39, 40
  in U.S. Constitution,   59-60
Representatives, House of
  in Constitution,   58
  origins of committee system in,   110
  and presidential election of 1800,   86
  and presidential election of 1824,
    134, 142
  and 'salary grab' bill,   123
  small size of,   60
Republican party (of 1850s),   202
Republicanism, theory and faith of,
  and antipartyism,   159
  and business enterprise,   172